Doublehead

Last Chickamauga Cherokee Chief

Doublehead

Last Chickamauga Cherokee Chief

Rickey Butch Walker

Published by:
Bluewater Publications
1812 CR 111
Killen, Alabama 35645
www.BluewaterPublications.com

Table of Content

Doublehead: Last Chickamauga Cherokee Chief

Introduction

Prior to the birth of Doublehead in 1744, the area of the Muscle Shoals of north Alabama was the ancestral hunting grounds of the Cherokee. By the 1770's, Doublehead with the assistance of his warriors would rule the area of the Great Bend with an iron fist for some 40 years. During the Chickamauga War beginning with the signing of the Treaty of Sycamore Shoals in 1775, he would fight the northern encroachment of white settlers from his stronghold in the southernmost portion of the Tennessee Valley shoals. Doublehead would become one of the most influential Chickamauga leaders with the tribes making up the Indian confederacy.

Doublehead was very independent from other Chickamauga leaders including the great war chief Dragging Canoe. He would make his own decisions in the isolation of the Muscle Shoals and had complete control of his war against the Cumberland settlements. He made his raids without asking for permission or guidance from other Chickamauga leaders. Doublehead was the last Chickamauga Cherokee Chief to cease hostilities and to live along the Muscle Shoals in the Great Bend of the Tennessee River of north Alabama.

Indian Tribes of the Chickamauga Confederacy

From the 1600's through the early 1800's, five American Indian tribes claimed the area of the Muscle Shoals which included the Yuchi (Euchean), Upper Creek (Muskogee), Shawnee (Algonquin), Chickasaw (Muskogee), and Lower Cherokee (Iroquois). Portions of all these Indian tribes including the Delaware (Algonquian) became a part of the Chickamauga Confederation that fought against the settlement of their hunting grounds in the Cumberland River Valley.

The tribes that made up the Chickamauga Confederacy consisted of the Yuchi, Delaware, Upper Creek, Shawnee, Chickasaw, and Lower Cherokee. Some members of all the tribes making up the confederacy would live in Doublehead's Town at the upstream end of the Muscle Shoals. Doublehead and his Chickamauga alliance would be the last Indian people to occupy and control this valuable piece of Tennessee River real estate. Even though there were previous conflicts among the Indian tribes that occupied the area of the Muscle Shoals, Doublehead would work with all of these tribes including the Chickasaw and form alliances with the remaining remnants in order to organize the strongest historic Indian confederacy to ever occupy the Tennessee Valley's Great Bend.

It would be the last twelve years of his life that Doublehead would become a peace seeking warrior. He made shady deals with government officials to his own personal benefit which caused a dislike of Doublehead by many of his fellow Cherokees. Prior to his death, Doublehead became a very wealthy businessman but would realize a widespread decline in his respect among the Upper Cherokees. The loss of his feared Chickamauga warrior status would embolden his own Cherokee people to carry out Doublehead's assassination, which would lead to another division of the tribe. In 1809, some 1200 of Doublehead's family and friends would leave the Cherokee tribe for lands west of the Mississippi River and would become known as the "Old Settlers or Cherokees West".

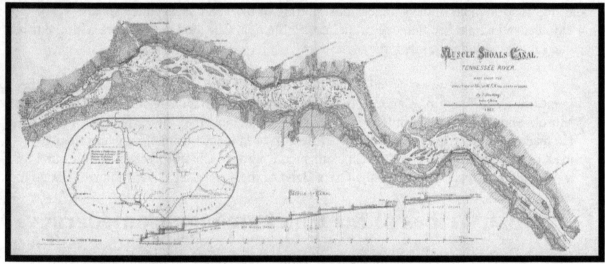

Muscle Shoals prior to the Building the Dams

Yuchi (Euchean)

Many people in north Alabama are not familiar with one of the most historic tribes to inhabit our area; however, the Yuchi were here at the time DeSoto traveled through our part of the country in 1540. They consider themselves the "First People" and are some of the most pure traditionalists among Indian people. According to the *Journal of Muscle Shoals History*, *"...the Cherokees were not the first Indians to live at the Muscle Shoals on the Tennessee River. This honor belongs to the mound builders, who were followed by the Euchees (Yuchi), a tribe having a unique language and no migration legend. They may have lived at the Shoals in pre-historic times. The Euchees were probably living at the*

2

Shoals when Desoto (1540) came through Alabama and were definitely there in 1700 when discovered by some traveling Canadians... Shortly after they were discovered by the Canadians in 1700, the Euchees departed from the Shoals and moved to the mountainous regions of what is now East Tennessee" (Watts, 1973). Another contingent of Yuchi migrated south along Black Warriors' Path and settled near the mouth of Euchee Creek and the Chattahoochee River in present-day Russell County, Alabama.

John R. Swanton in his book, *The Indians of the Southeastern United States*, shows the Yuchi (Euchees) living along Elk River and the Tennessee River at the mussel shoals in the early 1700's. For some reason, part of the Yuchi migrated to the Hiwassee River in east Tennessee and the rest migrated south to the Chattahoochee River on the Alabama-Georgia border. After fighting the Cherokee in east Tennessee, many of these northern Yuchi also migrated south to the Chattahoochee River Valley; however, a few Yuchi remained in the Tennessee Valley maintaining friendly relations with Doublehead and the Lower Cherokee, who sought the alliance of all regional tribes.

According to Tom Hendrix's book, *"If the Legends Fade"*, his great-great-grandmother was Yuchi, and she was born in the Tennessee Valley about the time Doublehead and his people were controlling the area. *"Her name was Te-lah-nay, which means Woman with Dancing Eyes. She was born above the shoulder bone in the valley of the Tennessee River in the 1800's. Her tribe was the Yuchi, and she was my great-great-grandmother"* (Hendrix, 2000). The shoulder bone Hendrix refers to is now under the backwaters of Wilson Lake about midway between Wheeler Dam and Wilson Dam on the Tennessee River. This shoulder bone is now an underwater island about four to five feet under the backwaters of present-day Wilson Dam, and lies slightly north of the middle of the river and just east of a line drawn from Gargis Hollow to Four Mile Creek. The underwater island is in the shape of a shoulder blade bone with the small end facing downstream.

Some of the Yuchi intermarried with the Cherokee and assisted Doublehead in establishing his domain and Indian alliance along the Big Bend. The Yuchi were considered the "First People" of the Muscle Shoals area of the Tennessee River. They were known as the children of the sun. As recorded by Terra Manasco in the book *"Walking Sipsey"* (1992*), "It was the Uchee, who called themselves the Children of the Sun, who first used this site to Walk the Rainbow. Inducing themselves into a trance of blue-blackness formed by a series of sacred number patterns, a cord of white light would shoot out from their navels and arc out into the universe. It was upon this cord that they Walked the Rainbow and visited many worlds. The symbols carved on Kinlock's rocks are the magic symbols used in the trance as well as recreations of spirits encountered beyond the Rainbow."* The Kinlock site was sacred to the Yuchi and Chickamauga and today is still considered sacred by those mixed Indian descendants that still call north Alabama home. The Kinlock Rock Shelter was part of Doublehead's territory located in the Warrior Mountains some 30 miles south of his home on the Muscle Shoals in present-day Lawrence County, Alabama.

Kinlock Rock Shelter

Delaware (Algonquian)

Doublehead, as did Dragging Canoe, built alliances with surrounding tribes including the Delaware in efforts to stop white settlement on their sacred hunting grounds. Through intermarriage, the Delaware became members of Doublehead's extended family. Doublehead's third wife was a Delaware Indian probably from the northern part of Kentucky along the Ohio River. His Delaware wife was thought to be born about 1750 and they had two daughters named Corn Blossom who was born about 1770 and Kstieieah born about 1775. His marriage to the Delaware woman was an appropriate way to establish a friendly relationship with her people who controlled a great portion of the Ohio River Basin. The Delaware alliance with the Chickamauga was helpful to Doublehead in controlling the northern portion of Tennessee and Kentucky. The hunting areas from the

4

Cumberland River to the Ohio River were assessable to all factions of the Chickamauga which included the Yuchi, Delaware, Shawnee, Upper Creek, and Lower Cherokee.

The Delaware, known as Leni Lenape meaning "Real People" or "Human Beings", originated around the Delaware River Basin, but they were forced westward by white encroachment into their homelands. By the 1750's, many of the Delaware were living in the Ohio River Valley. The Delaware were considered by some historians to be one of the oldest tribes in the northeastern United States, and the parent tribe of the Cherokee people who migrated from the north and settled in the mountainous Appalachian region of the Southeast. The Cherokee and Delaware had many cultural similarities.

In 1780 a group of Delaware hunting south of the Cumberland River were met by a party of men from Fort Nashborough. The men noted that the group of Delaware was moving south into Alabama as seen in the following:

In the latter part of January some of the men in pursuit of game through the woods were surprised to find traces of a party of Indians. These they were able to identify by the moccasin prints and also because the toes of the tracks turned inward, a characteristic of the savage foot. Following on apace the hunters found them encamped on a branch of Mill Creek in Davidson County, a few miles south of the Bluff. The stream mentioned has since been called Indian Creek because of this incident. The whites returned at once to the Bluff (Fort Nashborough), and a delegation was sent down from the settlement to seek an interview, and discover if possible whether the intruders were only friendly visitors or on mischief bent. The whites had no interpreter, but after "heap much talk," combined with a variety of sign making it was found that they were of the Delaware tribe. Probably ignorant of the advent of the settlers they had journeyed hundreds of miles from their home in New Jersey for a quiet hunt in the reservation. Having been already for some time in the Caney Fork country, which at that time abounded in game, they remained only a few days near the settlement, after which they quietly took their leave going south into Alabama (Albright, 1909). This particular group of Delaware was moving into the area of the Tennessee River controlled by Doublehead.

The different factions of the Chickamauga made raids that overlapped into the territories of each tribe making up the confederacy. Doublehead and his war parties made raids into Delaware territory against white settlers on the Rolling Fork section of the Salt River Basin in northern Kentucky and even assisted the Delaware in their fight against white encroachment into the Ohio River Valley. Even though the Delaware were not documented inhabitants of the Muscle Shoals area of the Tennessee River Valley, they also considered the Cumberland River Valley their hunting grounds. The Delaware were documented taking part in raids on the Cumberland settlements within the territory claimed by the Lower Cherokee. During some of the Cumberland raids, the Delaware faction of the Chickamauga was particularly brutal by cutting up some of their victims and scattering the remains in the yard around their log cabins. Some of the Delaware warriors would take the heads of victims as war trophies. These were some of the same brutal tactics used by Doublehead and his warriors.

Dragging Canoe, in his speech to the delegation after the Treaty of Sycamore Shoals in 1775, mentions the Delaware as a vanishing people being destroyed by the encroaching white settlers. At this time, he said the Delaware tribe was only a remnant of its once great nation. Eventually the Delaware were defeated in 1794 by General Anthony Wayne at the Battle of Fallen Timbers, where over 100 Cherokee warriors fought with the Delaware but lost to the superior American forces. By June of the same year of this defeat, Doublehead signed a peace agreement known as the "Treaty of Philadelphia" with President George Washington. Doublehead probably saw the handwriting on the wall and knew that his days were numbered if he did not make the change from war to peace.

The Delaware had tried to stop further white settlement of their new Ohio lands in order to protect their homes and save their people from destruction. They were not successful and many were later forced on to the lands of the Cherokee Nation in Oklahoma. In the middle 1790's, the Delaware appeared to abandon the Chickamauga and were not particularly noted as taking part in raids on the Cumberland settlements. The Delaware became more involved in saving their people and homes along the Ohio River Basin.

Creek (Muskogee)

The Creeks befriended Chickamauga Chief Doublehead and became one of his strongest allies. They fought to the bitter end and were eventually defeated by General Andrew Jackson in March 1814. The Creeks utilized the friendly territory Doublehead controlled at the Muscle Shoals and followed him as their leader on many raids. Their hunting and raiding parties passed east of their enemy, the unfriendly Chickasaw stronghold of the upper Tombigbee River towns. The Creeks assisted Doublehead in establishing villages along the Great Bend of the Tennessee River and many times accompanied him on raiding parties into the Cumberland settlements. At times as many as 700 Creek warriors would follow Doublehead on the warpath. With the assistance of friendly Creeks, Lower Cherokees, Shawnees, Yuchi, Delaware, mixed-bloods, relatives, and friendly whites, Doublehead enforced his supreme control of the Great Bend and his followers were known as the Chickamauga. In his days as a Chickamauga warrior, not one Cherokee, Creek, or any other warrior would challenge Doublehead's authority.

6

The boundary line between the Creeks and Cherokees remained in question for many years with the Creeks denying that a boundary existed in the Muscle Shoals area of the Tennessee River; however, as seen in the following by Phil Hawkins, Jr., the Creeks wanted to unite the tribes into a confederacy. Also, Hawkins identifies Shoal Town where Doublehead and Katagiskee had a large settlement that extended a mile and half southward from the river along Shoal Town Creek.

In 1802, at the treaty of Fort Wilkinson, it was agreed between the parties that the line was from the High Shoals on Apalatche, the old path (High Town Path), leaving Stone Mountain to the Creeks, to the shallow ford on the Chattahoochee.

This agreement was in presence of the commissioners of the United States and witnessed by General Pickens and Colonel Hawkins. On the 10th October, 1809, a letter was sent from the Cherokees to the Creeks and received in February in the public square at Tookaubatche, stating the line agreed upon at Fort Wilkinson, and that all the waters of Etowah down to the ten islands below Turkey Town these lands were given up to the Cherokees at a talk at Chestoe in presence of the Little Prince, and Tustunnuggee Thlucco Chulioah, of Turkeystown, was the interpreter.

In August, 1814, at the treaty of Fort Jackson, the Creeks and Cherokees were invited to settle their claims, and Colonel Meigs was engaged for three or four days in aiding them to do so. The result was they could not agree, but would at some convenient period agree. This was signed by General Jackson, Colonel Hawkins, and Colonel Meigs.

At the convention with the Creeks, in September, 1815, the Cherokees manifested a sincere desire to settle their boundaries with the Creeks, but the latter first declined and then refused. Tustunnuggee Thlucco, being asked where their boundary was west of Coosa, said there never was any boundary fixed and known as such between the parties, and after making Tennessee the boundary from tradition, and that the Cherokees obtained leave of them to cross it, the policy of the Creeks receiving all destroyed red people in their confederacy, the Cherokees were permitted to come over and settle as low down on the west of Coosa as Hauluthee Hatchee, from thence on the west side of Coosa on all its waters to its source. He has never heard, and he has examined all his people who can have any knowledge on the subject, that the Cherokees had any pretensions lower down Coosa on that side. He does not believe, and he has never heard, there was any boundary agreed upon between them. Being asked by Colonel Hawkins his opinion where the boundary should be, he says it should go up Hauluthee Hatchee, passing a level of good land between two mountains, to the head of Itchan Hatchee, and down the same to Tennessee, about 8 or 9 miles above Nickajack.

In the year 1793 the Cherokees had a settlement at the Muscle Shoals (Shoal Town on Big Muscle Shoals), **Doublehead and Katagiskee were the chiefs**, *and the Creeks had a small settlement above the Creek path on Tennessee. The Cherokee settlement extended southwardly from the shoal probably a mile and a half* (Shoal Town). *The principal temporary agent for Indian affairs south of the Ohio was early instructed in 1777 to ascertain the boundary line of the four nations, and instructions were given accordingly by him to Mr. Dinsmore and Mr. Mitchell to aid in doing it. Several attempts were made, but all proved abortive, owing to the policy of the Creeks, which was to unite the four nations in one confederacy and the national affairs of all to be in a convention to be held annually among the Creeks, where the speaker for the Creeks should preside.*

*At every attempt made among the Creeks when these conventions met, the answer was, "**We have no dividing lines, nor never had, between us**. We have lines only between us and the white people, our neighbors." At times, when the subject was discussed in the convention of the Creeks, they claimed Tombigby, called by them Choctaw River (Choctan Hatchee), the boundary line between them and the Choctaws. Tustunueggee Hopoie, brother of the old Efau Hajo (mad dog), who died at ninety-six years of age, and retained strength of memory and intelligence to this great age, reported publicly to the agent, "When he was a boy his father's hunting camp was at Puttanchan Hatchee (Black Warrior)." His father had long been at the head of the Creeks, and always told him "Choctaw River was their boundary with the Choctaws." He never saw a Choctaw hunting camp on this side of the Black Warrior. Phil. Hawkins, Jr.* (Powell, John Wesley, et.al., 1887)

According to the above text, the Creek people claimed the territory all the way to the banks of the Tennessee River where Doublehead lived at Shoal Town. Both the Creeks and Doublehead's people lived in harmony along the mussel shoals until the year about 1795 without having disputes of land claims on the territory in the Great Bend. The Creek alliance that developed between Doublehead and the Chickamauga put fear in the hearts of encroaching settlers, military groups, and also the Upper Cherokees who did not question Doublehead's authority. As they had wanted for many years, the Creeks united in a loose confederacy with Doublehead to carry their war to the white settlers who were invading their frontiers, killing their people, and taking their lands. As the Creek alliance that Doublehead nurtured weakened, so did his power and authority. Doublehead was drawn into conflicts with the Creeks by government officials who ultimately were responsible for the downfall of both Doublehead and his supporters in the Creek Nation.

A cloud of impending doom for Doublehead's Creek alliance began to spread over the Tennessee Valley after Doublehead agreed to peaceful relations with the United States government during a 1794 meeting with President George Washington in Philadelphia. The break in friendly relations with the Creeks was due in part to the response Doublehead

8

received from Governor William Blount telling him to control the Creeks living in his territory if he wanted to maintain peace. The issue with the Creeks played a major role in Doublehead's acceptance by the government officials, who at the time were a lesser of two evils. The bribes offered to Doublehead by the government were of assistance in maintaining peace, controlling the Creeks, and encouraging him to give up Cherokee lands.

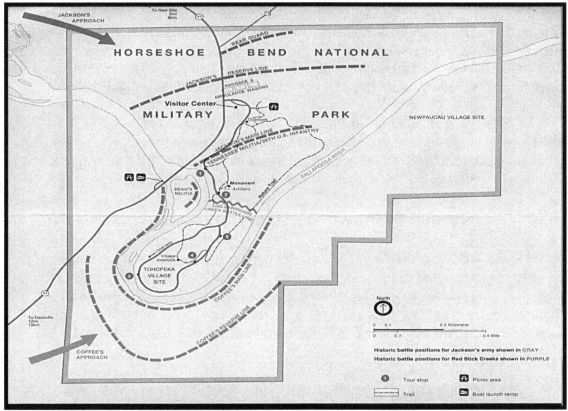

Horseshoe Bend National Military Park

Tension with the Creeks was also due to the Cherokees allowing the United States government to increase the number of federal roads and trails passing through Indian territory as seen in this excerpt from the book, "*The Old Southwest*" as follows, *"Among the Creeks a deep dissatisfaction stemming from numerous and diffuse sources was seething. In part, the roots of Creek uneasiness related to the opening and expansion of so many roads and trails — activities viewed by many of their leaders as an evil omen. Immigrants were already taking advantage of the widening of the Federal Road from the Chattahoochee River to Mims' Ferry on the Alabama, and the Secretary of War had ordered General Wade Hampton to open a wagon road from Muscle Shoals to Fort Stoddert along a route surveyed by Edmund P. Gaines"* (Clark and Guice, 1989).

Some seven years after the death of Doublehead on March 27, 1814, the Cherokees would join forces with General Andrew Jackson to defeat the Red Stick Creeks at Horseshoe Bend on the Tallapoosa River. Jackson and his army of some 3,300 men including a large contingent of Cherokee warriors attacked some 1,000 Creek warriors at a fortified bend of the Tallapoosa River. Just a few years earlier, some of these same Cherokee warriors were in the Chickamauga Confederacy fighting the whites side by side with the Creeks they were now attacking. Over 800 Upper Creeks died in the battle defending their families and land they loved. Near the beginning of the Creek War at Fort Mims some 700 Creeks died and over 800 died at Horseshoe Bend. This country has never in our history witnessed such a large loss of American Indian lives in single battles.

The death of Doublehead and defeat of his Creek alliance at Horseshoe Bend was the beginning of the end and great downfall for all Southeastern Indian people. Total Indian removal from the Southeastern United States to the west of the Mississippi River was not many years in the future from the defeat of the Red Stick Creeks.

Shawnee (Algonquian)

Some years after the Cherokee and Yuchi moved from the Great Bend, bands of Shawnee migrated south and took possession of the deserted country along the Muscle Shoals of the Tennessee River. The Shawnee migrated south from the Ohio and Cumberland River Valleys to take up residence in present-day north Alabama. The Shawnee were of Algonquin stock and originated north of the mussel shoals of the Tennessee River.

The Cherokee became very angry at the Shawnee intrusion upon the lands of the Tennessee Valley to which they still claimed as their primary hunting grounds. Eventually the Cherokee declared war against the Shawnee who were occupying their ancestral home lands. After many years of warfare, the Cherokee formed an alliance with the Chickasaw, and the two tribes after a war of "five hundred moons" drove the Shawnee not only from the Tennessee Valley, but from the Cumberland Valley, forcing them to seek new homes beyond the Ohio River. This Cherokee and Chickasaw war against the Shawnees came to an end about 1721.

After years of hostilities with the Cherokee, Doublehead and his Chickamauga people developed friendly relationships with the Shawnee. Some Shawnee were noted as living in north Alabama with the Lower Cherokee at Doublehead's Town. Many historians agree that some intermarriage occurred between Doublehead's family and the Shawnee people. In addition, the Shawnee were also intermarrying with the Creek people.

In 1810 the great Shawnee Tecumseh came through Alabama advocating a united Indian confederacy. He was considered by many historians as being half Shawnee and half Creek.

Tecumseh

*Tecumseh (Tekoomsē: "Shooting Star" or "Panther Across The Sky") was born about March 9, 1768, probably just outside Chillicothe, present-day Ohio in Old Town, 12 miles east of Dayton, Ohio in Greene County. His father was Pucksinwah, a minor Shawnee war chief of the Kispoko ("Dancing Tail" or "Panther") branch of the tribe. His mother Methoataske, who was believed to be either Muscogee Creek, Cherokee, or Shawnee…When his parents married, **their tribe was living somewhere near modern Tuscaloosa, Alabama. They had lived in the region among the Creek tribe** since being driven from homes in the Ohio River Valley by the Iroquois based in New York and Pennsylvania during the 17th-century Beaver War.*

At age 15, after the American Revolutionary War, Tecumseh joined a band of Shawnee who were determined to stop the white invasion of their lands...Tecumseh became the leader of his own band of warriors...and took an active part fighting along with his older brother Cheeseekau, an important war leader who essentially raised Tecumseh and Tenskwatawa after their parents' early deaths.

*In early 1789, Tecumseh traveled south with Cheeseekau to live among, and fight alongside, the **Chickamauga faction of the Cherokee**. Accompanied by twelve Shawnee warriors, they stayed at Running Water in Marion County, Tennessee, where Cheeseekau's wife and daughter lived. There **Tecumseh met Dragging Canoe**, a famous leader who was leading a resistance movement against U.S. expansion. Cheeseekau was killed while leading a raid, and Tecumseh assumed leadership of the small Shawnee band, and subsequent Chickamauga raiding parties.*

Tecumseh returned to Ohio in late 1790, having fathered a Cherokee daughter before leaving (according to Cherokee oral tradition). Afterward, Tecumseh took part in several battles, including that of the 1794 Fallen Timbers. The Indians were defeated by the Americans, which ended the Northwestern Indian Wars in favor of the Americans (Sugden, 1998). After the Battle of Fallen Timbers, Tecumseh continued his struggle against white encroachment and tried to unite all the southern tribes as he had seen Dragging Canoe and Doublehead accomplished with the Chickamauga Confederacy.

The Shawnee had joined forces with the Chickamauga to fight a common enemy who were moving into their hunting grounds, farming their lands, and building houses and towns in their country. A small group of Shawnee warriors were loyal to Doublehead and lived in his town at Brown's Ferry. As many as 300 Shawnee warriors would join Doublehead's alliance and accompany him on raids against the land hungry white settlers.

Chickasaw (Muskogee)

At the beginning of the 1780's, the Chickasaw were a major faction of Doublehead's Chickamauga confederacy, and were on friendly terms because Chickasaw Chief George Colbert married two of Doublehead's oldest daughters. George Colbert claimed that Doublehead was living at the Muscle Shoals by his permission.

After the conflict with the Shawnees ended, the Chickasaws moved east to the Chickasaw Old Fields on Chickasaw Island in the Tennessee River south of present-day Huntsville, Alabama. According to Professor Henry Sale Halbert (January 14, 1837-May 8, 1916), "*around the mid 1700's, the Chickasaw's formed the settlement in the Chickasaw Old Fields, which angered the Cherokees very much against their former allies. A great battle was fought in the Chickasaw village in 1769, in which the Chickasaw were victors, but their victory was gained at such a great loss that they retreated from the country, but the Chickasaw's continued their claims to lands on both sides of the Tennessee River."*

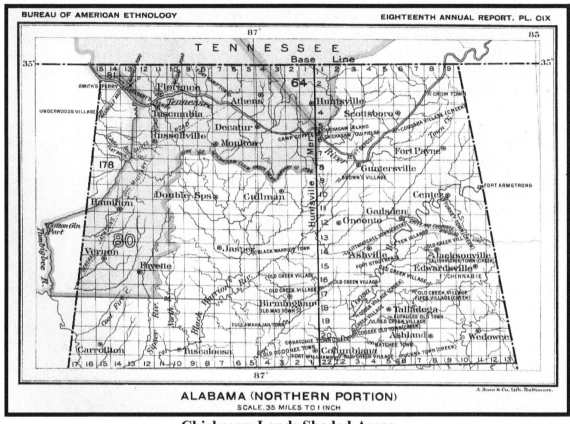

ALABAMA (NORTHERN PORTION)
SCALE, 35 MILES TO 1 INCH

Chickasaw Lands Shaded Areas

In the Chickasaw Boundary Treaty of January 10, 1786, the government established a boundary they viewed as belonging to the Chickasaw people; however, according to Phil Hawkins, Jr., the Chickasaws and Cherokees did not have clearly defined borders in the area along the Muscle Shoals: *In the treaty of this date with the Chickasaws the lands allotted them eastwardly shall be the lands allotted to the Choctaws and Cherokees to live and hunt on. In the conference which took place between the commissioners of the United States and the Chickasaws and Cherokees, it was apparent that their claims conflicted with each other on the ridge dividing the waters of Cumberland from those of Duck River and around to the Chickasaw Old Town Creek on Tennessee, thence southwardly, leaving the mountains above the Muscle Shoals on the south side of the river, and to a large stone or flat rock, where the Choctaw line joined with the Chickasaws. The journal of occurrences at the time was lodged with the papers of the old*

13

Congress, and probably was transferred to the office of Secretary of State. On the 7th of January, 1806, in a convention between the United States and Cherokees, on the part of the former by Mr. Dearborn, the United States engaged to use their best endeavors to fix a boundary between the Cherokees and Chickasaws, beginning at the mouth of Caney Creek, near the lower part of the Muscle Shoals, and to run up the said creek to its head, and in a direct line from thence to the flat stone or rock, the old corner boundary, the line between the Creeks and Cherokees east of Coosa River (Powell, et. al., 1887). The Chickasaws did not recognize the 1806 boundary and, at the death of Doublehead, demanded that the intruders on their lands at the Muscle Shoals be removed.

The Chickasaw stronghold was the upper Tombigbee River towns in northeastern Mississippi where they had defeated French incursions into their territory on three separate occasions by the mid 1700's. The stronghold of the Chickasaw in the upper Tombigbee River Valley lasted from the time before Desoto in 1540 all the way to Indian removal in the 1830's.

Shortly after the fight with the Cherokee in 1769, the Chickasaws moved west from the Chickasaw Old Fields beyond Caney Creek in the western portion of present-day Colbert County, Alabama. As the Chickasaws moved down the Tennessee River toward Mississippi, Doublehead and his followers moved into and occupied the Muscle Shoals. After conflicts over the mussel shoals ceased, the newly established United States government recognized the Chickasaw land claims east to Chickasaw Island in the middle of the river and north along the Flint River into the State of Tennessee encompassing the upper drainage of Elk River. From the Chickasaw Old Fields in the Tennessee River to the south, the Chickasaw claims followed the Huntsville Meridian to the Tennessee Divide, and then west along the High Town Path to Haleyville, Alabama. The boundary line then ran south along the Byler Ridge that separates the waters of the Warrior River to the east and the waters of the Tombigbee River Drainage to the west, and then due west into Mississippi as authorized by the Chickasaw Boundary Treaty of January 10, 1786, as seen in the map above; however, Doublehead and his Chickamauga warriors also claimed the area by occupation.

The Chickasaw were the first tribe of the Great Bend to abandon the Chickamauga confederacy in January 1781. At this time, the great Chickasaw Chief Piomingo and General James Robertson of the Cumberland settlements agreed to terms of peace. However, a few Chickasaws remained loyal to the Chickamauga confederacy and lived at Doublehead's Town near Brown's Ferry. These loyal Chickasaws continued to make raids with Doublehead and the Chickamauga.

14

Lower Cherokee (Iroquois)

Professor Henry Sale Halbert stated that, *"the Cherokee's belong to the Iroquois family, as is evidence by their language. Under the name Taligewi, they are first mentioned in the Delaware Migration Legend and lived in the upper Ohio Valley. After a long war, they were expelled from their country and driven southward. After moving southward, the maximum boundaries of the Cherokees once included southwest Virginia, the western part of North and South Carolina, north Georgia, east Tennessee, and the Tennessee Valley of north Alabama.*

Tradition and archaeology agree the Cherokee were occupants of the Tennessee Valley in North Alabama in prehistoric times. How long they have lived in this area is not known, but some time before 1650, (after Desoto's visit in 1540) they abandoned this region, and retired beyond the Cumberland and Sand Mountain, but reserving their abandoned country as a hunting ground".

Lower Cherokees under the leadership of Doublehead were living on the land along the Muscle Shoals at the time it was recognized as belonging to the Chickasaws by the United States on January 10, 1786; therefore, the Cherokees and Chickasaws had overlapping claims to the Great Bend of the Tennessee River until the Turkey Town Treaty of September 1816. Even though the claims overlapped, Doublehead controlled the Muscle Shoals of the Tennessee River from 1770 until his death in 1807.

During Doublehead's reign of the Lower Cherokee faction of the Chickamauga at the Muscle Shoals area, four major trading routes came from the east into the southern portion of the Tennessee Valley: 1) The High Town Path from Olde Charles Town, South Carolina ran the Tennessee Divide through Lawrence County, Alabama south of the shoals; 2) Coosa or Muscle Shoals Path traversed from Ten Islands on the Coosa River to Ditto's Landing south of Huntsville, Alabama through the Moulton Valley to Tuscumbia Landing; 3) Chickasaw Trail, came from the Chickasaw Old Fields to Moulton, to Russellville, then to Cotton Gin Port on the Tombigbee; and, 4) the South River Road, traveled by Reverend Patrick Wilson in 1803, followed the south side of the Tennessee River and passed adjacent to Doublehead's Town.

The Gaines Trace which was also a trade route from the Muscle Shoals at Melton's Bluff in Lawrence County, Alabama to Cotton Gin Port on the Tombigbee River was laid out by Captain Edmund Pendleton Gaines in December 1807, just four months after the death of Doublehead on August 9, 1807. Captain Gaines was married to Barbara Blount, the daughter of Governor William Blount of the Southwest Territory. Governor Blount was primarily responsible for making peace with Doublehead (Walker and Marshall, 2005).

Nina Leftwich states in *Two Hundred Years at the Shoals*, *"Both the French and the English contended for the Indian trade along the western waters; the French planted a post at Muscle Shoals before 1715. Because of the increasing importance of trade with the whites, the Cherokees planted villages near the Muscle Shoals area in the last quarter of the eighteenth century. There was Doublehead's village on the Tennessee and a large settlement* (Shoal Town) *at the mouth of Town Creek, extending a mile along the river and far up the creek"* (Leftwich, 1935).

Doublehead moved to the Lower Cherokee village described above, which is Shoal Town, located on Big Muscle Shoals of the Tennessee River between Big Nance (Path Killer's) Creek, Shoal Town Creek, and Blue Water Creek. He lived at Shoal Town from 1802 until his death on August 9, 1807. At Shoal Town, Doublehead had a large trading post or store that sold merchandise to the Chickasaws, Creeks, Shawnees, Cherokees, Yuchi, and white settlers leasing Doublehead's Reserve.

Tom Hatley also discusses early trade with the Cherokees along the Tennessee River, *"This **river road** was scarcely traveled in the years before 1715, because of the intercolonial and intercultural hostilities especially in the direction of Spanish Florida — which engaged the English during the first decade of the century....Though the colonists may have overestimated the bindings of trade, there is no doubt that joint Cherokee and Carolina trade expanded greatly, along with the burgeoning commerce of Charlestown, right up to the 1750's. Though rice had supplanted deerskins in export value, deerskin loadings remained high at the Charlestown docks, and a significant percentage of these were of Cherokee origin. During 1747-48 the value of shipments of deerskins (and other tribal commodities) roughly equaled the combined total of indigo, beef and pork, lumber, and naval stores....On the other hand a Charlestown alliance with the* (Lower Cherokee) *tribe would finally give Carolinians access to the long-sought **Tennessee River road** to the Mississippi"* (Hatley, 1995). The road Hatley is referring to is the South River Road adjacent to the Muscle Shoals and by Doublehead's home located in Doublehead's Town at the Brown's Ferry crossing of the Tennessee River.

Doublehead and the Lower Cherokees in the Big Bend of the Tennessee River Valley and the Chickasaws in the upper Tombigbee River watershed of northeastern Mississippi benefitted from English trade from Olde Charles Town. The majority of these traders were Scots-Irish men who had Indian wives while among the Cherokee and Chickasaw. For Doublehead it was no different, since his first two daughters married the same half-blood George Colbert who was the son of a Scots trader and lived at the Natchez Trace crossing of the Tennessee River. Doublehead's second two daughters married an Indian trader by the name of Samuel Riley and they lived near South West Point close to the junction of the Clinch River and Tennessee River in east Tennessee.

16

Chickamauga

The Chickamauga was a confederacy that was a combination of Yuchi, Delaware, Creek, Shawnee, Chickasaw, Lower Cherokees, mixed-bloods, and white sympathizers. Most of the white sympathizers were British agents of Scots-Irish ancestry who were supplying the Chickamauga with arms and ammunition in order to defeat the American colonists rebelling against the mother country England. John McDonald, one of the more famous British/Spanish agents, married a Cherokee half-blood Anne Shorey and lived at the mouth of Chickamauga Creek. Other agents/traders also had Indian wives and most were very loyal to their wife's people.

The Lower Cherokee of the Chickamauga faction split from the main Cherokee Nation primarily because of the tribe giving up large tracts of sacred hunting grounds in north middle Tennessee and Kentucky in 1775. The treaty relinquishing Cherokee claims to these hunting grounds was known as the Treaty of Sycamore Shoals or Henderson's Treaty. The treaty was strongly opposed by Dragging Canoe, Doublehead, John Watts, Jr., and other members of the Lower Cherokee faction of the Chickamauga; and, therefore was the primary reason for the start of the Chickamauga War.

The Chickamauga controlled most of northern Alabama and a large portion of middle and east Tennessee and northwest Georgia. The Upper Cherokee controlled most of north Georgia, western Carolinas, and a portion of east Tennessee. Dragging Canoe ruled over the Chickamauga in the five lower towns with his stronghold located on the Tennessee River at Nickajack Town west of Chattanooga, Tennessee. Over 100 miles to the southwest of Chattanooga at the Muscle Shoals of the Tennessee River, Doublehead reigned over the Chickamauga in the Great Bend Towns from present-day Decatur, Alabama to Florence, Alabama.

The first and the greatest Chickamauga chief, who led and strengthened the southeastern Indian alliance until his death, was Dragging Canoe. After Dragging Canoe died on March 1, 1792, half-blood John Watts, Jr. took over as chief of the Chickamauga; however, Watts did not enjoy the complete loyalty of the federation that had been established by Dragging Canoe. Doublehead filled the role as the supreme authority of the Chickamauga and ruled without submitting to the orders of other leaders in the federation. His great strength was the respect of the Chickasaw and the complete loyalty of the Creek faction of the Chickamauga. As a Chickamauga leader, Doublehead was not only feared by white settlers and politicians, but also by each tribal faction of the Indian confederacy and including the Upper Cherokees. He backed up his stature by vicious blood thirsty attacks on his enemies encroaching on his aboriginal hunting grounds and homelands.

Besides the Lower Cherokee, the Creeks were the largest force among the Chickamauga and were extremely loyal to Doublehead. The Creeks helped him establish himself as supreme ruler of the Muscle Shoals and Tennessee River Valley. The other major force of the Chickamauga was the Shawnee who seemed to show some loyalty to John Watts, Jr., but several Shawnee lived in Doublehead's Town at the head of the shoals. Another faction who fought with Doublehead on the Cumberland was the Chickasaws and a few of the Chickasaws also lived in Doublehead's Town. The Chickasaws also had their differences with the Creeks and some Cherokees, and they were the first tribe to officially abandon the confederacy at the beginning of 1781 by signing a peace treaty with the Cumberland settlements. Other members of the Chickamauga included the Delaware, Yuchi, Scots-Irish mixed bloods, and sympathetic whites who were related to the tribe through intermarriage or were British agents. Many of the mixed bloods, such as Bob Benge, did atrocious deeds in order to prove their loyalty to the Chickamauga.

The Chickamauga was a great Indian force to be reckoned with until the government began eroding its base by turning factions against each other. General James Robertson first turned the Chickasaw away from the Chickamauga Confederacy at a peace conference with Piomingo. Colonel Return J. Meigs and Governor William Blount finally convinced Doublehead to turn against his strongest faction of the Chickamauga-the Creeks. By the end of 1795, Doublehead appears to have split from his fellow Creeks, and thus his feared warrior status took a gradual and then rapid downfall ending in his assassination by his own people on August 9, 1807. However, the Creeks continued their relentless attacks on white settlers until their defeat at Horse Shoe Bend by General Andrew Jackson in March 1814. This decisive battle which was supported by the Cherokees spelled doom for all the southeastern Indian tribes and their eventual removal west of the Mississippi River by the late 1830's.

18

Doublehead's Family Tree

Genealogy is many times controversial and subject to disagreement, and this text on Doublehead's extended family is no different; therefore, this is a generally accepted family line most of which is based on factual knowledge with some information based on folklore. The following information was taken from Family Tree Maker, Roots Web Ancestry, archival microfilm, and numerous historical resources which have been utilized in organizing and writing this book. In addition, some of the information was incorporated from Kenneth Barnett Tankersley's _Native American Studies_ from Northern Kentucky University (2004-5), Joel Mize's _Unionists of the Warrior Mountains_ (2005), and William Lindsey McDonald's _Lore of the River_ (2007).

Archival microfilm from official government documents and letters of the time period were used and are probably the most accurate genealogical records. Many times, the dates of birth and sometimes death are at best educated guesses unless specifically recorded in archival documents; therefore, there is room for disagreement unless these dates are specified in time period historical literature. Also many generations of Indian descendants carried the same name for several different individuals and generations, and the Indian names of the same person were spelled as the person writing thought the sound of the name should be written; therefore, these two conditions create a lot of confusion in Indian genealogy.

Family History-Doublehead's Cherokee Ancestry

Doublehead was born about 1744 and died on August 9, 1807. He was also known as Talo Tiske, Tal Tsuska, Dsugweladegi, or Chuqualatague and was the son of Great Eagle (Willenawah or Tifftoya of Tanassee) and grandson of Moytoy. Great Eagle, who married AniWadi Woman, was born between 1711 and 1720. Among Great Eagle's children and Doublehead's siblings were:

Red Bird I

I.	Red Bird Carpenter, the oldest brother of Doublehead, was born about 1734 and was noted as first born of the Great Eagle. Red Bird and Doublehead married sisters-Susan and Creat Priber. Red Bird was given the white name of Aaron Brock. Other Cherokee names noted for Red Bird and his son by the same name (John Brock) were Tsisquaya, Dotsuwa, Totsuwha, Tochuwor, and Toochalar. The elder Red Bird was murdered along with his friend Cripple Willie by Ned Mitchell and John Livingston in early 1797. Arrest warrants were eventually issued and confirmed in letters from the Governor of Kentucky James Garrard and the Governor of Tennessee John Sevier between February 10, 1797, and April 1797.

Red Bird Historic Marker

T he first Red Bird lived through the Chickamauga War and probably fought with his younger brother Doublehead. Not only were Doublehead and Red Bird brothers, they also had the same in-laws by marrying the Priber sisters. Both men were from highly regarded Cherokee families and their children by the Pribers had the same blood as brothers and sisters being double first cousins. After the war, Red Bird wanted to live in peace and hunt his ancestral lands that he had fought to preserve, but the greed of some white men would be his demise.

Red Bird II

The younger Red Bird was born about 1755 and died after 1845. Red Bird II also fought with his father and Doublehead in the Chickamauga War and became a supporter of Doublehead after the war by signing treaties they had negotiated. He signed the Treaties with the Cherokee on October 25, 1805, and October 27, 1805, along with his uncle Doublehead. Young Red Bird also signed the Cotton Gin Treaty of January 7, 1806, along with two of his uncles, Sequechee and Doublehead. In addition, two of Red Bird's cousins, John Jolly and Taluntuskee, also signed the Cotton Gin Treaty. Red Bird and his uncles Doublehead and Sequeechee signed a letter on August 9, 1805, encouraging other Cherokee chiefs cooperate with the government in order to get needed trade items and implements. Red Bird, his uncle WawHatchy, and John Jolly signed the treaty of December 26, 1817, while living in Cherokee Territory in Arkansas; therefore, the young Red Bird migrated west probably with the 1,131 Cherokees in 1809 after the murder of his uncle Doublehead.

In his last will and testament signed on December 7, 1844, John Brock Red Bird Carpenter (Atsilagolanv-Fire Raven) stated he was 90 years old with no known living blood relatives. He left his estates in Kentucky, Tennessee, Virginia, and Missouri to John White, Burrell McLemore, and John McLemore. Red Bird stated all his brothers and sisters are now dead including Aaron, Jake, Mahalla, Jesse, Mary, and James, *and "it is time for me to join them along with our mother, Susan Priber, and our father"* (Red Bird). Susan was a sister to Doublehead's first wife, Creat Priber.

Wurteh

II.   Wurteh (Gi-Yo-Sti-Ko-Yo-He), oldest sister of Doublehead, was born about 1736 and married John Watts. John Watts was born about 1720 and was a Scots-Irish/Cherokee trader who lived in the Overhill Cherokee Towns on the Little Tennessee River. His father was George Watts and his mother was thought to be Cherokee Indian. Trader John Watts was the official government interpreter for the Cherokee Indians until his death in 1770.

John Watts was an Indian trader with the Cherokee prior to 1750 and also acted as an interpreter for them in dealing with the government. He was white trader who served Captain Demere as the interpreter during the building of the British Fort Loudon in 1756 through 1757. During this time, he was accused of stirring up trouble between the Cherokees and the white settlers. In a letter from Littleton to Demere, Littleton says, "I'm well convinced that this talk proceeded from something that was told the Indians by John Elliot and John Watts. Watts speaks their language well. Elliott and Watts is a couple of dangerous people" (Brown, 1938).

John Watts was first hired by Christian Gist to work for the Virginia Land Company. He was known as a Virginia trader and they worked out of Olde Charles Town, South Carolina. Both Watts and Gist became the grandfathers of Sequoyah. In addition, he was the father of Chief John Watts, Jr., who became the second chief of the powerful Chickamauga Confederacy.

John and Wurteh had at least six half-blood children of Scots-Irish and Cherokee lineage. The children of John and Wurteh were quarter Scots-Irish and three quarters Cherokee: Nannie Watts, Wurteh Watts, John Watts, Jr., Malachi (Unacata) Watts, Garrett Watts, and Thomas (Big Tom) Watts.

Nannie Watts

A. Nannie Watts (one-quarter Scots-Irish and three quarters Cherokee) was born about 1748 and married George Lowery, who was full-blooded Scots-Irish and was born in Scotland in 1740. They had seven children who were five eighths Scots-Irish and three eighths Cherokee. These children would pass for white as easily as they would be counted as Cherokee.

George and Nannie's children were: 1) Major John Lowery born about 1768, died in 1817, and married Elizabeth Shorey (mixed); 2) Major George Lowery, Jr. born on the Little Tennessee River in Tennessee about 1770, died October 20, 1852, and married Annie Fields and Lucinda (Lucy) Benge; 3) Sallie Lowery was born about 1776 and married a Baldridge, Gourd, Jr., Rope Staydt, and Jack Cersingle; 4) Elizabeth Lowery was born about 1777, died May 18, 1839, at Calhoun, Tennessee, and married a Walker; 5) Jennie Lowery was born about 1780; 6) Aky Lowery was born about 1782; and, 7) Nellie Lowery was born about 1782.

Wurteh Watts

B. Wurteh Watts had the same first name as her mother and was quarter Scots-Irish and three fourths Cherokee. She was born about 1750 in Tasagi Town in the old Cherokee Nation in east Tennessee.

Wurteh Watts-First Marriage

Wurteh Watts first married Robert Due, who was full Scots-Irish, and they had one son John Jolly (Ahuludegi) who was five-eighths Scots-Irish. John Jolly moved west to join the Old Settlers in 1818 and shortly after his arrival was elected Chief of the western Cherokees after the death of his half-brother Tahlonteeskee Benge in the Spring of 1819.

1. John Jolly (Ahuludegi, Ooluntuskee) was one-quarter Cherokee and three fourths Scots-Irish. He was born about 1763 and died December 1838. In 1810, John Jolly adopted Sam Houston (The Raven), who was born March 2, 1793, in Rockbridge, Virginia and died July 24, 1863, in Huntsville, Walker County, Texas. In 1830, Sam married Tiana Rogers, a Cherokee woman who was the niece of John Jolly. As a young man, Sam lived on Hiwassee Island with his adopted family of John Jolly and stayed several years with the Cherokees in Tennessee. Sam eventually moved to Arkansas where his

22

adopted father John Jolly lived and later to Texas where he helped win their independence and became the President of the new republic of Texas.

John Jolly married Sarah who died about 1824. John and Sarah had six children: 1) Girt Jolly was born in 1795, died in1825, married Naomi; 2) Rachel Jolly was born about 1816; 3) Sallie Jolly was born about 1826 and married Isacc Upton; 4) Coleesta (Golista) Jolly was born about 1820 in Arkansas and married Looney Price; 5) Price Jolly was born about 1822; and 6) Betty Jolly was born about 1824. John Jolly also married Elizabeth Emory and they had two children: John Jolly, Jr.; and, William Jolly.

The following story of John Jolly written by James A. Bullman was published in "The Lunch Counter" on Sunday, April 13, 2008: *John Jolly was born in Tennessee (Ta ni si) of a mixed family. His father a Scots, his mother (half) Cherokee. Not much can be found about John Jolly's early years. It is known that he had a trading post on Hiwassee Island at the meeting point of the Hiwassee River and the Tennessee River and that he was considered wealthy. At this time, a young white boy, who had been born in Virginia, showed up. After this boy's father died his family had moved to Tennessee. They started a farm and a store. The young lad of 15 had rebelled against the work and his overbearing brothers. The boy ran to Hiwassee Island and the Cherokee.*

This boy was Sam Houston, the same Sam Houston of Texas fame. The young Sam Houston was adopted by John Jolly as his son. Jolly gave him the Cherokee name Raven (Go La Nu). The Cherokee lifestyle suited young Houston. He adopted Cherokee dress and learned the Cherokee language. In 1818 Houston became a federal agent with the help of John Jolly's influence, later governor of Tennessee and later still, president of the Republic of Texas.

The population of Hiwassee Island ranged from 180 to 300 people with cattle, horses and hogs. John Jolly having more money than most lived in a two story frame house and had his trading post. Jolly's brother was Tolontuskee (Tahlonteeskee); one of several Cherokee chiefs who voluntarily moved west to what would become Arkansas.

In the treaty of 1805 John had signed a treaty giving up much Cherokee land; again on Jan 7, 1806 John signed another treaty again giving up Cherokee land. The treaty of 1817 promised land in the west equal to land given up in the east. The problem with this treaty was it did not guarantee the Cherokee rights to the new land in the west.

Chief John Jolly (Ooluntuskee)

In 1817 (actually moved in 1809) John's brother (Tahlonteeskee) moved west with his followers and settled in what is now central Arkansas along the Arkansas River. In 1818 John Jolly and his people joined Tolontuskee on the Arkansas River. The 1817 treaty had given most of Northwest Arkansas to the Cherokee who willingly moved west but Cherokee rights to the land were not spelled out clearly.

In time John Jolly's homestead in Arkansas became a prosperous venture with a log h ouse, many cleared fields, orchards and cattle raising facilities. A missionary named Cephas Washburn had built a school near Jolly and depended on his support for continued success. Indian agents and government officials visited many times hoping to use Jolly's influence. John Jolly has been described as an easy going person who dressed in the manner of white settlers, understood English and may have also understood French. John was also known as a spokesman for his people.

In 1819 with the death of his brother Tolontuskee, John Jolly became the principal civic chief. As principal civic chief John Jolly dealt with civil affairs. He was also leader of domestic affairs for the Arkansas Cherokee people. He also represented the Arkansas Cherokee with the U.S. Government.

In 1824 the Cherokee in Arkansas reorganized the tribal government to reflect the U.S. government and John Jolly was made president by general consensus. As leader of the Arkansas Cherokee, John Jolly was always in the forefront when it came to treaty rights, taking on both the U.S. government and Arkansas territorial authorities. When the governor of Arkansas asked about sale of Cherokee lands in Arkansas he was told bluntly by Jolly that no Cherokee land was for sale and the U.S. government still owed the Cherokee money under the terms of the 1817 treaty.

For most of his time in Arkansas, Jolly used every diplomatic trick he could find to fend off white settlers and the U.S. government as both wanted the Cherokee out of Arkansas. In 1828 the Cherokee in Arkansas finally gave up their land and farms and were forced to Indian Territory, present day Oklahoma. John Jolly died in December 1838 near what is now Webbers Falls, Oklahoma (Bullman, 2008).

Wurteh Watts-Second Marriage

Wurteh Watts' second husband was Nenetooyah (Bloody Fellow) and they had no children.

Wurteh Watts-Third Marriage

Wurteh Watts' third husband was Trader John Benge, a Scotsman, who was born about 1734 in Albemarle, Virginia. John Benge's father was Thomas Benge, and his mother was Martha Martin. They had six children who were five eighths Scots and one-fourth Cherokee. Wurteh Watts' sons would fight with their great uncle Doublehead in the Chickamauga War.

2. Richard Benge was born before 1764 and was killed by Robertson in 1813. He married Wo-Di-Yo-Hi and they had five children: 1) Tsa-Wa-Yu-Ga Benge was born about 1808; 2) Nancy Benge was born about 1810 and died after 1837; 3) Peggy Benge was born about 1812; 4) Richard Benge, Jr. was born about 1814 and married Polly Watts; and, 5) Patsy Benge was born about 1806, died about 1855, and married a Shaver, who was born about 1800.

3. Robert (Bob, Bench, Colonel, Captain) Benge was born about 1766 probably at the village of Toquo, on the Little Tennessee River in Monroe County, Tennessee. Some historians say the Robert Benge married Black Fox's daughter, and some say he married Jennie Lowery and they had eight children: 1) Eliza; 2) Chief John (Wagon Master) Benge was born about 1787, and he married Run After (Ganelugi) McLemore and Quatie Conrad. John Benge led the "Benge Detachment" during removal to the west; 3) Mary (Polly, Ooloosta) who was born about 1790 and married John Baldridge; 4) Robin; 5) McLemore; 6) Young; 7) Pickens; and, 8) Sarah.

During his years on the war path, Bob Benge personally took some 45 scalps. He was ambushed and killed by Lieutenant Vincent Hobbs on April 9, 1794, at Stone Gap, Virginia. Robert Benge's red headed scalp was delivered to the Governor of Virginia Henry Lee III, then presented to President George Washington, and wound up in the Smithsonian on display for many years.

4. Martin (Utana, The Tail) Benge was named after his mother's family Martin. He was born about 1768 and died 1838 in Virginia. He married Eliza Lowery a sister to his brother's wife, Jennie Lowery. Martin lived for a while at Wills Town in DeKalb County, Alabama.

Some genealogists say that there were two cousins of Robert (Bench) and Martin (The Tail) who had the same names, and they were the men who married Jennie and Eliza Lowery. This is a possibility since many Indian people had the same names, and the same names were carried through many different generations.

5. Tahlonteeskee (Taluntuskee, Tashliske, Talohuskee, Talluhuskee) Benge was born about 1770 and died in the Spring of 1819. He lived to Shoal Town in present-day Lauderdale County, Alabama in the Big Bend of the Tennessee River. In the summer of 1808, he sought permission from President Thomas Jefferson to take some 1,131 Chickamauga Cherokees to Arkansas. His group became known as the "Old Settlers or Cherokees West" and left in 1809 primarily because of they were relatives, friends, or loyal supporters of Doublehead. Taluntuskee also stated that he feared assassination like his uncle Doublehead had received because he had signed some of the same treaties and received benefits as Doublehead. After moving west of the Mississippi River, Tahlonteeskee became Chief of the western Cherokees or Old Settlers.

6. Lucinda "Lucy" Benge was born about 1776 in Cherokee Nation, Tennessee and died on October 10, 1846, at Greenleaf Plantation, Tahlequah District in Cherokee County, Oklahoma. She first married John Brown (Drowning Bear, Yonaguska) who was born about 1762 and died November 20, 1858. Her second marriage was to half-blood Cherokee Major George Lowery, who was born about 1770 and died October 20, 1852. George was the uncle to Bob Benge's wife Jennie Lowery and Martin Benge's wife Eliza Lowery. Lucy and George had several children: 1) James Lowery; 2) Charles Lowery; 3) Archibald Lowery; 4) Washington Lowery; 5) Susan Lowery was born on February 25, 1793, and married Andrew Ross; 6) George Lowery III; 7) Lydia was born in 1803 and married Milo Hoyt; 8) Rachel Lowery; 9) Anderson Pierce Lowery; and 10) John Lowery.

Major George Lowery, II

Major George Lowery, one of the most distinguished citizens of the Cherokee Nation. He was born at Tuskegee Village on the Little Tennessee River near Tellico Blockhouse about 1770. He was one of the Cherokee delegations

26

headed by John Watts who visited President Washington at Philadelphia in 1791 or 1792. He was captain of one of the Light Horse companies appointed to enforce the laws of the Nation in 1808 and 1810; a member of the National Committee organized in 1814, and one of the delegations that negotiated the treaty of 1819 in Washington...and was elected assistant principal chief..., an office he held for many years. At the time of his death he was a member of the Executive Council. He died October 20, 1852, at the age of eighty two. The National Council being in session at the time, on hearing of his death, passed resolutions providing for his interment in a burying ground near Tahlequah and for funeral services on the occasion... His funeral services were preached on Thursday by the Rev. S. A. Worcester. His passing brought sorrow throughout the Cherokee Nation (Worcester, 1853).

Major George Lowery, II

7.   Joseph Benge

Wurteh Watts-Fourth Marriage

Wurteh Watts' fourth husband was Colonel Nathanial Gist who was born October 15, 1733 in Baltimore, Maryland. Nathaniel Gist died at about 80 years old in Kentucky as reported by Samuel C. Williams (1937). *"On his Kentucky (land) grant Colonel Gist established his home, "Canewood," which was to become noted for the beauty of its embellishment and for its hospitality. He died there about the close of the War of 1812."* Nathaniel was the son of Christopher Gist and Sarah Howard and was of Scots-Irish lineage.

Nathanial Gist (son of Christopher Gist) first appeared among the Cherokees as a messenger of Governor Dinwiddie in 1775. Following the French and Indian War, he formed a trading partnership with Richard Pearis and lived in the Cherokee Country for several years. During that time, he took as his wife, Wurteh...and became the father of Sequoyah (Brown, 1938).

...by a Kentucky family it is claimed...Sequoyah's father was Nathaniel Gist, son of the scout (Christopher Gist) who accompanied (George) Washington

on his memorable excursion to the Ohio. As the story goes, Nathaniel Gist was captured by the Cherokee at Braddock's defeat (1755) and remained a prisoner with them for six years, during which time he became the father of Sequoyah. On his return to civilization, he married a white woman in Virginia, by whom he had other children, and afterward remove to Kentucky, where Sequoyah, then a Baptist preacher, frequently visited them and was always recognized by the family as his son (Mooney, 1900).

Other historical documents indicate that Nathaniel Gist was an agent serving under British Commander Cameron who was supplying the Cherokees with arms and ammunition to fight the white settlers and American soldiers. The following was given by Samuel C. Williams (1937):

Too, as we shall later see, in the following year Gist wrote to the Cherokees reminding them that he had on this occasion, in 1776, warned them, before they went to war against the whites, against the step...When, after the three contemporaneous attacks on the upper country settlers at Island Flats, on the Watauga and in Carter's valley, and in the latter part of the same year Colonel William Christian began his retaliatory campaign against the Cherokees, his instructions from Governor Patrick Henry were to insist upon the Indians "giving up to justice all persons amongst them who had been concerned in bringing on the present war, particularly Stewart [Stuart], Cameron and Gist."

When Christian, on the march towards the Cherokee towns, reached the French Broad River, Gist came in from the Indian side under a flag of truce to the camp of the colonel. He reported that 1,000 of the Cherokees from the Carolina side of the mountains had joined the Overhills, who would not give battle until the troops crossed the Little Tennessee. Christian wrote to Governor Henry (Oct. 15, 1776) "I judge the flag was only an excuse for him to get with me. I believe he is sorry for what he has done. I did intend to put him in irons, but the manner of his coming I believe will prevent me. The officers tell me that the camp is in great confusion about him; some think that there are many favorable circumstances attending him; many are for killing him—of the last the greatest part. I spoke but little to him and don't know whether he wants to go back or not."

Two of the soldiers under Col. Christian left accounts of this incident. Benjamin Sharp stated that the border men "were so exasperated at him that almost every one that mentioned his name would threaten his life, yet Christian conveyed him through the settlements unmolested, and he went to the headquarters of Washington, where I presume the former friendship was renewed. He became a zealous Whig." John Redd stated that "when Gist first came in to Christian he was

28

viewed in a very suspicious light; he was thought to be a spy. But the prejudice against him soon wore off and he became very popular."

Gist went to Virginia and promptly laid a memorial before the governor and the council of state. The order entered by the council, Dec. 17, 1776, as is follows:

"Capt. Nathaniel Gist having presented a memorial to the Governor lamenting the suspicions which he fell under with several of his countrymen, as having acted an inimical part against America by aiding and abetting the Cherokees in their late hostile conduct and desiring his excellency and the council would make inquiry into the same, as a preparatory step either to his acquittal or consign punishment, the board accordingly considered the several depositions transmitted by Colonel Christian to the governor and which had been laid before the general assembly, and moreover examined Colonel William Russell, Major Evan Shelby and Isaac Thomas, upon oath; and, upon the whole matter are of opinion that Captain Gist is a friend of his country and was acting in that character most effectually when he was suspected of encouraging the Indian hostilities."

It no doubt gratified Gen. Washington to have the record of an old friend thus cleared; and on Jan. 11, 1777, Gist was appointed a colonel of a regiment in the continental line. The newly-made colonel was sent south by Washington to use his influence in bringing the Cherokees into the promised treaty at Fort Patrick Henry, Long Island. Arriving at the island on March 28, Gist sent by an Indian messenger a talk to the chiefs, a copy of which is to be found in the Library of Congress, Manuscript Division (Williams, 1937).

Therefore, Gist was living among the Cherokees at the time that George Gist was conceived and probably born in 1776. Most all historical documents agree that Nathaniel Gist was the father of Sequoyah and even some important Cherokee leaders of the time as seen in the following:

The Tassel (Kahn-yah-tah-hee), uncle of the Indian consort of Gist, replied:" Here is my friend and brother (pointing to Colonel Gist) whom I look upon as one of my own people. He is going to leave me and travel into a far country, but I hope he'll return. Here is one of my people, the Pigeon, that will accompany him, but I do not know of many more that will. He was once over the great water where he could not see which way he was going; but this journey will be all by land and he will think nothing of the fatigue."

Sequoyah

At the end of the treaty negotiated at Fort Patrick Henry in 1777, above the signatures, appears this "memorandum before signing": "The Tassel yesterday objected against giving up the Great [Long] Island opposite to Fort Henry to any person or country whatever except Colonel Gist, for whom and themselves it was reserved by the Cherokees. The Raven did the same this day in behalf of the Indians and desired that Colonel Gist sit down upon it when he pleased, as it belongs to him, and them, to hold good talks on." Colonel Gist aided while on the treaty ground in celebrating the first July 4 anniversary ever held in Tennessee (Williams 1937).

Wurteh Watts and Colonel Nathaniel Gist had one son George Gist, also known as Sequoyah, who was three eighths Cherokee and five eighths Scots-Irish.

8. George Gist (Sequoyah) was born about 1776 just outside Fort Loudon in Tuskegee Village on the Little Tennessee River, in Monroe County, Tennessee. He married Sally Waters and they had the following children: 1) Teesey, 2) George II, 3) Polly, and 4) Richard. Sequoyah also married Utiyu (Uckteeyah) Langley and they had Eyagu, Oolootsa, and Guneki. Sequoyah died in Mexico in the summer of 1842 looking for lost Cherokees.

John Watts, Jr.

C. John Watts, Jr. (Young Tassel, Kunoskeskie) was born about 1752 in Wills Town, Alabama and died in 1808 at Wills Town. He was elected Chief of the Chickamauga Cherokee after the death of Dragging Canoe on March 1, 1792. He was married to Wurtagua. She was born about1760 and was the daughter of Attakullakulla and Ollie. He married the second time to Kay-I-Oh born about 1765, daughter of Hanging Maw and Betsy. John Watts, Jr., and Kay-I-Oh probably one daughter. 1) Joseph Watts was born June 25, 1765 and died April

30

14, 1874. 2) Nancy Watts was born about 1780 and was killed by whites on June 16, 1793.

Chief John Watts was described by Governor Blount as, "unquestionably the leading man in his Nation. He possessed a talent for making friends, red and white." William Martin, son of General Joseph Martin, said of him, "He was one of the finest looking men I ever saw, large of stature, bold and magnanimous, a great friend of my father's." Major G. W. Sevier states, "He was a noble looking Indian, always considered a generous and honorable enemy", and other pioneers paid high tribute to, "his engaging personality" (Brown, 1938).

Malachi Watts

D. Malachi Watts (Unacata, Uninagadihi, White Man Killer) was born about 1754 and died about 1804. He married Ann or Maw and they had several daughters: 1) Frances Watts married a Garrett; 2) Sally Watts married a Benge; 3) Ann Watts married a Dabbs; 4) Sarah Watts married Willie Alsobrook; 5) Jemima Watts married a Wood; 6) Polly Watts married a Phillips; and, 7) Elizabeth Watts married Clement Phillips.

Garrett Watts

E. Garrett Zachariah Watts was born January 8, 1756, and died February 6, 1838. Garrett married Annie (Annis) Selp who was born in 1766 and died in 1855. They had thirteen children: 1) Garrett Watts, Jr., born about 1788; 2) Solomon Watts 1795-1870; 3) Clinton Watts 1807-1861; 4) John Zachariah Watts, born about 1785; 5) William Jefferson Watts born about 1787; 6) Nancy Watts born about 1790; 7) Malachi Watts was born January 9, 1793, and died December 16, 1871; 8) Martha Matilda Watts born about 1800; 9) Vincent Vinson Watts was born January 12, 1805, and died May 10, 1879; 10) Mary H. Watts born about 1805; 11) Annie (Annis) born on January 9, 1809; 12) Jefferson J. Watts, 1815-1817; and, 13) Malinda born about 1803.

Thomas Watts

F. Thomas Watts (Big Tom) was born about 1764 in Virginia and died in 1832 in Benton, Alabama. He had four children: 1) John Watts, born about 1799 and died about 1848; 2) Ludwell P. Watts, born April 24, 1808, died about 1877, and married Mary Myrick; 3) Vinson Thorington Watts, born October 3, 1812, died July 24, 1883, in Greenville, Butler County, Alabama, and married Martha

Ann Harris; and, 4) Agnes Watts, born about 1817, died about 1855, and married Phillip Voeglin.

Old Tassel

III.   Old Tassel (Utsidsata, Corn Tassel, Onitositah, Thistle Head, Coatohee, Kaiyahtahee), Chief of the Tsalagi, was married to Hanging Maw's sister, born about 1738 and died at Chilhowee, Tennessee in June 1788. He was murdered while attending peace talks held by James Hubbard, an officer of Colonel John Sevier. Old Tassel and Hanging Maw's sister had Doublehead Tassel; Daughter married Chisholm, and Little/Young Tassel.

Doublehead Tassel

A.   Doublehead Tassel, born about 1760 and was murdered by John Kirk, Jr. along with his father Old Tassel in June 1788.

Daughter

B.   Daughter of Old Tassel married Ignatius Chisholm the son of John D. Chisholm. She was the mother of Jesse Chisholm of the famed Chisholm Trail of the west.

Little/Young Tassel

C.   Little/Young Tassel was born in1758.

Old Tassel would fight with his brother Doublehead in the Chickamauga War and had the highest respect of Creek Chief Alexander McGillivray. He would forge the way for his younger brother Doublehead to command large numbers of Creek warriors and earn their complete loyalty and respect. McGillivray was extremely upset on hearing the news of his friend and ally Old Tassel.

Prior to his murder by John Sevier's men, Old Tassel told that he had fought against John Sevier several times and actually tried to kill Sevier. Old Tassel had a letter written to Sevier and said, *"Tell John Sevier these words. Many times we have fought and Old Tassel has tried to kill you. But always Old Tassel has been able to say of John Sevier, he is a good man: He speaks the Old Beloved Speech. I sorrow because for a little while I doubted John Sevier. Now, because you have sent goods, I know that John Sevier does indeed speak the Old Beloved Speech.*

John Sevier is a good man." It appears that Old Tassel's trust in the words of John Sevier cost him his life.

Standing Turkey

IV.   Standing Turkey (Gvnagadoga) was born about 1738 and died about 1785. He was the great nephew of Old Hop and succeeded his uncle as chief of the Cherokee Nation for a brief period. Old Hop, also known as Standing Turkey, died in August 1761 in Chota, the Overhill Towns Cherokee Capital, on the Little Tennessee River in Monroe County, Tennessee.

The young Standing Turkey was chief of the Cherokee Nation for only a short period in 1761. It was the young Standing Turkey who led a four day assault on Fort Loudoun on the Little Tennessee River in 1760. He went to Loudon with Henry Timberlake in 1762-1763 and signed the Royal Proclamation of 1763 which was an agreement with the Crown of England to allow no more white people or settlements west of the Appalachians. In 1782 he was one of a party of the Chickamauga on a diplomatic mission to the Spanish at Fort St. Louis in Missouri to get arms and to receive permission to emigrate west from the Governor of Spanish Louisiana.

Standing Turkey-Doublehead's Brother

Standing Turkey, also known as Cunne Shote or Kunagadoga, succeeded his uncle, Kanagatucko, or Old Hop, as First Beloved Man of the Cherokee upon the latter's death in 1760. Pro-French like his uncle, he steered the Cherokee into war with the British colonies of South Carolina and Virginia in the aftermath of the

*murders of several Cherokee leaders held hostage at Fort Prince George at the
edge of the Lower Towns of the Cherokee in what is now western South Carolina.
He held office until the end of the Anglo-Cherokee War in 1761, when he was
deposed in favor of Attakullakulla.*

*He was one of three Cherokee leaders to go with Henry Timberlake to
London in 1762-1763, the others being Ostenaco and Pigeon. In 1782, he was one
of a party of Cherokee which joined the Lenape (Delaware), Shawnee, and
Chickasaw in a diplomatic visit to the Spanish at Fort St. Louis in the Missouri
country in see king a new avenue of obtaining arms and other assistance in the
prosecution of their ongoing conflict with the Americans in the Ohio Valley. The
group of Cherokee by Standing Turkey sought and received permission to settle in
Spanish Louisiana, in the region of the White River* (Tanner, 1978).

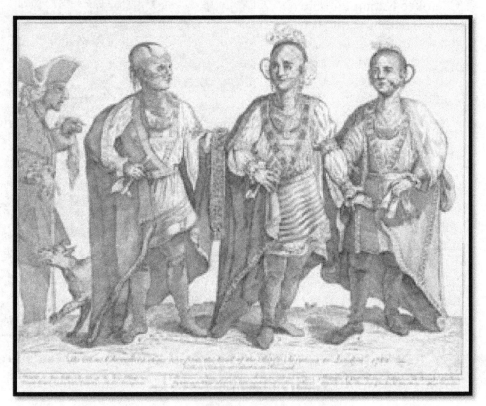

Standing Turkey, Pigeon, and Ostenaco

Standing Turkey, the brother of Doublehead, and members of the
Chickamauga confederacy were accompanied by factions of the Lower Cherokee,
Delaware, Shawnee, and Chickasaw to seek arms and ammunition to carry on their

34

war against white settlers encroaching on their ancestral hunting grounds and homelands. According to the above reference in the year 1782, Doublehead's confederacy was still strong and contained factions of all the tribes even though Chickasaw Chief Piomingo had signed a peace agreement in 1781 with General James Robertson of the Cumberland settlements. It is not sure how many rifles and the amount of ammunition, powder, and military supplies the Chickamauga confederacy received from the Spanish. Standing Turkey died within three years after his meeting with members of the Chickamauga confederacy and the Spanish. The circumstances of Standing Turkey's death are not known, but for sure he was fighting with his brother Doublehead against the Cumberland settlers.

Doublehead

V.   Doublehead (Tal-tsuska) was born about 1744 and died August 9, 1807. (See Doublehead's family below)

Pumpkin Boy

VI.   Pumpkin Boy (Eyahchutlee, Iyahuwagiatsutsa) married Chaueukah, born about 1746. He was shot and killed by John Sevier's men after being spotted during a scouting encounter at Ish's Station in 1793. He was scouting for the raid that was to take place at Knoxville; however, it wound up being Cavett's Station where Doublehead took out his revenge for Pumpkin Boy's death. Pumpkin Boy and his wife had one daughter, Catherine.

Catherine Pumpkin Boy

A. Catherine Pumpkin Boy married a Spencer. On June 8, 1838, Catherine gave a sworn testimony of Doublehead's estate at the time of his death. She states that she lived with her uncle Doublehead's family about 12 years and was about 19 years old when Doublehead was killed.

Sequechee

VII.   Sequechee (Sequechu, Sequichee) was born 1748 and died about 1816. In a letter dated August 9, 1807, Captain Addison B. Armstead of Hiwassee Garrison specifically mentioned Sequechee as Doublehead's brother. Sequechee also signed the Cotton Gin Treaty of January 7, 1806, along with his nephew Red Bird and his brother Doublehead. Sequechee also signed a letter with his brother Doublehead and his nephew Red Bird on August 9, 1805.

Nancy

VIII. Nancy (Nani) who married the Badger, born about 1750. Nancy's death is not known, but she was mentioned in a letter from John D. Chisholm from Darnelle Rock on the Arkansas River on June 28, 1812. In microcopy 208, roll 5, and number 2846, the following statement identifies that Nancy is still alive: *"Lost nearly all my property. Two Negroes ran away in possession of big Nance, Doublehead's sister. I have been constantly with Talluhuskee and his party."* Big Nance Creek in present-day Lawrence County, Alabama, was named after Doublehead's sister, Nancy.

WahHatch

IX. Wah-hatch (Wah-hatih, Wah-hatihi, WawHatchy, WahHatchie, Warhatchee) was mentioned by his niece Catherine Spencer, daughter of Pumpkin Boy, that he was the brother of Doublehead in an affidavit given June 8, 1838. He was also mentioned by his nephew Bird Tail Doublehead, son of Doublehead, as a brother of his father in an affidavit given June 21, 1838. His date of death and birth is not known. WawHatchy signed a treaty with the Cherokee on December 26, 1817, while living in Arkansas Cherokee Territory. There is a community in Lauderdale County, Alabama just north of Florence called Wah-hatchie. The community is the namesake of Doublehead's younger brother and lies within the old Doublehead's Reserve.

Ocuma

X. Ocuma was born about 1750 and married John Melton, an Irishman, about 1780. According to microcopy 208, roll 7, and number 3229, she wrote a letter to Colonel Return J. Meigs about her husband John Melton dying on June 7, 1815 (See letter under John Melton section). According to Anne N. Royall's *Letters from Alabama 1817-1822*, they had several children with most marrying white people. John and Ocuma Melton's children were half Irish and half Cherokee, and therefore were Celtic-Indian mixed blood members of the Cherokee Nation.

Charles Melton

A. Charles Melton founded the town of Meltonsville in east Alabama after the Turkey Town Treaty of 1816 took the lands at Melton's Bluff from the Cherokees. Oliver D. Street in *Indians of Marshall County* refers to Charles Melton as an Indian from Melton's Bluff who settled Meltonsville in Marshall County, Alabama. Charles moved east after the Turkey Town Treaty of September 1816 abolished his claims at the "Bluff". In the Spring of 1816, Charles ran a trading post at Melton's Bluff and on a few occasions traded with General John Coffee who was surveying for the treaty cessions.

David Melton

B. David Melton signed the deed on November 22, 1816, that gave General Andrew Jackson all the Cherokee land at Melton's Bluff. The lands claimed by David Melton's family were given to Jackson in the first legal deed to white people in present-day Lawrence County, Alabama. Jackson kept the plantation until 1827.

Lewis Melton

C. Lewis Melton was the father of Moses Melton, according to microcopy 208, roll 3, and number 1689. Moses Melton had equal shares to land with Charles Hicks that was located just west of Melton's Bluff. Moses Melton, the grandson of John Melton, is listed in the Cotton Gin Treaty of 1806 as an Indian.

Elick Melton

D. Elick Melton signed a letter with The Gourd asking for Negro Fox to be returned to the Cherokees after members of the Burleson family attacked and killed three of their Cherokee people. These Cherokee men were killed at Mouse Town which was located on the border of present-day Lawrence County and Morgan County, Alabama at the mouth of Fox's Creek and the Tennessee River.

Thomas Melton

E. Thomas Melton is found in the 1820 United States Census of Lawrence County, Alabama. He is also mentioned as a son of John Melton in William Lindsey McDonald's, *Lore of the River* (2007).

James Melton

F. James Melton, according to Colonel James Edmonds Saunders, *Early Settlers of Alabama* (1899), was hired as a keel boat guide for an early Lawrence County, Alabama land speculator known as Malcolm Gilchrist. Today, the Gilchrist estate is one of the largest tracts of private property in the county. Also, Ms. Barbara Melton a fifth great granddaughter of James Melton still lives in Moulton, Lawrence County, Alabama.

Merida Melton

G. Merida Melton is also found in the 1820 United States Census of Lawrence County, Alabama. Merida is also mentioned as a child of John Melton in William Lindsey McDonald's, *Lore of the River* (2007).

Rhea's Wife Melton

H. Rhea's wife was the daughter of John Melton and Ocuma. Her name is not given, but on January 12, 1818, Anne N. Royall's *Letters from Alabama 1817-1822* talks about John Melton's son-in-law Rhea. Rhea, a white man, stated that he had guided boats through the Shoals for some 15 years. On January 14, 1818, Royall also tells about John Melton's half-blood daughter (Rhea's Wife) leaving Melton's Bluff for lands in the west. Royall says that Rhea's wife left Melton's Bluff last fall for Indian Territory in Arkansas which would have been the Fall of 1817.

Ulauhatchy

XI. Ulauhatchy was listed as a brother of Doublehead in a sworn testimony by Doublehead's son, Bird Tail Doublehead on June 21, 1838.

Doublehead's Family Genealogy

Doublehead was born in the Cherokee Nation around 1744 in Stearns, McCreary County, Kentucky. He was described by Colonel Return Jonathan Meigs in a letter to Benjamin Hawkins on February 13, 1805.

"He is a man of small stature, compact and well formed, very dark skin, small piercing black eyes, the fixture of which when engaged in conversation are as immovable

38

as diamonds set in metal and seem to indicate clearly that he comprehends the subject and in his reply to an address will omit nothing that has been said. He is occasionally guilty of intemperance and then off his guard, and if he considers himself insulted the explosion of his passion resembles that of gunpowder."

Creat Priber-First Marriage

Doublehead was believed to be married at least five times and possibly more. His first wife was Creat (Drags Blanket) Priber, half German and half Cherokee, who was born between 1735 and 1740 in a Cherokee town at Tellico Plains in Monroe County, Tennessee. Creat Priber was the daughter of Christian Gottlieb Priber (Anglo-German) who was born on March 21, 1697, and Clogittah (Cherokee) who was the daughter of the great Cherokee Chief Moytoy. Clogittah was born between 1705 and 1720 and died about 1790. Clogittah was the aunt of Doublehead; therefore, Creat Priber was Doublehead's first cousin.

Christian Gottlieb Priber

Christian Gottlieb Priber, the father-in-law to Doublehead, was such an important figure among the Cherokee, it is necessary to discuss his life and beliefs that were carried out to some degree by Doublehead and the Chickamauga. Priber believed in a united Indian alliance and attempted to establish a confederacy with the Creek Nation as the Chickamauga eventually succeeded. Doublehead in some degree accomplished his father-in-law's dream by commanding a strong alliance of Creek warriors during the Chickamauga War. Doublehead's older brother Red Bird married Susan Priber who was the daughter of Christian G. Priber.

Christian Gottleib Priber, a Utopian Socialist (Black Robe or Jesuit), was born in Saxony, Germany on March 21, 1697. On June 13, 1735, he petitions London to be allowed to leave the country on the next ship to Georgia in America. He left a wife and four children in Saxony when he was forced to leave the country, they would not go with him. Priber said, *"I was married to Christiane Dorothea Hoffman in Zittau, Germany and we had four girls together. She was a portrait painter and very educated woman. Her father was the rector of the Classical College, a senator and noted printer. I had wanted to bring my wife and children with me when I left Germany, but her father wouldn't allow it."*

Priber arrived in Charles Town and applied for land in Amelia Township, stating he was a family of six persons in the province, including a wife, a servant and four small children from Saxony, Germany. On February 27, 1736, he petitions the state of South Carolina for a warrant of survey to buy land. He is a wealthy man who is dressed very well. He was an odd ugly little man who speakes languages fluently including Latin, French, German, English, Greek, and Spanish. In December of that same year, he sold all of his worldly goods, clothes, wigs, spatter dashes of fine Holland, shoes, boots, guns, pistols, powder, a silver repeating watch, a sword with a silver gilt hilt, English seeds, beds, and a fine chest drawer. He was preparing to go to the Cherokee Nation which he did after being granted the land. He went to the Commissioner of Indian Trade Captain Charles Russell with Henry Spacks, John Pearson and George Chicken and traveled to the Cherokee Nation in 1736 where he took up residence in Great Tellico.

Through his good works and marriage to Cloggitah, Moytoy's daughter, Priber established himself firmly in the confidence of the Cherokees. In deference in the red men's taste for stately ceremonial, he had devised an impressive new ritual for the crowning of the emperor and a variety of imposing titles for the other chiefs who constituted the nobles of the court, reserving for himself the title of secretary of state or prime minister.

Priber founded an empire, crowned Moytoy Emperor, and declared himself the prime minister. He declared Moytoy the Emperor and gave high sounding titles to all the chief warriors. He called them the His Majesty's Red Court. He made himself the Imperial Majesty's Principle Secretary of State. He signed all letters to the British with this title, which infuriated them. He stated that the Europeans should get out of America or he would throw them out. He was constantly at his task of remaking the world.

Over the next several months, trader James Adair grew to like the man. Adair was then sent south to trade with the Creeks, but asked Priber to continue correspondence with him. Priber agreed, but after the attempts to capture him by the English, he lost trust in Adair and told the Cherokee that Adair was the devil's clerk and to destroy any letters arriving from him. Over a short period of time, he had become an Indian. The tribe had adopted him as a great beloved man. He learned their language with ease and became their teacher and counselor. Priber was probably one of the smartest men to live among the Cherokee and would be considered genius.

Priber claimed to be a Jesuit acing under orders of his superior in Germany to bring steady industry, an organized government, and civilized living to the Cherokees. He has a strong memory, stronger than anyone Adair has ever met. He learns their language in about a month. When he arrives, the Cherokee are often ambushing the French. They often bring back scalps, booty and prisoners whom they sometimes torture. Many times the Cherokee would adopt captives into the tribe. Many of the French adoptees promoted the French cause when becoming a Cherokee.

Antoine Bonnefoy, captured along the Ohio River in 1741, escaped the next year and managed to find his way to French Fort Toulouse (Montgomery, Alabama). He had been Priber's second secretary and had desired to go on a hunting party. He kept a journal of his experiences, in which he told how the Cherokee truly felt about the French and English and what influences Priber had on them.

Bonnefoy is amazed that Priber speaks French fluently. Priber tells Bonnefoy and the others with him that he is sorry about their misfortune, but it may prove to be their happiness, and he would explain it to them. Priber tells Bonnefoy to call him Pierre Albert, took him into his cabin and told him what he wished him to understand. Bonnefoy wants to know what this happiness is that he had spoken of earlier. Guillaume Potier and Jean Arlut were prisoners with Bonnefoy. Priber says it will take time and he will tell Bonnefoy and the others later. He did say that he wished for all three of them to join his society. Priber offered to include Bonnefoy in the Republic and Bonnefoy played along.

The English were soon out to get Priber. They were convinced that he was an agent to turn the Cherokee's against them and favor the French. Priber actually did not attempt to turn the Cherokee against the English, he only taught them the use of weights and measures and how they were getting short changed in trading. He also taught them to play the French against the English to obtain better prices for the goods they traded.

The governments of South Carolina and Georgia are greatly concerned about Christian G. Priber and his government. They were concerned most about him allowing the French and black slaves to live freely and as equals in the kingdom of his paradise. British Commander Oglethorpe's true enemies are the Spanish who control Florida and also the French, so he suspects Priber of being in touch with the Spanish also.

There was another more serious problem with Priber. He was teaching the Cherokees that they must hold on to all their land and never cede another inch to the Europeans. Priber believes in establishing an empire by having peace between all Indians and having them drive the white man back to Europe. Prior to signing a peace agreement with President George Washington, Doublehead had exactly the same beliefs as his father-in-law Priber. Soon there were stories being brought back by the traders and hunters about how the Cherokee would soon drive the English off the continent.

Then the governor of South Carolina received a letter from Priber. It gave him a severe shock. It was an official communication from Great Tellico, capital of the Cherokee Nation and in effect, it informed his Excellency the Governor, it was polite, but firm, that the sooner he and his English got out of America the better, because America belonged to the Indians and the Indians intended to keep it. The letter was signed, "Christian Priber, Prime Minister."

The South Carolina governor said, "The French envy our American colonies. Their choice of the man Priber as their emissary was genius, although the man was a stranger to the mountains and wilds, as well as to their language, his sagacity has won through and given him the proper place among them. He is slowly forming a red empire and that to the great danger of our southern colonies." Therefore, the Carolina governor ordered Ludovick Grant to arrest him. He went into the Town House to see if it could be done, but when he attempted it, Priber laughed at him insolently and indicated the Indians would not permit it. Grant was extremely angry and could hardly control himself from shooting Priber.

The governor of South Carolina in Charles Town then sent messages to Priber trying to draw him away from town to take him, but Priber would not fall for it. The governor then sent South Carolina agent, Colonel Joseph Fox, who actually attempted to seize him. The English Board of Trade offered to pay Fox 402 pounds in 1739 to get Priber. He and his men escaped with his life only because Priber himself intervened to save him. Fox's arms were stronger than his mind and seized Priber in the great square of their state house. Fox gave a large oration on the occasion and when finished, a head warrior rose up. He found himself surrounded by thousands of Indians. He immediately stopped and let go of Priber's arm.

The head warrior told him to stop, as the man he intended to enslave had been made a great beloved man, and was now one of their own people. *"How dare you enter into our Emperor's Court and seize his prime minister and you being a foreign authority. You cannot even support a charge of guilt against him. The red people know his honesty, we know the secretary's heart and it would never permit him to tell a lie."*

Priber had told them, "I am a foreigner and owe no allegiance to the British and only traveled through their country in a peaceful manner, paying for anything I got. I feel sorry for the poverty and insecure state of the Cherokees. I have traveled a great way and lived among the Cherokees as brothers. I have tried to preserve our freedoms by opening a water communication between us and New Orleans. My motive was only to do well and bring up sufficient numbers of Frenchmen to teach us the use of gunpowder. I urge the tyrannical design of the English commissioner toward our principle secretary appears to be leveled against him, not because of having done any ill will toward the English, but his crime must be his love for the Cherokee. If that is reckoned to be such a heinous crime in the eyes of the English, they send one of their military men to enslave me. It just further confirms all the honest speeches I have so often spoken."

An old warrior then stood up and said, "You should go to your superiors and tell them the Cherokee are desirous of continuing a peaceful union with the English as freemen and equals. We hope to receive no further uneasiness from them, for consulting their own interests, their reason dictated. Send no more bad papers to our country on any account and do not reckon us to be so base as to allow you to take any of our friends out of our presence and into slavery." After the warrior spoke, Priber insisted on providing Fox an escort for he feared for his safety after riling the Indians up to such an extent. The Cherokee then allowed Fox and his men to leave, but Fox was afraid of being killed; therefore, the Cherokee guards escorted him far away from the Nation before leaving Fox, who safely returned to South Carolina.

Over the years, Priber adopted some of the very things that he had taught against. He soon owned a black slave. He thought back on the things he had accomplished and the things he wanted to accomplish. He had a town set up at the foot of the mountains for a place of refuge for criminals, debtors, and slaves. Priber had been working on getting the Cherokee National Capital moved from Great Tellico closer to the French. He had been working on convincing Moytoy to move the capital to Coosawattee because it is situated on what he feels is better land. Coosawattee is in Creek territory, but Priber justifies this by saying the land belonged to the Cherokees before the Creeks.

After seven years of living with the Cherokees and convincing them to set up an alliance with the Creeks, Priber was making his way to Mobile to unite the Creeks with the Cherokees in his Republic. During the trip to Mobile, Priber was accompanied with a few hand-picked Cherokees. They traveled by land to the great river of the Muskogee and there took canoes. He was joyous on the occasion and could hardly contain himself. The empire was about to expand into a powerful force with this unification. He wanted to unite all the southern tribes of Indians including the Chickasaw, Creek, Yuchi, Shawnee, Choctaw, and western Mississippi Indians into a Republic as a model to be set up in Europe at a later date.

The English had tried many tricks on Priber to get him out of the way and to put a stop to his empire building. It took them six years to lure him far enough away from his headquarters so that they could ambush and kill him which would end his republic of paradise. He landed one evening at Tallapoose Town at nightfall. His black slave jumped from the canoe into the river to make his escape and the English traders shot him dead. Priber was seized by English traders among the Creeks, convinced the Creeks of his dangerousness, and took him to Georgia, where he was imprisoned for the remainder of his life. The traders bound him and carried him to Fort Augusta where Captain Kent was in command. Kent apologized to Priber for the traders rough treatment and then sent him on to Fort Frederica.

Oglethorpe was told that Christian Priber was captured in route to Fort Toulouse. Oglethorpe was told that Priber was a monster, teaching the Indians the grossest of immoralities. He is surprised to find Priber to be a polished gentleman in his manners and of a rare courage. Priber tells Oglethorpe he is Jesuit acting under orders of his superior to introduce habits of steady industry, civilized arts, and a regular form of government among all the southern tribes, with a view to the ultimate founding of an independent Indian state. Oglethorpe knows that the English all refuse to believe Priber is a Jesuit, but he also knows their reputation for scholarship, devotion and courage.

Oglethorpe's first impression of Priber was that of an Indian. He came in wearing only a shirt and flap as the Cherokee's wore. His hair was cut off except for a small patch of hair on the crown. He could have passed for an Indian, except the man was very educated and highly intelligent. Priber even had tattooed his face in the manner of the Cherokees. The man was polite and gentlemanly in bearing. Oglethorpe is fascinated with this odd little man.

Priber tells Oglethorpe, "All I am is a poor Jesuit Priest acting under orders from my superior. He asked me to introduce habits of industry, art and a regular form of government to these poor people. Before leaving Germany, I served as a government counselor of the Supreme Court in Zittau, Germany in 1732. I traveled over 500 miles by mountain trails to reach the Cherokees. I taught the Indians the use of weights and measures. I tried to help them not be taken advantage of in trade by the Europeans and that is what I am guilty of. I also helped them learn the use of gunpowder and iron works. The Europeans want to exploit the Indians for their own greed." Oglethorpe knew that Priber would still be a free man if what he taught the Indians had not interfered with the greed of the English.

On May 30, 1743, according to the South Carolina Gazette excerpt in Charles Town, Oglethorpe has written letter from Fort Frederica in Georgia to South Carolina acting governor William Bulletin: *"The Creek Indians finally brought Mr. Priber here as a prisoner. It is a very unusual nature, he is a small ugly man, but he speaks nearly all languages flowing, particularly English, Dutch, French, Latin and all types of Indian languages. He speaks very blasphemous against all religions, but particularly against the Protestants. He is guilty of building a city at the foot of the mountains for all criminals, debtors, and slaves to live."*

After Priber is captured, a treaty is signed in Charles Town with the Cherokee. The Cherokee agree to trade only with the English, to return run-away slaves and expel non-English whites from their territory. In return, the English sent them large amounts of guns, ammunition, and red paint. After Priber's abduction, the warriors at Great Tellico kept up a hostile attitude against the English for many years.

Oglethorpe still suspects that Priber was consorting with the French and the Spanish. The governor tells Oglethorpe that he is not to be kept in the same place as a felon, he is a foreigner and must be treated with honor. He was not placed in a common prison with other felons, but kept in a military fort, because he was a foreigner. Oglethorpe writes the governor of South Carolina saying, *"Priber is an odd man who proposed to establish the "kingdom of paradise" in the Cherokee Nation. I am impressed with the writings of Priber and they are the finest ever written about the Cherokee."* His manuscripts, a book he was writing, and a Cherokee alphabet, were destroyed by the English government at Fort Frederica. Oglethorpe was impressed that Priber spoke Cherokee, Creek and some other Indian languages.

Oglethorpe states, "Priber's book speaks of all kinds of licentiousness. It is extremely wicked. It is very methodical and full of learned quotations. In his book he brags on all his triumphs and glories, thinking highly of himself. He speaks profanely against all religions, especially anything other than Catholicism. He believes the English have printed his book and taken credit for his society and that it is being practiced in all of Europe. He says his nation would have become a Utopia if his government had survived, but it would have spelled the end to the colonization dreams of England and the English have never allowed any one to stand in their way when bent on opening up a new country. He tells how he had studied law at the University of Erfurt where he published his inaugural dissertation in October 1722 on The Use of the Study of Roman Law and the Ignorance of the Law in the Public Life of Germany."

Priber enjoyed considerable freedoms in his prison barracks. He entertained the intelligentsia of Frederica. His best friends were Doctor Frederick Holtzendorff from Brandenburg and Lutheran pastor Johann Ulrich Drietzler. He helps Drietzler translate the Lord's Prayer and some Bible verses into the Cherokee language. His cell in the barracks served for some time as a literary salon. Oglethorpe has allowed Priber to collect quite a library in his cell, but his papers are confiscated and destroyed. Priber does not know of this destruction. Oglethorpe later allows Priber's wives and children to come to Fort Frederica and live with him until his death. He died in 1751 and there is no evidence he was ever a Jesuit Priest.

On March 22, 1743, there was a fire in the powder magazine which was near the barracks. Priber was in his cell reading when his guards ran and unlocked his door and yelled for him to make his escape before the magazine exploded. The guards then ran. If the magazine exploded, shells would rain down everywhere and probably knock the barracks down. The magazine exploded, but did not do much damage and the guards soon returned. They found him squatting in the middle of the room with both hands covering the top of his head.

"You ignorant old fool," one of the guards yelled. "You could have been killed. Why didn't you run?" Priber said, "I've learned when in imminent danger that is the best position to get in."

The guards know the man is extremely intelligent, but having no common sense. They call him the educated fool. He often plays the devil's advocate with the soldiers stationed in the barracks. He speaks profanely of all religions, especially the Protestants. He has come to believe that his manuscripts were stolen by the English and is now being used back in Europe as a model for all of the world's governments. His guards learn to respect the strange little man in their midst. They are amazed at his memory. He can remember every soldiers name after only hearing it once.

He came down with a fever in 1744 and died. Christian Gottleib Priber rests in an unmarked grave in Frederica, Georgia today. Some historians indicate he was buried on Saint Simon's Island off the coast of Georgia.

When missionaries begin to arrive, they are surprised at how much the Cherokees already know about the Bible. Priber had taught them all of the Bible stories and the missionaries found the Cherokees the easiest tribe to convert because of this.

Doublehead and Creat

Doublehead's oldest brother Red Bird was married to Susan Priber who was thought to be a sister to Creat. Creat was said to have died from severe abuse and beatings by Doublehead. Doublehead was known as a wife abuser and was known to kill another wife to whom he had a violent relationship. She was a sister to James Vann's wife and was one of the reasons that Vann agreed to be the leader of the assassination group that would kill Doublehead.

Doublehead and Creat were thought to have five children who were one quarter German and three fourths Cherokee. They were Tuckaho, Tuskiahooto, Saleechie, Nigodigeyu, and Gulustiyu.

Tuckaho Doublehead

1. Tuckaho Doublehead was born about 1758 in Tellico Plains, Tennessee, and married Margaret Mounce, who was born 1768 and was from Cherry Fork, now Helenwood, Tennessee. Tuckaho died in 1800 in Eloping, Shasta, California. Tuckaho and Margaret had two children, a girl and a boy.

Tuskiahooto Doublehead

2. Tuskiahooto (Tusgiahute) Doublehead was born about 1760 in Tellico Plains and married George Colbert, who became the Principal Chief of the Chickasaw Nation. She died in 1817, and George seemed to never get over her loss. According to the description in the Treaty with the Chickasaws in 1834, George buried his beautiful wife 60 yards south of their dwelling house at Colbert's Ferry. George Colbert, known as Tootemastubbe-The Ferryman by his Indian friends, was born about 1764 and died January 7, 1839, in Indian Territory. Tuskiahooto, reputed to be one of the most beautiful Indian princesses in all the land, rests in an unmarked grave on a beautiful and serene hillside overlooking the south bank of the Tennessee, River. Today, the area is protected as part of the Natchez Trace Parkway at Colbert's Ferry in present-day Colbert County, Alabama.

Saleechie (Standing Fern) Doublehead

3. Saleechie (Salitsi) Doublehead was born about 1762 in Monroe County, Tennessee, and she also married George Colbert, and died February 1, 1846, in Oklahoma, Indian Territory. George and Saleechie (Standing Fern) had seven children who were one eighth German, three eighths Cherokee, one quarter Scots-Irish, one quarter Chickasaw : 1) Samuel "Pitman" Colbert, born about 1797, married Sarah McGillivray, and he died February 26, 1853, in the Choctaw Nation in Indian territory (Pitman was said to have been adopted by George and Saleechie); 2) Jane Colbert was born prior to 1800 and married Charles Frazier and had five children-Jane Frazier was born 1811, Andrew Jackson Frazier was born 1815, Mary Frazier, Maxwell T. Frazier, and Emily Frazier. She died about 1827 in the Chickasaw Nation, Mississippi; 3) Susan "Sukey" Colbert, born about 1810 at Colbert's Ferry, and first married John Mclish, and then the second marriage was to Robert McDonald Jones. She had one son by Mclish whose name was Benjamin Franklin McLish, born in 1830. She had three children by Jones-George Washington Jones was born 1840, Frances Jones was born 1842, and Joseph Jones was born before 1856. She died January 13, 1860, in Hugo, Choctaw Nation of Indian territory; 4) George Colbert, Jr. was born before 1818 and died in 1879; 5) Levica "Vicy" Colbert was born before 1818 and died in January 1846, in Indian Territory. Vicy first married William Duncan and had one son named John Duncan. John Duncan married Mary Hargett and they had Mary Elizabeth (born 1845), unknown daughter, Jonathan Duncan (born 1824), William Duncan (born1838), Morketts Annie (born 1840), Lucinda (born 1841), and Sara Emmiline (1844). Her second marriage was to Doctor James McDonna and they had one daughter; 6)

Chickasaw Chief George Colbert

Vina Colbert was born before 1818; and, 7) John Colbert was born before 1818 and married Rachel Perry and they had three children-Aley Colbert, Kittie Colbert, and Alfred Colbert. John Colbert died before 1834.

Chickasaw Chief George Colbert was the double son-in-law of Doublehead. He took two of the daughters of Chickamauga Chief Doublehead and Creat Priber as his wives-Tuskiahooto and Saleechie. By the Chickasaw Boundary Treaty of January 10, 1786, most of area north of the High Town Path and west of the Flint River in Madison County, Alabama became Chickasaw land; however, Doublehead was permitted to stay in this area of north Alabama because his daughters'- Tuskiahooto and Saleechie - marriages to Chickasaw Chief George Colbert. George Colbert's two Cherokee wives were said to be among the most beautiful women in the region.

George Colbert was the son of a Chickasaw woman Minta Hoye and James Logan Colbert, who was a Carolinian of Scots descent and lived with the Chickasaws at a young age. Some think that James Logan Colbert was born in the Carolinas, traveled with Indian traders at a young age, and stayed with the Chickasaws. George was born on the west side of Bear Creek where it empties into the Tennessee River in the present-day northeastern most corner of Mississippi. In December 1801, the United States Government agreed to build cabins for travelers, a store, stables, a large dwelling house, a new ferry boat, and other facilities for George to operate a ferry where the Natchez Trace crosses the Tennessee River in present-day Colbert County, Alabama.

Tuskiahooto, George's principal wife, lived at Colbert's Ferry, while Saleechie ran an inn on the Natchez Trace in present-day Tupelo, Mississippi. After Tuskiahooto died, George moved to Tupelo, Mississippi in 1817 and began his plantation activities. In the treaty of 1834, George made sure to include his wife's burial site in the reserve that was set aside for his personal use.

Nigodigeyu Doublehead

4. Nigodigeyu Doublehead was born about 1764 probably in Tellico Plains, Tennessee. She married Samuel Riley who was born about 1747 in Maryland and became an Indian trader. Samuel died in March 1819 at Blue Springs in Roane County, Tennessee. Samuel and Nigodigeyu had five children who were one eighth German, three eighths Cherokee, and one half Scots-Irish: 1) James Riley, born about 1792, married Jenny Shields and they had four children-Lewis Riley, Susan Riley, Malinda Riley, and Nannie Riley. His second marriage was to an unknown woman and they had one son Jonathan Riley. James died about 1824 in Alabama; 2) Catherine Riley, born about 1800, married Andrew Lacey and they had six children-Ensley Lacey, Amanda Lacey, Eliza Lacey, Mary Lacey, Alexander Lacey, and Catherine Lacey; 3) Martha Riley, born about 1802, married John Hall and they had three children-Elizabeth Hall, Ellen Hall, and Martha Hall;4) Nelson Riley, born about 1803, first married Mary Cordell and had two children-Martha Jane Riley, and Louisa Riley. His second marriage was to Elizabeth Thompson and they had seven children-Ellen Riley, Margaret Riley, Julius Riley, Joseph Riley, Mary Ann Riley, Perry Andre Riley, and Charles Riley. Nelson died between 1848 and 1851; and, 5) Madison Riley, born about 1808.

Gulustiyu Doublehead

5. Gulustiyu Doublehead was born about 1770 in Tellico Plains, Tennessee. She also married Samuel Riley and they had 11 children who were one eighth German, three eighths Cherokee, and one half Scots-Irish: 1) Richard Riley, born about 1791, married Dianna Campbell and had two children-Jennie Riley (born 1817) and Elizabeth Riley. Richard died April 26, 1824, at Creek Path, Alabama; 2) Nancy "Nannie" Riley was born about 1792 and married John McNary and they had one daughter Margaret McNary (born 1802). Nannie died before 1805; 3) Mary "Polly" Riley, born about 1793 in Roane County, Tennessee, married Samuel Riley Keys and they had three children-William Keys (born 1790), Isaac Keys (born 1794), and Samuel Riley Keys, Junior (born 1819). Mary (Polly) died March 8, 1829, in Jackson County, Alabama; 4) Elizabeth Riley, born July 5, 1794, married Isaac Keys and they had three children-Letitia Keys, Nannie Keys, and Isaac William Keys. Elizabeth died March 1857 in Indian Territory, Oklahoma; 5)John Riley, born about 1790, married Susan Walker and they had eleven children-Sallie W. Riley, Rebecca McNair Riley, Felix Riley, Jennie C. Riley, Nannie Riley, Perloney Riley, Susan Riley, Samuel Riley, Malinda Riley, Laura Riley, and John McNary Riley. John died February 14, 1845, Oklahoma; 6) Eleanor "Nellie" Riley,

born about 1796, married Charles Coody and they had ten children-Archibald Coody (1822), Engevine Coody (1824), Richard Coody (1826), Rufus Coody (born 1828), Madison Coody (born 1830), Charles Coody, Junior (born 1832), Sallie Coody (1834), Elizabeth Coody (born 1836), Nancy "Nannie" Coody (born 1838), and Samuel Coody (1840). Eleanor died June 1851; 7) Lucy Riley, born about 1796, married Owen Brady and they had ten children-Samuel Riley Brady, Elizabeth Brady, Malinda Brady, Charles Brady, Earl Brady, James Monroe Brady, Isaac Lewis Brady, Lucinda Brady, Rachel Brady, and Sallie Brady; 8) Sallie Riley, born about 1798, married William Keys and they had seven children-Lewis Keys, Diana Keys, Levi Keys, Mary Keys, Monroe Calvin Keys, Elizabeth A. Keys, and Looney Keys. Sallie died about 1871; 9) Louisa Riley, born about 1799, married Dennis Biggs and they had five children-Napolean Bonaparte Biggs, Sallie Biggs, Minerva Biggs, Elizabeth Biggs, and John Biggs; 10) Luney Riley, born November 12, 1800, married Rachel Stuart and they had ten children-Eliza Riley (born 1820), Belinda George Riley, Samuel King Riley, John Riley, Mary Jane Riley, Rufus Riley, Lucy Riley, Sallie Riley, Ellen Riley, and Randolph Riley. Luney became a judge and died February 28, 1883, Nowata, Oklahoma; 11) Rachel Riley, born about 1801, first married Daniel Milton and they one son John Milton. She then married James McDaniel and they had three children-Elias McDaniel, Charles McDaniel, and Joseph McDaniel. Rachel and James arrived at Indian Territory on May 16, 1834. They were removed in wagons and steamboats by Lieutinent J. W. Harris. One member of the family died on the way to Indian Territory. Rachel died after 1851.

The children of Samuel Riley and grandchildren of Doublehead were baptized as Christians and were listed in a "Register of Persons Baptized by the Reverend Evan Jones. A. M. in the Cherokee Nation on the 22nd of April 1805."

Mary the Daughter of Samuel Riley was baptized by me the day and date above Evan C. Jones. Richard the son of Samuel Riley was baptized by me the day and date above Evan C. Jones. Eleanor the daughter of Samuel Riley was baptized by me the day and date above Evan C. Jones. Elizabeth the daughter of Samuel Riley was baptized by me the day and date above Evan C. Jones. Catharine the daughter of Samuel Riley was baptized by me the day and date above Evan C. Jones. Sarah the daughter of Samuel Riley was baptized by me the day and date above Evan C. Jones. Luce the daughter of Samuel Riley was baptized by me the day and date above Evan C. Jones. James the son of Samuel Riley was baptized by me the day and date above Evan C. Jones. Lunithe the son of Samuel Riley was baptized by me the day and date above Evan C. Jones. Nelson the son of Samuel Riley was baptized by me the day and date above Evan C. Jones. Louiza the daughter of Samuel Riley was baptized by me the day and date above Evan C. Jones.

Samuel Riley was also the double son-in-law of Doublehead. He came into Cherokee country as an Indian trader and developed a remarkable relationship with the Cherokee people. As was the practice with many traders, he took two Indian wives who were the daughters of Doublehead and Creat Priber-Nigodigeyu and Gulustiyu. He obviously found favor with Doublehead and eventually settled on a tract of land that was given to Doublehead in a secret agreement with the government. He lived near Southwest Point near present-day Kingston, Tennessee where the Clinch River empties in the Tennessee River in Roane County, Tennessee. At this location, Samuel operated a ferry that had also been given to Doublehead as a bribe to get him to agree to the treaties of October 25 and 27, 1805, and that bribe cleared the way for a Federal Road through Georgia. After a United States garrison was established in 1792 at Southwest Point, Riley was hired as an interpreter. Of course, the 16 children of Samuel Riley and his wives were the grandchildren of Doublehead. Samuel Riley was granted a reservation for life by the United States Government.

With one double son-in-law (George Colbert) and two daughters in the western portion of the Tennessee River territory and another double son-in-law (Samuel Riley) and two daughters in the eastern portion of the Tennessee River territory, Doublehead was able to know what was happening in a vast section of the river valley. Through these marriages of four of his daughters, Doublehead basically controlled an area of the Tennessee River from Mississippi through north Alabama and into the middle of east Tennessee. After his assassination in 1807, some 1,131 of his family and loyal supporters moved west of the Mississippi River to Arkansas.

Cherokee Woman-Second Marriage

Doublehead's second wife was an unknown Cherokee woman by whom he had at least two children. It is probable that Doublehead killed her for telling James Vann about his deals with the government and for being unfaithful. Doublehead returned home from being away for six months and found his wife was a few months pregnant; therefore, he reasoned he was not the father. In addition, she was the sister-in-law of James Vann who was his enemy and used information on Doublehead to justify an eventual assassination. Doublehead reasoned that his wife had told Vann about his business affairs and secret deals with the government that led Vann and other Cherokees to plan his assassination; therefore, Doublehead killed his pregnant wife. They had two children-Two Heads, and Doublehead.

Two Heads Doublehead

6. Two Heads Doublehead was the daughter of Doublehead and was born about 1768. Two Heads married John Foster and they had one daughter Jennie Doublehead Foster who was born about 1777 and died about 1812. Jennie first married James Clement (Wa-Wli) Vann, who was born February 1765 and died February 21, 1809. Jennie's second marriage was to John Anthony Foreman, who was born about 1780 and died about 1807.

Doublehead Doublehead

7. Doublehead Doublehead was born about 1770 and is probably the reason many confuse the younger Doublehead with the old original Doublehead that died August 9, 1807.

    According to William Lindsey McDonald's book, Lore of the River (2007), *"It's a popularly held belief that some of Lauderdale County's more prominent citizens are descents of Doublehead. These are other suggestions that Doublehead had several sons and that one, in fact, bore his name. This possibly could account for some confusion in the early records that show Doublehead's name on documents which were prepared several years after his death in 1807."*

    The quote below maybe one of the references that William L. McDonald was referring to concerning a Doublehead after the death of the original on August 9,1807, and maybe his son Doublehead Doublehead. Based on the information below, some of the places listed as the home site of Doublehead may actually be those of his son Doublehead Doublehead.

    *"James Jackson came to America in 1799, settled first in Philadelphia, and in 1801 he followed relatives to Nashville, Tennessee. He was educated in Ireland as a civil engineer, he first engaged in surveying in Nashville, later he was involved in the mercantile trade. An old map of Nashville, 1807 shows his two story house, with nineteen others comprising the residential district of Nashville. In 1814, at the land sale he became one of the organizers of the Cypress Land Company. He bought extensive tracts of land in Lauderdale County and was one of the founders of Florence. He acquired a large plantation in the forks of the Big and Little Cypress Creeks which he purchased from the **Indian Chief, Double Head**, whom he permitted to still occupy his wigwam. This Indian home was only a short distance from the large house he proceeded to build. In 1821 he came to Lauderdale County, Alabama, and engaged in planting, and at his home "The Forks of Cypress" he dispensed a princely hospitality."*

52

Postcard: Forks of Cypress

Delaware Woman-Third Marriage

Some historians describe the Cherokee as originating from the Delaware Indians in the Ohio River Valley. A small faction of the Delaware was documented to migrate into north Alabama and make raids into the Cumberland settlements. Some speculate that Doublehead married his third wife who was a Delaware Indian in order to have an alliance with the tribe. His Delaware Indian wife's name is not known but she was born about 1750. They had two daughters, one was named Corn Blossom and the other Kstieieah. Pawalin is a Delaware word for corn blossom which was the name of their first daughter. Both of these daughters of Doublehead died and are buried in Kentucky.

Corn Blossom Doublehead

8. Corn Blossom (Pawalin) Doublehead was born about 1770 in Tellico Plains, Tennessee, and she died August 13, 1810. She married George Jacob (Big Jake) Troxell, who was born about 1759 and died July 1, 1843. They had seven children: 1) Peter Jacob Troxell, who was born about 1781 and died August 13,

Corn Blossom Doublehead Troxell

1810, married first Standing Fern about 1801 and second marriage to Jane Stevenson on January 17, 1804; 2) Catherine (Katy) Troxell was born about 1783 in Loudin County, Virginia and died about 1814. She married Jonathan Blevins who was born about 1779 and died March 21, 1863, and is buried in Hatfield Cemetery, Scott County, Tennessee; 3) Mary (Polly) Troxell was born about 1785 in Wayne County, Kentucky and married Tarlton Blevins on November 21, 1807; 4) Margaret Troxell was born about 1789 and married James Bell on July 13, 1808. He was born about 1788 in Buckingham County, Virginia and died in April 1854 in Wayne County, Kentucky; 5) Elizabeth (Betty) Troxell was born about 1796 and married James Vaughn on September 17, 1808; 6) Sarah Troxell was born about 1798 and married Thomas Bell on February 9, 1818; and, 7) William Troxel was born about 1800 and died May 15, 1892, in Jackson County, Alabama. He married Catherine Farris.

Kstieieah Keziah Doublehead

9. Kstieieah Keziah Doublehead was born about 1775 and died about 1850. Kstieieah was listed in a sworn testimony on Doublehead's estate as an aunt of Catherine Spencer (Pumpkin Boy's daughter) on June 8, 1838. She married Thomas Jefferson Dishman and they had the following children: Lewis Dishman; and James Robert Dishman who married Estelle Stone. Kstieieah was buried at Slickford in Wayne County, Kentucky. The county was named for General Mad Anthony Wayne.

Nannie Drumgoole-Fourth Marriage

Doublehead married his fourth wife Nannie Drumgoole (The Pain, OoWahWanSede) about 1794. She was the daughter of Alexander Drumgoole, a mixed blood, and Nancy Augusta Hop, the full blood daughter of Old Hop and Sugi (Sookie).

54

She was born about 1779 in Crow Town, Alabama, and christened in Guntersville, Marshall County, Alabama and died July 23, 1850, in Bradley, Polk County, Tennessee. Nannie and Doublehead had two children, who were Bird Tail and Peggy.

Nannie was married the second time in 1799 to half-blood John Foreman, who was born about 1783. He was the son of Scots-Irish trader John Anthony Foreman, who was born in Scotland about 1765, and his mother was Susie Gourd, a full blood Cherokee. Nannie and John had five children: Richard "Dick" Foreman; John "Jack" Foreman, who was born about1801; Elizabeth "Betsey" Foreman, who was born about 1802 and married Edley Springston; Johnson Foreman; and, James Foreman, who was born about 1807. At the time of her death, Nannie had four living children who were by her side and 73 grandchildren.

Bird Tail Doublehead

10. Bird Tail Doublehead was born about 1795 and died about 1857 at the age of 62. He married a Timson and they had two children: Lucy Doublehead was born about 1851 and died after 1906; and, Bird Doublehead was born about 1852 and died after 1937.

    Bird Tail Doublehead's second wife was Nakie and they had thirteen children: 1) Rebecca Doublehead, born between 1825 and 1835; 2) Susannah Doublehead, born about 1830; 3) Hen-il-lee Henry Doublehead, born 1835 and 1845; 4) Eli E-law-we Doublehead, born 1835; 5) Jim Doublehead, born between 1836 and 1842; 6) Josiah Tah-Lee Tsoo-Ska Bird Doublehead, born between 1836 and 1842; 7) Betsie Quatie Jew-Nah-Sto-Di Doublehead, born between1836 and 1842; 8) Tsa-Wa-Nee Doublehead, born between1835 and 1845; 9) Annie Ah-Nee Tah-Le-Jew-Sco Doublehead, born 1838 and 1844; 10) Sar-Mee Samuel Doublehead, born between 1838 and 1844; 11) Wal-Lee Doublehead, born 1838 and 1845; 12) Gah-le-Cha Kah-le-Tsa Doublehead, born 1838 and 1845; and 13) Skake Doublehead, born about 1845.

    Bird Tail Doublehead and his half-brother Tassel were sent to school by their father. Doublehead paid Thomas Norris Clarke of Kingston, Tennessee for boarding his two sons and sending them to school. Shortly after Doublehead was assassinated, Tassel died and Bird Tail left within two years. Bird Tail and his half-brother James Foreman killed Major Ridge soon after he arrived west of the Mississippi River.

Peggy Doublehead

11. Peggy Doublehead was born about 1800 and died around 1834. On April 3, 1824, Peggy married William Wilson in Madison County, Alabama. William Wilson was born in 1796, and he and Peggy had four children: 1) Elzrah Wilson, born May 22, 1822, died August 6, 1902, and married David Hicks, who was born July 13, 1830; 2) Jane Wilson, born about 1828; 3) Gilbert Bird Wilson, born about 1829 in the Cherokee Nation East, and died August 29, 1894. Gilbert Bird Wilson married Ellen and they had three children-Delilah Wilson born in 1860, William Wilson born in 1862, and Ida Wilson born in 1869; and, 4) George Wilson, born about 1832, was named after his grandfather George Wilson that married Ruth Springston, a half-sister to Nannie Drumgoole.

William and Peggy had a land grant in Madison County, Alabama that was reservation number 128. Their reserve was on the Flint River adjoining the Madison County line and surveyed on December 11, 1820, with Giles McAnulty and Aaron Armstrong being the chain carriers. Giles became Peggy's brother-in law after he married Alcy Doublehead. Very close to Peggy and William Wilson's reserve, William's brother Thomas Wilson had reservation number 131 that was located on the north side of the Tennessee River near the old Cherokee boundary line and the Hurricane Fork of the Flint River in Madison County, Alabama.

Kateeyeah Wilson-Fifth Marriage

Doublehead married the fifth time to Kateeyeah Wilson about 1797. Kateeyah's father was thought to be George Wilson (half Cherokee and half Scots-Irish) and her mother was Ruth Springston (half Cherokee and half Scots). Ruth Springston was the daughter of William Springston and Nancy Augusta Hop; therefore, Kateeyah was a niece to Nannie Drumgoole, since Nannie and Kateeyah's mother, Ruth, were half-sisters. Kateeyah was a sister to Thomas Wilson and William Wilson. She was born around 1760, and her step-daughter, sister-in-law, or cousin Peggy married her brother, William Wilson. Kateeyeah and Doublehead had four children, who were three quarters Cherokee and one quarter Scots-Irish: Tassel, Alcy, William, and Susannah.

Tassel Doublehead

12. Tassel Doublehead was born about 1798 and died at the age of nine years old about August 23, 1807. According to an affidavit given by his half-brother Bird Tail Doublehead on June 21, 1838, Tassel died two weeks after his father

56

Doublehead was murder on August 9, 1807. Tassel died in Kingston, Tennessee (South West Point located at the junction of the Clinch River and Tennessee River) at the home of Thomas Norris Clark who was boarding Bird Tail and Tassel for their father Doublehead for $100.00 per year. After Doublehead was murdered, Clark went to Muscle Shoals and took many slaves and horses of Doublehead. He quit sending the boys to school and made them work in the fields plowing and farming activities. The circumstances of Tassel's death are not known.

Alcy Doublehead

13. Alcy Doublehead was born about 1800 and died after 1838. Alcy married Giles McAnulty/McNulty who helped survey her half-sister Peggy's reservation. Giles McAnulty was on a list of persons entitled to a reservation for life under the treaty with the Cherokees of February 27, 1819. Alcy and Giles also had reservation number 132 on the Hurricane Fork of the Flint River adjoining Thomas Wilson. William Wilson, Thomas Wilson, and Kateeyeah Wilson, Doublehead's third wife, were siblings. Alcy and Giles had seven children: 1)Elzira McNulty, born about 1823, married Richard Carey Mann and died about 1902; 2) George Washington McNulty, born about 1826, married Rebecca and died before 1896; 3)Elisa McNulty, born about 1826, married John Vickery and died April 3, 1885; 4) John McNulty, born about 1828; 5) Sallie McNulty, born about 1830; 6) Armstead Blevin McNulty, born about 1832; and, 7) Mary McNulty, born about 1836, married a Miller and died after 1896.

William Doublehead

14. William Doublehead born about 1802. Very little is known about William Doublehead; therefore, he was probably the orphan son that Colonel Return J. Meigs mentioned in the letter below as being dead. By 1810 which may be the year of his death, William would have been only eight years old. But it is more accurate that William's death was between 1807 and 1810. He was probably named after his mother's brother William Wilson.

Susannah Doublehead

15. Susannah Doublehead was born about 1805 and died after 1838. Susannah first married George Chisholm and, later according to local lore, she married a McBride of Morgan County, Alabama.

Prior to Doublehead's assassination, he asks Colonel Return J. Meigs to take care of his children in case of his death. In microcopy 208, roll 5, and number 2540, from Doublehead's Reserve, Colonel Return J. Meigs writes the Secretary of War concerning Doublehead's young children. The letter was sent October 3, 1810. *"Doublehead ask him to look after his affairs in case of his death. Doublehead left two sons (one now dead) and two daughters now orphans without father or mother."* It should be noted that Tassel Doublehead died about August 23, 1807, the same year and month his daddy Doublehead was assassinated; therefore, it appears that over three years after Tassel died another of his last three sons is reported dead by Colonel Return J. Meigs and is probably William Doublehead.

Chickamauga War

Dragging Canoe-First Chickamauga Chief

From the time they were just reaching puberty, Dragging Canoe and Doublehead led other rebellious Cherokee youth on raiding parties against white settlers. A war over the loss of Cherokee hunting grounds and homelands raged for the entire life of Dragging Canoe and most of Doublehead's lifetime. As young boys growing up in their native lands, fighting the encroachment of white settlers was a way of life.

Chickamauga Chief Dragging Canoe

In his early years, Doublehead rode and fought with the great Chickamauga Chief Dragging Canoe, the son of Attacullaculla (Little Carpenter), Principal Chief of the Cherokee Nation. From the time of his youth, Dragging Canoe wanted to accompany war parties. At the age of about twelve years old, Dragging Canoe subsequently got his name by dragging a canoe to the water in order to go on a raid. Dragging Canoe became a great influence with other Cherokee youth such as Doublehead and organized the great Chickamauga Indian Confederacy. Initially, Dragging Canoe would establish his command stronghold near the mouth of Chickamauga Creek near Chattanooga, Tennessee; thus, the name Chickamauga was given to this rebellious group of warriors. Doublehead would follow Dragging Canoe and move to the extreme southwestern portion of the ancestral hunting grounds of the Cherokee along the Muscle Shoals of the Tennessee River in north central Alabama to carry on the war against white settlement of their lands. Both Dragging Canoe and Doublehead would be wounded during their conflicts with the settlers and soldiers.

The British agents would be their greatest supplier of arms and ammunition to carry on their war against the white settlers taking their lands and killing their people. At the beginning of the Chickamauga War, the main trade route with the British was from Olde Charles Town to the Tennessee Valley. The primary supply route was along the High Town Path to the area around Turkey Town (Gadsden, Alabama) and Brown's Village (present day Guntersville, Alabama). But as the Revolutionary War progressed, the High Town Path route was basically cut off and most Chickamauga supplies came from Pensacola, Florida.

Loss of Cherokee Lands

In 1763, the Cherokee War, known as the French and Indian War, between the French and British ended with the British victorious in controlling most of the eastern North America. In addition to ending the war, a Proclamation Line of 1763 was established to protect the Indians west of the Appalachians and to halt encroachment on their lands. Doublehead's brother Standing Turkey had signed the Royal Proclamation when he went to England with Henry Timberlake; however, the Proclamation Line did not prevent settlers from invading Indian lands west of the Appalachian Mountains, the very heart of Cherokee Country.

Eventually, the Cherokee were forced into making land cessions west of the Appalachians. In 1768, 1770, 1772, and 1773, treaties were made between the British government and the Cherokee Indians. The Cherokee were pressured to give up land claims in South Carolina, Georgia, Virginia, West Virginia, Kentucky, and Tennessee. The Treaty of Sycamore Shoals, in 1775, took Cherokee lands through the middle of Kentucky and Tennessee. The 1775 treaty was the major reason the Lower Cherokee broke from the nation and organized the Chickamauga to fight against the white settlers moving into their hunting grounds.

Now, with the door to settlement opened, settlers poured into the area north of the Little Tennessee River to the heart of the once powerful Cherokee Nation. As the settlers moved in from the north and east, the Lower Cherokees under the leadership of Dragging Canoe and Doublehead began moving south and west. By the 1750's, the Lower Cherokees were occupying eastern Alabama. By 1770, the Chickamauga under the leadership of Doublehead was firmly established in the area of the mussel shoals along the Big Bend of the Tennessee River in the north-central portion of Alabama.

The Cherokee decline and loss of lands continued after the Revolutionary War partly because of their alliance with the British. The Middle, Valley, and Overhill Towns of the Cherokee were practically destroyed by military movements led against the Cherokees by men such as Colonel William Christian and Colonel John Sevier. Eventually in 1780, the armies of John Sevier and Arthur Campbell destroyed the Overhill Towns including the Cherokee Capital of Chota. By this time, Dragging Canoe and a large

60

number of his followers were occupying the five lower towns along the Tennessee River in Alabama. In addition, Doublehead and a thriving population of mixed Chickamauga warriors were occupying the Great Bend of the Tennessee Valley along the Muscle Shoals.

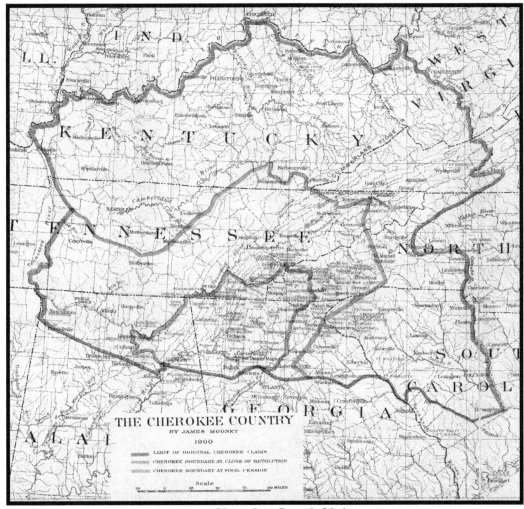

Cherokee Land Claims

The Lower Cherokee faction of the Chickamauga moved south under the leadership of Dragging Canoe and his warriors who resisted loss of their hunting grounds and homelands by white encroachment. These Chickamauga Cherokees under Dragging Canoe settled from Chattanooga to the south and west in five villages referred to as the "Five Lower Towns on the Tennessee"-Lookout Mountain Town, Nickajack, Running Water, Long Island Village, and Crow Town. It is well documented that warriors of the Creek and Shawnee factions of the Chickamauga had access to the five lower towns. In addition, Doublehead established several Chickamauga towns along the Great Bend that were occupied by warriors from the different tribes that made up the Chickamauga Confederacy.

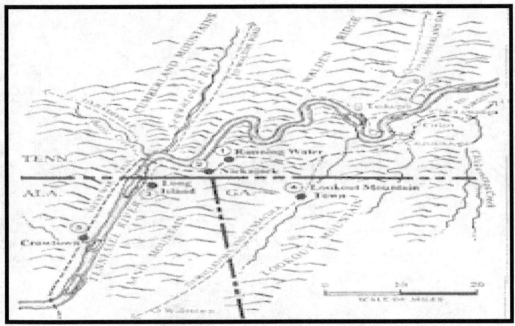

Dragging Canoe's Stronghold
Five Lower Towns of the Chickamauga

Henderson's Treaty

On March 17, 1775, Henderson's Treaty (sometimes known as the Treaty of Sycamore Shoals) gave up large tracts of Cherokee land in Kentucky and middle Tennessee to the Transylvania Company. At Sycamore Shoals on the Watauga River, near Elizabethton, Richard Henderson and his party bought a vast tract of territory, containing seventeen to twenty million acres, from the Cherokee without permission of the Crown (Belue, 1996).

According to Ted Belue's book, "The Long Hunt", "Dragging Canoe, a negotiator for the Chickamauga and son of Attakullakulla, stood aloof and angry during the proceedings. At the close of the day he stamped his foot, glowering with exasperation, and pointed west, warning Henderson that Kanta-ke (Kentucky) was still their hunting ground and the buffalo were still their cattle. Not only were the followers of Dragging Canoe great warriors, but they were also great hunters.

Sycamore Shoals Treaty Meeting

Why did Dragging Canoe, Doublehead, and other young Chickamauga men have such a love for the land in middle Tennessee and Kentucky that they would fight to death to preserve their hunting grounds? The answer was given by a white writer as follows:

From the expulsion of the Shawnees to the coming of the white settlers in 1779 the region now embraced in Middle Tennessee was indeed a hunter's paradise. Through its valleys and over its hills roamed countless herds of buffalo, deer, and elk. Within its forests and canebrakes bears, wolves, panthers, bob-cats, foxes, and other wild animals in great numbers found a home. Besides the food necessary for each they must also have salt. The provision made by nature for this essential was the saline water of the sulphur springs with which the country yet abounds. In times of overflow these springs left on the surrounding ground a slight deposit of salt, and over this the beasts would tramp and lick until often long trenches or furrows were made, sometimes over several acres. Thus were formed the "licks" which played so important a part in determining the location of early forts. Sulphur springs and the accompanying "licks" were especially numerous in Sumner and Davidson Counties. To this fact, together with the close proximity of these counties to the Cumberland River is largely due their selection as a location by the pioneers. The big sulphur spring in the bottom now within the corporate limits of Nashville, no doubt determined the location of that city.

To the licks in the region now embraced in Sumner and Davidson came at regular intervals the animals from over a large territory, and these in their journeys to and fro formed beaten paths or trails, all centering in this locality like the spokes of a wheel. As with the ancients all roads led to Rome, so with the conquerors of this boundless and uninhabited wilderness, all traces led to central licks which spots were destined to become the scene of earliest activity. Hunters, both Indian and white, roaming at will through the forests came upon these narrow paths, and turning about threaded them to the end. Here these mighty Nimrods fell upon and mercilessly slaughtered the game, large and small, which was usually found assembled in great abundance. After feeding upon the flesh of the slain animals, they carried away the hides or pelts from which they made clothing for themselves and their families...(Albright, 1909).

Now you have the answer to the question above! Both Dragging Canoe and Doublehead knew that their old ways of living would be gone when the animals they depended upon for survival were taken by the greed of the white long hunters. To these great Chickamauga leaders, the only response was to fight for their lives as well as those of their people.

Dragging Canoe's Speech

Dragging Canoe was greatly opposed to the 1775 treaty as evidenced in his speech: *"Whole Indian nations have melted away like snowballs in the sun before the white man's advance. They leave scarcely a name of our people except those wrongly recorded by their destroyers. Where are the Delaware? They have been reduced to a mere shadow of their former greatness. We had hoped that the white men would not be willing to travel beyond the mountains. Now that hope is gone. They have passed the mountains, and have settled upon Tsalagi (Cherokee) land. They wish to have that usurpation sanctioned by treaty. When that is gained, the same encroaching spirit will lead them upon other land of the Tsalagi. New cessions will be asked. Finally the whole country, which the Tsalagi and their fathers have so long occupied, will be demanded, and the remnant of the AniYvwiya, the Principal People, once so great and formidable, will be compelled to seek refuge in some distant wilderness. There they will be permitted to stay only a short while, until they again behold the advancing banners of the same greedy host. Not being able to point out any further retreat for the miserable Tsalagi, the extinction of the whole race will be proclaimed. Should we not therefore run all risks, and incur all consequences, rather than to submit to further loss of our country? Such treaties may be all right for men who are too old to hunt or fight. As for me, I have my young warriors about me. We will hold our land"* (Mize, 2005).

One of Dragging Canoe's warriors was none other than Doublehead. After the Treaty of Sycamore Shoals, Dragging Canoe told Henderson, *"You have bought a fair*

64

land, but there is a black cloud hanging over it. You will find its settlement dark and bloody." Doublehead followed Dragging Canoe on attacks against white settlers moving in to claim Cherokee lands as their own and he kept the promise Dragging Canoe made to Henderson until 1795. For the rest of his life, Dragging Canoe with the assistance of other tribal factions of the Chickamauga resisted white encroachment and carried out his dark and bloody promise.

Dragging Canoe launched his first attack of the Chickamauga War against the east Tennessee settlements in 1776. The Chickamauga attacks consisted of a series of raids, ambushes, skirmishes, and some full-scale frontier battles with the settlers. The start of the 1775 Chickamauga campaign was a continuation of the struggle against white encroachment into Indian territory by American frontiersmen from the colonies east of the Appalachian Mountains.

The Chickamauga War actually started in the summer of 1776 between the Chickamauga and frontier settlers along the Watauga, Holston, Nolichucky, and Doe Rivers in east Tennessee. Eventually the war spread into Virginia, North Carolina, South Carolina, and Georgia. By 1780 after the first permanent settlements were made by General James Robertson and his followers on the Cumberland River around the Nashville area, the Chickamauga War spread to those stations established in middle Tennessee, Kentucky, and a few skirmishes in Alabama. Dragging Canoe, Doublehead, and their warriors fought in conjunction with factions of the Chickamauga from a number of other Indian tribes both in the south and in the north.

John McDonald

Initially, Dragging Canoe's 500 warriors traveled south and settled on the bank opposite of Chickamauga Creek across from the home of John McDonald, a British agent, establishing Chickamauga Town, the first in a series of "Lower Towns" of disaffected, mostly younger Cherokees and their families. Their selection of a town site was no coincidence. Dragging Canoe knew that McDonald had supply lines from his British contacts in Pensacola. With the American Revolution brewing, the Chickamauga and the British now had common enemies. McDonald, an ensign in the British Army, could provide the Chickamauga with guns, ammunition, and other supplies that they could no longer get from the French or the Americans (Brown, 1938).

Scottish trader John McDonald is perhaps best known for being the grandfather of Cherokee Principal Chief John Ross…His primary home in the Cherokee Nation was not in Rossville, but on the waters of Chickamauga Creek, where the Brainerd Mission was later located. It is from this location in the Revolutionary War era that the fierce Chickamauga Chief Dragging Canoe was supplied with British weaponry to make war against the Americans…the Cherokees were seen as a barely containable force that could help tip the balance of power in early America one way or the other, and McDonald was seen as a possible fulcrum-for-hire, right at the center (Bishop, 2010).

Chickamauga Town

McDonald immigrated to South Carolina from Scotland in the 1760s and by 1770 he had married Ann Shorey, daughter of Ghigooie, a Cherokee of the Bird Clan. Though Ann's father had been Englishman William Shorey, she had been reared fully as a Cherokee after Shorey died on Lt. Henry Timberlake's journey back to England in 1762 (Moulton, 1978). By 1771, John and Ann McDonald settled on Chickamauga Creek, some 15 miles south of its junction with the Tennessee River. McDonald was appointed assistant superintendent or "deputy and commissary" of Indian Affairs for the British, under John Stuart (Brown, 1938).

McDonald was soon not only supplying Dragging Canoe, Doublehead, Bloody Fellow, and other Chickamauga with supplies but also actively helping to coordinate attacks against the frontier settlements in Georgia and the Carolinas, even to the extent of leading Cherokee raiding parties (Pate, 1969). The British began to use the Chickamauga Town as a headquarters for their operations in the Southwest, stockpiling food and supplies there and using the area as a rallying point for all tribes hostile to the Americans.

But all of this came to an abrupt end in April, 1779, when General Evan Shelby led an American attack against Chickamauga Town and the surrounding villages. The army burned all the buildings and destroyed the commissaries of McDonald and the other British agents, laying waste to the stores of food and plundering everything that could be carted

66

off for sale, such as ammunition, furs, and horses (Brown, 1938). (This is the sale from which Sale Creek gets its name.)

"I ... enclose you a letter from Colonel Shelby stating the effect of his success against the seceding Cherokees and Chuccomogga," Thomas Jefferson (1779) reported to George Washington following the attack. "The damage done them was ... burning 11 towns, 20,000 bushels of corn collected probably to forward the expeditions ... and taking as many goods as sold for $125,000".

The Chickamauga warriors were not present during the attack (Pate, 1969). When they returned they decided to relocate again, even farther from the whites, west of Lookout Mountain, forming what would become known as the "Five Lower Towns" of Nickajack, Running Water, Long Island Town, Crow Town, and Stecoe, or "Lookout Mountain Town" (Brown, 1938).

Though the Americans had officially declared the Revolution over on April 11, 1783, the Chickamauga fought on from their new base at the Five Lower Towns, and by 1784, McDonald returned to help them, setting up shop at Running Water, a town situated at a Creek crossing on the Tennessee River, just west of Lookout Mountain (Brown, 1938). McDonald and several others living at Running Water were within twenty miles of Chicamoggy (Chickamauga). A certain Alexander Cameron who was living with McDonald was being supplied with goods and ammunition from Savannah or Augusta. Cameron in the course of the war was a murderer and robber, and frequently went out with the Indians, murdering women and children.

About 1788, McDonald moved together with his family to Turkey Town, and continued trade with the Chickamauga. The Little Turkey was the Principal Chief of the Cherokee Nation and resided in that town. The town was also much closer to the old abandoned French Ft. Tolouse, and there was talk being circulated that it might be re-garrisoned by the Spanish or that a new fort would be garrisoned just north, near the current site of Ft. Payne, Alabama. Turkey Town, near the present location of Center, Alabama on the Coosa River, was where John Ross was born, in 1790. At this time, McDonald was corresponding with William Panton of Panton, Leslie & Co., a British supplier of trade goods that had become allied with the Spanish interests (Bishop, 2010).

Death of Dragging Canoe

In east Tennessee after the Revolutionary War in 1783, the upper Cherokee were a people trying to make peace and survive in a country controlled by a newly established government of the United States. Devastated by war, disease, and land hungry American settlers, their days east of the Mississippi River were numbered. However, Dragging Canoe and his warriors of the Lower Cherokee faction of the Chickamauga continued the fight until his death. After Dragging Canoe died, Doublehead continued his war for three more years. It was a war against land hungry white settlers, and a fight that both Dragging Canoe and Doublehead knew and prophesied would be futile in the end.

After successful raids on the Cumberland settlements by his brother Little Owl and a mission to unite other major tribes in the area, Dragging Canoe participated in a huge all-night celebration and scalp dance at Stecoyee. By the next morning of March 1, 1792, Dragging Canoe was dead. A procession of honor carried his body to Running Water, where he was buried. By the time of his death, the resistance of the Chickamauga and Lower Cherokee faction had led to a grudging respect from the white settlers, as well as the rest of the Cherokee Nation. Dragging Canoe was even memorialized at the general council of the Cherokee Nation held in Ustanali in June 1792 by his nephew Black Fox (*Inali*):

"The Dragging Canoe has left this world. He was a man of consequence in his country. He was friend to both his own and the white people. His brother (Little Owl) is still in place, and I mention it now publicly that I intend presenting him with his deceased brother's medal; for he promises fair to possess sentiments similar to those of his brother, both with regard to the red and the white. It is mentioned here publicly that both red and white may know it, and pay attention to him."

Doublehead-Last Chickamauga Chief

Prior to the death of Dragging Canoe, Doublehead operated from the Great Bend towns almost completely independent of the rest of the Chickamauga leaders. He loved his small war parties that he dominated with complete control and authority. In addition, Doublehead's brutality included butchering some of his victims with the most noted act of eating Lieutenant William Overall and a Burnett man. He also participated in the mutilation of his white settler enemies that were encroaching into his sacred hunting grounds. By these atrocious acts, Doublehead put fear into the hearts of both his white enemies and fellow Chickamauga warriors.

After Dragging Canoe's death in 1792, Doublehead moved into a more powerful position among the Chickamauga and carried on the war against the encroaching settlers until June 1795. Prior to Dragging Canoe's death, Doublehead had already lost his older brothers Red Bird, Old Tassel, and Standing Turkey. In 1793, his younger brother Pumpkin Boy would be shot dead at Ish's Station by Colonel John Sevier's men while Doublehead was carrying the fight to the frontier settlers. Doublehead considered no superiors among the Chickamauga and was the last Chickamauga chief to cease hostilities against the land hungry white settlers.

In the year of 1769, the Cherokees attacked the Chickasaws at Chickasaw Island in the Tennessee River south of present-day Huntsville, Alabama. Even though the Chickasaws claimed victory in the Battle of Chickasaw Oldfields, they began migrating west. At the same time, the Lower Cherokee faction of the Chickamauga under the leadership of Doublehead began moving into the lands of the Great Bend that had previously been occupied by Chickasaws. By the early 1770's, Doublehead and the Chickamauga were occupying the Tennessee River towns from present-day Guntersville, Alabama to the mouth of Bear Creek near the present-day Mississippi State line in the western portion of the Great Bend. According to the Cherokee Treaty of March 22, 1816, *"The Cherokee Nation extended as far west as a place on the waters of Bear Creek (a branch of the Tennessee River), known by the name of the Flat Rock, or Stone."*

Great Bend Towns

Following Dragging Canoe, Chickamauga Chief Doublehead migrated farther southwest along the Tennessee River into north central Alabama. Doublehead and his Chickamauga warriors helped establish the following villages in the Great Bend of the Tennessee River: Brown's Village on Brown's Creek near the Creek Path; Mouse Town (Monee town) at the mouth of Fox's Creek and Tennessee River; Doublehead's Town at Brown's Ferry, between Fox's and Mallard Creeks; Fox's Stand at the junction of the Browns Ferry Road and Black Warriors' Path; Melton's Bluff between Mallard and Spring Creeks; Cuttyatoy's Village on an island in the mouth of Spring Creek north of Big Head Spring; Gourd's Settlement near present-day Courtland, Alabama on Big Nance Creek; Shoal Town on Big Muscle Shoals between Blue Water Creek, Shoal Town Creek, and Big Nance Creek, just west of present-day Wheeler Dam; Oakville at the junction of Black Warriors' Path and the Coosa Path; Cold Water near mouth of Big Spring Creek or Coldwater Creek and Tennessee River; Doublehead's Village near Mhoon Town; and, Colbert's Ferry at the Natchez Trace crossing of the Tennessee River.

According to Two Hundred Years at Muscle Shoals, "Oka Kapassa was established as a Cherokee village about 1770 on the west bank of Coldwater, or Spring Creek, at its confluence with the Tennessee, about one mile west of the present Tuscumbia. This site was resorted to by neighboring Indians for the purpose of trading with the French who still persisted on the Wabash, and became the source of great vexation and numerous outrages to the Cumberland settlements about our present Nashville" (Leftwich, 1935). Coldwater was eventually destroyed by Colonel James Robertson's forces because of the numerous attacks and killings taking place in the Cumberland settlements around Nashville, Tennessee.

Eventually, the French were defeated in several battles by the British Alliance with the Chickasaws and Cherokees; however, toward the end of the 1770s, French influence greatly diminished and Doublehead begin trading with Scots-Irish frontiersmen who eventually intermarried with his family. These Scots-Irish traders were bringing in British items from Old Charles Town that were cheaper and of better quality.

From his Great Bend stronghold, the powerful Chickamauga Chief Doublehead controlled the Carolina trade and exerted the most influence along the Tennessee River from Mississippi, through north Alabama, and into the middle of east Tennessee. His influence dominated trade in the Great Bend of the Tennessee River Valley's historical landscape from 1770 to his death on August 9, 1807.

Chake Thlocko

Governor William Blount referred to Doublehead as the principal chief of the lower Tennessee River Indian towns along the Muscle Shoals. During his time in the Great Bend, Doublehead helped establish several Chickamauga towns along the Tennessee River with the help of the Creek, Shawnee, Yuchi, white sympathizers, relatives, and his loyal mixed bloods of Scots-Irish ancestry. With this motley mix of warriors, Doublehead ruled the great crossing place of the Muscle Shoals known to the Indians as Chake Thlocko, Big Ford or Great Crossing Place. The Great Bend of the Tennessee River is the southernmost loop of the river where it turns south out of Tennessee into Alabama and runs east to west across the northern portion of Alabama before turning north back into Tennessee and through Kentucky to the Ohio River.

Numerous Indian trails, basically unknown to the white settlers encroaching into Chickamauga country, crossed along some 37 miles of the Muscle Shoals on the Tennessee River. The trails crossed on a series of shoals which included: Elk River Shoals, the most upstream; Big Muscle Shoals; Little Muscle Shoals; Colbert Shoals; Bee Tree Shoals; and Waterloo Shoals, the most downstream of these rapids. The shoals were created by a geologic feature consisting of layers of chert (flint) outcroppings that were very resistant to erosion. This resistant rock formed stretches of rushing waters cascading over sharp rocky defiles which created very hazardous conditions for water travel. These shoals also had numerous sand bars and islands that only experienced Indian guides were able to safely navigate during high water levels and rainy seasons of the year. The Tennessee River at the shoals dropped 134 feet vertically within some 37 miles from Elk River Shoals to Waterloo Shoals and created corridors for trail crossings.

The trails that crossed Chake Thlocko were used for thousands of years by Indian inhabitants and were well known to Doublehead and his Chickamauga people. These trails

70

and roads provided easy routes east to the main Lower Cherokee towns, north to the Cumberland settlements, west to the Chickasaw towns on the upper Tombigbee, and south to the Creek towns including the Atlantic and Gulf Coast.

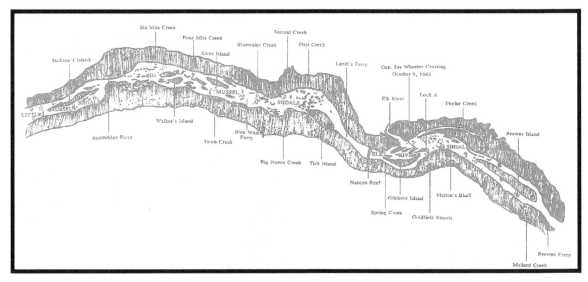

The Mussel Shoals of the Tennessee River

It was mainly the north-south routes that Doublehead's Chickamauga warriors used to conduct raids against the Cumberland settlements from the Muscle Shoals. The major northern routes to the French Lick included: 1). Mountain Leaders Trace crossed the Tennessee River at the mouth of Bear Creek at the Mississippi-Alabama state line became portions of the Natchez Trace; 2) Old Buffalo Trail ran from Tuscaloosa, Alabama and became portions of the Byler Road. After Doublehead upgraded the northern portion of the trail to a road, it became known as Doublehead's Trace and portions of present-day highway 101, to present-day Lawrenceburg, Tennessee, then to Nashville; 3) Sipsie Trail became known as the Cheatham Road from Tuscaloosa to Moulton, Alabama and was known as the Lamb's Ferry Road after establishing the ferry crossing of the Tennessee River to Rogersville, to Minor Hill, Tennessee, then to Nashville; 4) Black Warriors' Path from St. Augustine, Florida to Nashville, Tennessee was later called Mitchell Trace after a post route was established from Fort Mitchell in Russell County, Alabama to Fort Hampton in Limestone County, Alabama, to Elkton, Tennessee then north to French Lick; 5) Old Jasper Road lay along the corridor of present-day highway 41 through Jasper, Alabama, crossed the Tennessee River at Rhodes Ferry in present-day Decatur, Alabama, and followed portions of present highway 31 to the French Lick; and, 6) Great South Trail

71

crossed the Tennessee River at Ditto's Landing and became the Old Huntsville Road from Nashville to Tuscaloosa.

Doublehead and his warriors were not noted for taking prisoners unless he was accompanied by the Creek faction that would take prisoners deep into Alabama along the winding routes. During most of Doublehead's raids, scalps and horses were prized items to take and bring back to the shoals along these numerous trails that crossed Chake Thlocko. In addition, the rough Appalachian terrain to the east, Warrior Mountains to the south, and the Cumberland Plateau to the north of the Muscle Shoals added a protective but difficult barrier to access the Great Bend towns of Doublehead's Chickamauga.

Doublehead's Town

In the 1770's, Doublehead moved to the head of Elk River Shoals on the south bank of the Tennessee River in present-day Lawrence County, Alabama. His village was called Doublehead's Town and was at a river crossing known as Brown's Ferry, which was located at the upstream end of the Muscle Shoals. He lived at the Brown's Ferry site until 1802 when he moved to Shoal Town on the north side of the river near the mouth of Blue Water Creek in present-day Lauderdale County, Alabama.

Doublehead's Town was originally established and occupied by some 40 warriors and their families, but quickly increased in size to a considerable village. The town was a mixed community of Lower Cherokee, Creek, Shawnee, Chickasaw, Yuchi, and several mixed bloods who carried out many raids against the Cumberland settlements to steal horses and take a few scalps. Doublehead's Town was located just one mile east of the junctions of Brown's Ferry Road, South River Road, and Black Warriors' Path.

"Yet, Doublehead was without influence or position until about the year 1790, when he established a town on the Tennessee River at the head of the Muscle Shoals. An early map of the Cherokee country shows this village at a site near the south bank of Brown's Ferry below Athens. He later in 1802 moved it to the north bank of the river near the mouth of Blue Water Creek in Lauderdale County, Alabama…Inhabitants of Doublehead's Town, originally about 40 in number, were mostly cast-offs from other Cherokee and Creek villages. This motley bunch became infamous in Tennessee history as The Ravagers of the Cumberlands" (McDonald, 1989).

For a brief period, the Brown's Ferry at Doublehead's Town became known as Cox's Ferry. A man by the name of Cox, who was supposedly the son of Zachariah Cox, had apparently married Betsy, one of John Brown's Cherokee girls, and for a short period was known as Cox's Ferry. The Brown's Ferry Road crossed the river at Doublehead's Town and approximately one mile west intersected Black Warriors' Path and the South

72

River Road at Fox's Stand. During the surveys made by General John Coffee, the stand was run by Black Fox II, the son of the Principal Chief of the Cherokee Nation, Black Fox. Black Fox was principal chief of the Cherokees from 1801 through 1811, and Fox's Creek in Lawrence County, Alabama is named in his honor. Black Fox and Doublehead were friends and each signed treaties from which they received benefits.

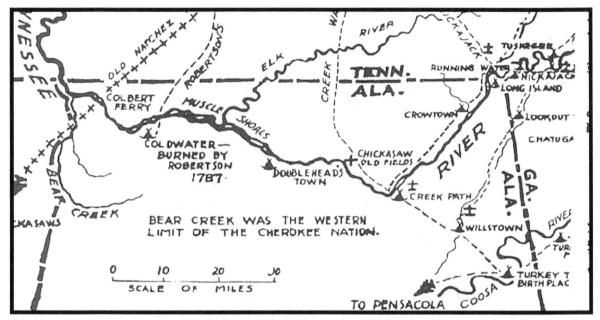

Doublehead's Town at Brown's Ferry

Adjacent to the west of where Brown's Ferry crossed to the south bank of the Tennessee River is a higher level ground that contained in excess of 40 homes of Doublehead's Town. The high ground on each side of the Brown's Ferry Road forms a peninsula that extends into the river flood plain and was an ideal location for buildings, pastures, and farmlands. Remnants of the old road bed, some ten feet deep in places, now disappears into the backwaters of Wheeler Lake. Still clearly visible at the town site, which is presently Tennessee Valley Authority property, is evidence of occupation including crude nails, broken ceramics, metallic pieces, garlic, and other domestic flowering plants.

Historical records indicate that Doublehead lived in his Chickamauga Indian town at Brown's Ferry from the 1770's through December 1801. According to *History of Alabama* by Albert James Pickett (1851), *"Dec. 1801: Emigrants flocked to the Mississippi Territory...constructing flat-boats at Knoxville, they floated down the river to the head of the Muscle Shoals, where they disembarked at the house of Double-Head, a*

Cherokee Chief...placing their effects upon the horses, which had been brought down by land from Knoxville, they departed on foot for the Bigby settlements." Based on this 1851 historical note, Doublehead was still living at Brown's Ferry until early 1802. The route the settlers utilized for bringing their horses to Brown's Ferry was along portions of the South River Road. From Doublehead's Town, the emigrants followed the Brown's Ferry Road to Gourd's Settlement (Courtland, Alabama) where it intersected with Gaines' Trace that led to Cotton Gin Port on the Tombigbee River.

In 1803, Reverend Patrick Wilson traveled along the southern side to the Tennessee River and followed the South River Road. The following excerpt describes the route, *"The expedition continued on the Natchez Trace to present-day* (Colbert County) *Alabama, where Wilson observed land controlled by the Chickamauga Cherokee, who, although interested in European American material culture, were highly resistant to territorial encroachment in the Tennessee Valley. Federal efforts to assimilate the Cherokee economically and culturally began in earnest in 1798 with the signing of the Tellico Block House Treaty. The United States government established gristmills and provided cottonseed, spinning wheels, and looms to the Cherokee. Federal agents were sent to teach farming techniques such as plowing and fence building. The "worm or angle" fences described by Wilson were zigzag fences made of split rails crossed at the ends.*

At the Muscle Shoals, east of present-day Florence, Alabama, the expedition left the Natchez Trace to follow the south bank of the Tennessee River. Here the party rested in a Chickamauga Cherokee town (Doublehead's Town) *administered by Tal Tsuska* (Doublehead), *a controversial and historically significant chief who controlled transportation routes, leased land to settlers, and led resistance against European American encroachment.*

Tal Tsuske and his followers controlled the Muscle Shoals area for many years. Wilson does not mention, however, that Tal Tsuske was the father-in-law of George Colbert...Continuing in Cherokee territory, Wilson's party traveled north, passing through "Watts or Wills Town," the capital of the Chickamauga... Wilson's narrative ends in Hiwassee, a Cherokee town no longer in existence." (Hathorn and Sabino, 2001) By the time of Wilson's expedition in 1803, Doublehead had already moved from his town at Brown's Ferry to the Chickamauga village known as Shoal Town on the north side of the Tennessee River near the mouth of Blue Water Creek. Also note, that Wilson observed that the Chickamauga Cherokees controlled the Big Bend area all the way to the Natchez Trace crossing of the Tennessee River.

Doublehead's Domain

Doublehead had influence from the southern portion of the Natchez Trace, up the Tennessee River to the middle of east Tennessee at South West Point, the mouth of the Clinch River. Since two of his daughters lived on Natchez Trace and two other daughters lived near South West Point, Doublehead's family dominated a large area along the Tennessee River.

Doublehead's first two daughters Tuskiahooto and Saleechie were the wives of Chickasaw Chief George Colbert, (Tootemastubbe, The Ferryman) and ran inns along the Natchez Trace. Tuskiahooto ran an inn at Colbert's Ferry in present-day Colbert County, Alabama, and Saleechie ran an inn in Tupelo, Mississippi. In addition, Doublehead's second two daughters Nigodegiyu and Gulustiyu lived with their husband Samuel Riley near South West Point which was located at the forks of the Clinch River and the Tennessee River in east Tennessee.

George Colbert's Home on Natchez Trace, Colbert County, AL

Doublehead exerted his authority, control, and influence over the Chickamauga towns along the Great Bend of the Tennessee River all the way to Mississippi because he and his warriors had helped establish these towns during the 1770's. Also, he became upset that his sister's son, John Watts, Jr., was elected chief over him after the death of the powerful Chickamauga Chief Dragging Canoe on March 1, 1792; therefore, he exercised his power with the assistance of a motley bunch of Lower Cherokee, Chickasaw, Upper Creek, Shawnee, Yuchi, Delaware, white sympathizers, Scots-Irish mixed blood warriors, and his relatives. Most of the whites and Scots-Irish mixed bloods were connected to the tribe by intermarriage and initially became affiliated with the tribe as traders.

Doublehead's War

Doublehead's personal war against encroaching settlers lasted for some 20 years from 1775 through June 1795. From the southwestern most portions of the Cherokee land claims along the Muscle Shoals, Doublehead made his own declarations of war against the white settlers moving into his hunting grounds. He decided when and where to attack whether it was only two, two hundred, or two thousand in his party. If they were with him, he was in charge. Occasionally, Doublehead would join Chickamauga forces from the five lower towns to conduct large scale raids into east Tennessee, but on most of these raids, Doublehead caused more controversy because he wanted to do things his way.

During his years on the war path, the Cumberland River was Doublehead's primary focus in order to protect his favorite buffalo hunting grounds. It was originally called the Warioto River by the Indians and the Shauvanon River by the French traders. But the early white settlers named it in honor of the Duke of Cumberland, the Prime Minister of England. For several years, these first white people who settled at the French Lick or Big Lick (Nashville) on the Cumberland River in 1780 paid Doublehead and the Chickamauga in their own blood.

Doublehead was considered the most ruthless, brutal, violent, and blood thirsty Chickamauga warrior to ever live. Even though his nephew Robert Benge personally took 45 scalps, historians agree that Doublehead far surpassed that mark. Some forty years of his life was spent on the warpath-killing, scalping, stealing, burning, and destroying. However, one day in June 1795, Doublehead ceased all hostilities against the white settlers and was never recorded on another raid. After his time on the warpath ended, he became a very shrewd and very successful businessman

In order to have an understanding of Doublehead and the Chickamauga raids made upon the frontiers of the Tennessee and Cumberland Rivers, several references were utilized for a better understanding of the dark and bloody suffering that was occurring on the side of white settlers. Doublehead's people were fighting for their families, their way of life, their homelands, and their sacred hunting grounds. White settlers were seeking the opportunities among unfamiliar people in a remote frontier that could be theirs for the taking but at some sacrifice. Many times that sacrifice would be their lives or the lives of family members.

Not all raids were documented and recorded by historians, therefore, many attacks may have occurred during the Chickamauga War. This section is about the documented raids made by the Chickamauga to hold their lands and preserve their way of life. Some of the sources include *Tennessee, The Volunteer State* (Moore, 1923), *The Annals of Tennessee* (Ramsey, 1853), *The Aboriginal History of Tennessee: up to the first settlement therein by the white people in the year 1768* (Haywood, 1973), *Civil and Political History of the State of Tennessee* (John Haywood, 1823), *The Civil and Political History of the State of Tennessee from its earliest...*(Haywood and Colyer, 1891), *The Story of the Cherokee Indians...*(Brown, 1938), *Andrew Jackson and Early Tennessee History* (Heiskell, 1918), *Early History of Middle Tennessee* (Albright, 1909), Historic Sumner County, Tennessee: with genealogies of the Bledsoe, Cage, and Douglass families and genealogical notes on other Sumner County families*(Jay Guy Cisco), *History of Old Sumner* (Puryear, 2011), and other historical and archival records.

Doublehead's Alliance

Doublehead continued to build an Indian alliance as his predecessor Dragging Canoe had done the day before he died. Doublehead, John Watts, Jr., Bloody Fellow, and "Young Dragging Canoe" (*Tsula*) continued Dragging Canoe's policy of Indian unity, including an agreement with Creek Chief Alexander McGillivray of the Upper Muscogee to build joint blockhouses or trading posts from which warriors of both tribes could operate. One trading post was at South West Point near the junction of the Tennessee and Clinch Rivers, one at Running Water west of Chattanooga and north of Nickajack, and one at Muscle Shoals. Doublehead's base of operations was at the mouth of Blue Water Creek on Big Muscle Shoals in order to be close to his Muscogee allies. At this site, Doublehead had a large trading post where the 100 mile long Doublehead's Trace from Franklin, Tennessee crossed the Tennessee River at the mouth of Blue Water Creek.

Doublehead's alliance was a loose confederacy of Lower Cherokee, Upper Creek, Chickasaw, Shawnee, Yuchi, Delaware and many mixed blood Scots-Irish warriors that he would command from his stronghold of the shoals in the Great Bend. Doublehead and his warriors lived along the Muscle Shoals that consisted of a series of six rapids covering some 40 miles of the Tennessee River. Beginning at the upstream or eastern end was Elk River Shoals, Big Muscle Shoals, Little Muscle Shoals, Colbert Shoals, Bee Tree Shoals, and Waterloo Shoals was the western most of these shoals. It was from his sanctuary along these Muscle Shoals of the Big Bend of the Tennessee River that Doublehead and his Chickamauga staged raids against white settlers to the north along the Cumberland River into Kentucky and east to Virginia.

From 1775 through the middle of 1795, Doublehead's Chickamauga warriors killed several hundred white settlers with a large number wounded, and over two thousand horses were stolen. Many more unknown white settlers were killed and not recorded or failed to be counted as casualties. In the following, documented raids and battles waged by Doublehead's Chickamauga, known as the "Ravagers of the Cumberlands", will be identified by place and date in chronological order. Doublehead may have not participated in each raid, but he was the leader of the Chickamauga at Muscle Shoals and continued to encourage the destruction of the Cumberland settlements until 1795.

Year of 1780-First Cumberland Settlements

Chattanooga

March 8, 1780—In the early days of 1780, General James Robertson and Colonel John Donelson were the leaders that began a movement west to establish a new settlement on the Cumberland River that would eventually become Nashville, Tennessee. General Robertson would take a group overland to the area, while Colonel Donelson's group would make the trip by water. The water route would take the group down the Tennessee River to the Ohio River, then up the Ohio to the Cumberland River, then up the Cumberland to the Big Lick (Nashville). The Donelson route was extremely dangerous, not only because of the treacherous rapids, but the group would go through the country of the Chickamauga and by some of the largest Indian towns on the Tennessee River. Not only would the Donelson party pass the town of Dragging Canoe, but also the town of Doublehead. Both of these war leaders of Chickamauga had declared in 1775 their intentions of stopping the encroachment of white settlers on their sacred hunting grounds.

In the early part of 1780, Colonel John Donelson's flotilla of some forty boats carrying 50 men and 130 women and children begin descending the Tennessee River toward Nashville. While in route west of Chattanooga, they were fired upon by a group of Chickamauga killing a young man by the name of Payne. Lagging behind the main group of voyagers was a boat of 28 persons that had smallpox and this group was captured and killed by the Chickamauga as seen in the following:

There was with the flotilla a boat carrying twenty-eight passengers, among whom an epidemic of smallpox had broken out. To guard against a spread of this disease to other members of the fleet agreement had been made that it should keep well to the rear, its owner, Mr. Stuart, being notified each night by the sound of a hunting horn when those ahead went into camp. Therefore, this unfortunate party was far behind while the events above mentioned were taking place. When they came down opposite the towns the Indians were on the shore in large numbers and seeing them thus cut off from the rest of the fleet swarmed out in canoes and with cold-blooded, murderous intent killed and captured the entire crew. Cries of the latter were distinctly heard by those in the boats ahead, but they were unable to stem the swift current and thus return to aid their perishing comrades.

But the Indians suffered a swift and righteous retribution for this wanton act of cruelty. They became infected with the disease of their victims, and for many months thereafter smallpox raged, not only among the Chickamauga, but in the tribes of their neighbors, the Creeks and Cherokees. When stricken with the malady and while the fever was yet upon them, the savages would take a heavy sweat in their huts. When driven to madness by the fever and heat, they would rush out and leap into the river, from the effects of which folly they died by scores. Old persons of to-day well remember the traditional accounts of a great and terrible mortality which prevailed among the savages after the capture of Stuart's boat (Albright, 1909).

The great Chickamauga Chief Dragging Canoe had survived the smallpox disease, but the scars remained on his body to the day he died. Thousands of native American Indian people were not as lucky and died of the horrible afflictions brought into their land by white settlers.

After the ordeal with the Stuart boat, the Chickamauga Indians again attacked some ten miles west of Chattanooga at the "Suck" and wounded four people including the infant of a Mrs. Peyton. The son of Jonathan Jennings, his comrade, and a Negro man jumped into the water to swim to shore. The black man drowned and the two boys were captured by the Chickamauga. The Jennings boy was ransomed by a friendly half-blood trader named John James "Hell-Fire Jack" Rogers and returned to his family at the French Lick. His comrade was killed and burned; therefore, by the time Donelson's group reached Nashville, he had 31 people killed by the Chickamauga.

Muscle Shoals

March 14, 1780--Doublehead and the lower Tennessee River Chickamauga were firmly in control of the eastern and western ends of the Muscle Shoals, which consisted of a series of six sets of rapids. *"When Colonel John Donelson and his company drifted down the Tennessee River in 1780, they encountered hostile Indians at both ends of the Muscle Shoals and at the lower end, five of their party was wounded."* This is one of the first confirmed conflicts with white settlers and the Chickamauga at Doublehead's bastion of the Muscle Shoals. The Muscle Shoals stretched from just west of present-day Decatur, Alabama to Waterloo, in western Lauderdale County, Alabama.

Nashville

May 1780—Nashville was one of the prime targets of Doublehead and his Chickamauga Warriors. The area around Nashville was the site of one of the largest mineral licks found along the Cumberland River, and therefore attracted great herds of deer, elk, and buffalo. Many of the licks along the river were described as the hub of a wagon wheel with its animal trails radiating out like the spokes. These buffalo, elk, and deer trails were worn deeply into the earth and many times were used as roads by both the Indians and white long hunters.

The lick at Nashville was known as the Big Lick or French Lick and a favorite hunting site of Doublehead. Several trails from the Muscle Shoals stronghold of Doublehead led directly to the licks on the Cumberland River. These trails included what would become known as the Natchez Trace, Doublehead's Trace, Sipsie Trail, Black Warriors' Path, and several lesser known routes. All these trails were used by several factions of the Chickamauga including the Chickasaw, Lower Cherokee, Upper Creek, Delaware, Shawnee, Yuchi, and others to attack the white settlers who were invading their hunting grounds. The Delaware faction would at times attack areas along the Cumberland from their stronghold in the Ohio River Basin.

One morning during the month of May, a hunter by the name of Keywood came running to the fort at the Bluff and reported that John Milliken had been killed on Richland Creek, five or six miles to the south. The two men were journeying toward the settlement and stopped at the creek for a drink. While they stooped down to drink, they were fired upon by a band of Chickamauga Indians hidden on the bank and Milliken fell dead. Keywood had escaped uninjured and made his way to the settlement to bear the news of the tragic death of his comrade.

A few days later, Joseph Hay was on the Lick Branch between the Bluff and Freeland's Station when a party of Chickamauga shot and scalped him. The Indians took his gun, hunting knife, shot pouch, and powder horn. He was buried east of Sulphur Spring.

Soon thereafter, a man named Bernard was at work clearing land when he was shot and killed. The Indians cut off his head and carried it with them. In the retreat of the Chickamauga, they encountered three young men, two brothers named Dunham and a son of John Milliken, who had already been killed. The Dunhams escaped to Freeland's Station, but the young Milliken was killed and his head also cut off and carried away.

80

Mansker's Station

June 1780—Mansker's Station, near Goodlettsville, Tennessee, was located 12 miles north of Nashville on the west side of Mansker's Creek between two large licks. The station was named after Casper Mansker who was born in 1746 and died in1820. Mansker was one of the early long hunters that came from the east in the late 1760's to take bear, deer, elk, and buffalo. Mansker killed 19 deer in one day that were traveling between the two licks.

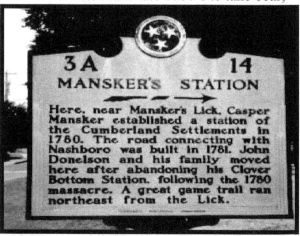

Two settlers by the names of Goin and Kennedy were clearing land between Mansker's and Eaton's Stations. They were fired upon, killed, and scalped by the Chickamauga. Later in the year, the Chickamauga killed Patrick Quigley, John Stuckley, James Lumsey, and Betsy Kennedy at Mansker's Station. Also, William Neely from Mansker's Station was killed near Neely's Lick and his daughter taken prisoner. She was held at a Creek town but released several years later.

Renfroe's Station

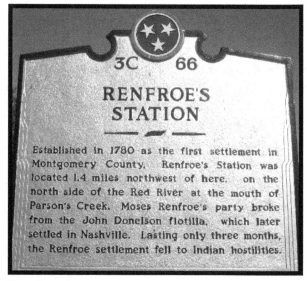

July 1780—Some twenty persons were killed over two days by Doublehead's Chickamauga warriors during their assault on Renfroe's Station at the mouth of the Red River. Two were killed in the initial attack and the rest left for the Bluff, but they came back and gathered belongings. Again they started for Eaton's Station or the Bluff, but made camp before reaching their destination. Early the next morning, they were attacked and scattered in the woods where each of them were hunted down and killed. Among those that died were Joseph Renfroe and Mr. Johns and his entire family of twelve.

Nashville

August 1780—Late in August 1780, Jonathan Jennings was killed near the river bank on a point above Nashville. At the time he was killed, Jennings was building a cabin on the tract of land upon which he had recently made entry. The Indians chopped his body into pieces and scattered the fragments over the surrounding ground.

A number of the settlers were killed by Doublehead's forces within what is now the city limits of Nashville, Tennessee. D. Larimer was shot, scalped, and beheaded near Freeland's Station. Isaac Lefeore met a like fate on the west bank of the Cumberland River.

Solomon Murry, Soloman Phillips, and Robert Aspey were fired upon while at work. Murry and Aspey were killed and scalped. Phillips was wounded but escaped to the fort at the Bluff (Fort Nashborough) where he died a few days later.

Benjamin Renfroe, John Maxwell, and John Kennedy were fishing on the river bank near the mouth of Sulphur Spring Branch. The Chickamauga made an attack on them and took the men prisoners. They killed and scalped Renfroe, but spared the lives of Kennedy and Maxwell.

Phillip Catron journeyed from Freeland's Station to the Bluff along a buffalo path that passed a thick cluster of undergrowth. While in the thicket, Cantron was shot but held to his horse and rode to the station. Even though he was severely wounded, he eventually recovered.

John Caffrey and Daniel Williams, two occupants at the Bluff (Nashville) Fort, went up river and on their return were shot in the legs. The two men escaped with only wounds because of assistance from John Rains and several of his companions who rushed from the fort to chase eight to ten Chickamauga as far as Sulphur Springs (Albright, 1908).

Eaton's Station

Summer 1780—Eaton's Station was named in honor of Amos Eaton who helped to build the fort. James Mayfield and a man named Porter were killed in plain view of their comrades near Eaton's Station. The men in the fort grabbed their rifles and gave chase, but the Indians escaped.

Colonel Richard Henderson's body servant and Negro cook, Jim, was killed by a party of Indians east of Nashville near Clover Bottom. The bottom was ten miles up the Cumberland from the mouth of Stones River. Jim and a young white man, a chain carrier in Henderson's surveying party, were about to begin a journey down the river by canoe from the camp to the Bluff. The Chickamauga was hiding in thick cane and fired upon the two men and killed Jim.

HEATON'S STATION

On this bluff in 1780, pioneers who came with James Robertson built Heaton's (also spelled Eaton's) station. It and two other forts (Nashborough and Freeland's) withstood all Indian attacks and saved the Cumberland settlements. On the river below were successively a buffalo ford, ferry, and Lock I. The home of Amos Heaton stood 100 feet north.

Ned Carvin had made an entry on land four miles east of Nashville and built a cabin in which he and his family lived. One day while hoeing in his garden beside the house, he was shot by the Indians and killed instantly. His wife and two small children escaped by a door on the opposite side of the cabin and hid in cane all night and the next morning made their way to Eaton's Station. A few days after, John Shockley and Jesse Balestine were killed while hunting in the woods not far from Carvin's Cabin.

Jacob and Frederick Stump, two Dutchmen, had built a cabin on White's Creek, three miles north of Eaton's Station. While both were engaged in clearing land, Indians fired upon them killing Jacob. His brother Frederick started to run toward Eaton's Station and barely escaped with his life.

Bledsoe's Station

Fall 1780—Around 1780 an early long hunter Isaac Bledsoe and his brother Anthony built Bledsoe's Station and establish a white settlement near a huge mineral lick. A band of Chickamauga went to Bledsoe's Station and killed and scalped William Johnson and Daniel Mungle. After killing these two men, the Indians killed all the cattle they could find and set fire to some of the out houses and fencing.

On the way up the Cumberland River, the same band met Thomas Sharpe Spencer with two horses loaded with bear meat and pelts. The Indians fired on Spencer slightly wounding him. He dismounted and ran through the woods until he got into Bledsoe's Fort. He complained little about his wound, but grieved long and loud over the loss of his horses and bear meat.

The Chickamauga killed a man by the name of Payne and wounded a Phillips at Asher's Station in Sumner County just west of Bledsoe's Station.

Clover Bottom

November 4, 1780—A party of some 200 Chickamauga killed Captain Abel Gower, his son Abel Gower, Jr., Randolph Robertson, and six other men. A free black man by the name of Jack Cavil was taken prisoner, eventually became a member of the Chickamauga, and lived at the Chickamauga town that took his name called "Nickajack or Nigger-Jack's Town".

Year of 1781

Freeland's Station

January 15, 1781—During the night some 150 Chickamauga, most of whom were Chickasaw and a contingent of Lower Cherokee, entered the fort and were fired upon by General James Robertson. The Indians killed Major Lucas and a black man before being repelled by vicious fire from the portholes. Over five hundred bullets were dug out of the fort walls that were fired by the Indians during the six hour battle. Several Indian causalities were obvious by the large amount of blood found after daylight.

Shortly after this attack General Robertson had a peace meeting with Chickasaw Chief Piomingo and both agreed to terms of peace. The Chickasaws had participated in several prior attacks, but after the meeting with Robertson, the alliance was broken with the Chickamauga. The Chickasaws actually became allied with Robertson and the Cumberland settlers. It is worthy to give the description of the old chief Piomingo as follows:

"Piomingo was a striking figure among the noted Indian rulers of his day. He is described as having been of medium height, well-proportioned in body, and as possessing a face of unusual intelligence. Though at the time of his visit to Bledsoe's Lick, more than a hundred years old, he strode the earth with the grace of a youth. His dress was of white buckskin, and his hair, which he wore hanging down his back in the form of a scalp lock, was, by reason of his great age, as white as snow. This was clasped round about on top of his head by a set of silver combs" (Albright, 1909)

The Chickasaw was the first tribe to officially abandon the Chickamauga and to break from Doublehead's alliance. Eventually in 1795, Doublehead himself would forsake the Creek faction that was his most powerful force of the Chickamauga confederacy. The Creek would continue attacks on settlers until the Battle of Horse Shoe Bend in 1814.

Bluff Station (Fort Nashborough)

April 1, 1781—About 400 Chickamauga, most of the Lower Cherokee faction under Doublehead's leadership set an ambush around the fort. The next morning, three Indians were sent out as decoys to lure the armed men out of the fort. The plan worked to perfection when about 20 of the settlers rode their horses out of the fort and chased the Indians into the ambush they had set. As the settlers dismounted, they were surrounded by hundreds of Indians. Captain James leiper, Peter Gill, Alex Buchanan, John Kesenger, Zachariah White, George Kennedy, and John Kennedy were killed.

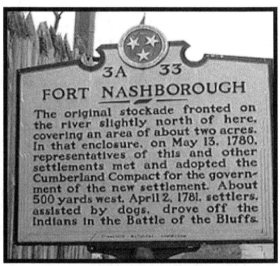

Kasper Mansker, James Manifee, Joseph Moonshaw, Isaac Lucas, and Edward Swanson were wounded.

Two things allowed most of the men to make it back to the fort. First, the settler horses spooked and many Indians tried to catch the animals. Second, Mrs. Robertson turned loose some 50 vicious dogs which attacked the Indians with such force they became overwhelmed. Mrs. Robertson later said, "*Thank God that he had given Indians a love of horses and a fear of dogs*".

A few days later just north of Nashville, the Chickamauga killed William Hood and Peter Renfroe.

Year of 1782

Kilgore's Station

Fall 1782—The Chickamauga ambushed and killed Josiah Hoskins and a young man by the last name of Mason.

Sumner County

Fall 1782—The Chickamauga killed William McMurry and wounded General Daniel Smith, who later became the Secretary of the territory and Senator from Tennessee.

Year of 1783

Rains' Station

Summer 1783—Chickamauga killed Roger Top and wounded Roger Glass.

Nashville

Summer 1783—Chickamauga killed Joseph, William, and Daniel Durham who were prospecting on Richland Creek. A few days later, they killed Joshua Norrington and Joel Mills. Betsy Williams was killed while riding a horse with her friend Patsy Rains. Miss Rains escaped to the safety of the Bluff. In addition, Joseph Nolan was killed while hunting and a few days later his father Thomas Nolan met the same fate.

Buchanan's Station

Summer 1783—In the Spring of 1783, Major John Buchanan built Buchanan's Station east of Nashville. The Chickamauga killed Samuel Buchanan and William Mulherrin while they were guarding the recently constructed fort. William Overall and Joshua Thomas were ambushed and killed while in route to Kentucky from the Cumberland settlements.

Nashville

Summer 1783—A band of Chickamauga Indians stole many horses around the Bluff and fled south with their booty. They were pursued by some 20 of the settlers under the command of Captain Pruett. He caught up with the Indians beyond the Duck River and recaptured the horses, but his group was counter attacked by the Indians who killed Moses

Brown, Daniel Pruett, and Daniel Johnson and retook the horses. Being outnumbered by superior numbers, Captain Pruett had several men wounded and his group made a retreat back to the Bluff.

Year of 1784

Many of Doublehead's raids were actually hunting excursions where parties of Indians and settlers came in contact and fought. Therefore, many people killed were due to conflicts over hunting territory. In the year 1784, the following skirmish was a direct result of hunting parties of settlers and Chickamauga coming in conflicts.

Nashville

May 1784—Cornelius Riddle was turkey hunting between Stones River and Buchanan's Station when he was shot and killed by the Chickamauga. They took his scalp and the turkeys he had killed.

Eaton's Station

Spring 1784—Phillip Mason and Nicholas Trammel had killed a deer near Eaton's Station and was in the process of cleaning the animal when Mason was wounded during an initial attack by Chickamauga. Trammel went to the station and got help and continued the confrontation with the Indians. Mason, Trammel, and Josiah Hoskins were killed in the fierce fire fight between the groups before each went their own way.

Drake's Creek

Summer 1784—George Espie, Andrew Lucas, Thomas Sharp Spencer, and a Johnson left the Bluff on a hunting trip on Drake's Creek. The creek had got its name in 1771 from long hunter Joseph Drake. The men were crossing the creek when they were attacked by a group of Chickamauga. Lucas was wounded and Espie was killed and scalped. Johnson and Spencer made a great stand until Spencer's arm was broken by a bullet. The two escaped to the Bluff and later Lucas made it back to safety.

Year of 1785

Nashville

Spring 1785—Another man by the name of Moses Brown built a fort near Richardson Creek some two and a half miles west of Nashville. During an attack by the

Chickamauga, Brown was killed and scalped. After his death, his family moved back to the Bluff. In addition, a man who was hired by William Stuart was killed on the farm near the forks of Mill Creek.

Summer 1785—Colonel Robertson, Colonel Weakly, and Edmund Hickman left the Bluff toward Piney Creek for the purpose of entering some tracts of land. They were attacked by a party of Chickamauga and Hickman was killed. Robertson and Weakly made it back to the fort at the Bluff.

Year of 1786

Clarksville

January 1786—The Chickamauga, mostly of the Lower Cherokee faction, killed Peter Barnett and David Steel and wounded William Crutcher.

Bledsoe's Lick

January 1786—The Chickamauga, primarily of the upper Creek faction, stole twelve of William Hall's horses that were very near his house. Fearing for his family's safety, the Halls moved to Bledsoe's Fort until the Fall.

February 1786—Ephraim Thomas, and John Peyton, John Frazier, Thomas Pugh, and Esquire Grant were hunting and surveying in Smith County. They were fired upon by about 60 Cherokees under the leadership of Hanging Maw. John Peyton, Thomas Peyton, Esquire Grant, and John Frazier were wounded and all their horses and equipment taken. All the party eventually reached the safety of Bledsoe's Fort.

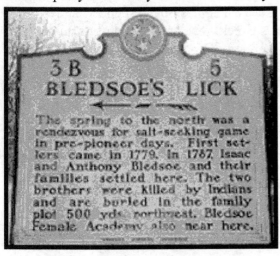

Year of 1787

Bledsoe's Lick

June 3, 1787—Bledsoe's Lick was named after Isaac Bledsoe a long hunter who in 1769 rode east from Station Camp Creek on a buffalo trace in what is now Sumner County, Tennessee. When Bledsoe came within two miles of the broad salt lick later named for him, his horse dashed into a galloping buffalo herd. He told Kasper

Mansker that the lick was covered with a moving mass of buffaloes, which he could not estimate by hundreds, but by thousands (Belue, 1996).

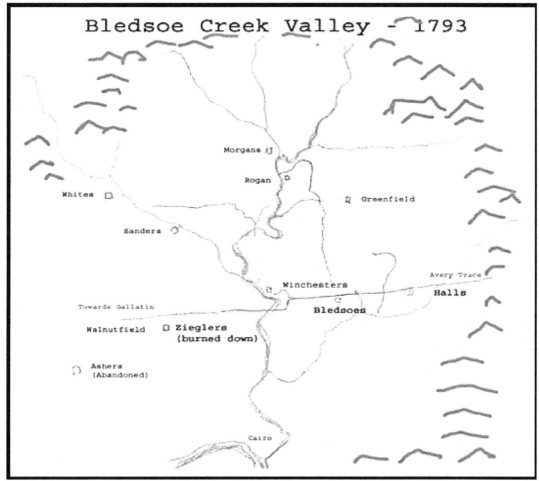

History of Old Sumner, Bill Puryear, 2011

The buffalo was one of the reasons Dragging Canoe, Doublehead, and other Chickamauga strongly opposed giving up their sacred hunting grounds in the area and the reason they fought so hard to keep white settlers from moving into the area. At the Treaty of Sycamore Shoals, Dragging Canoe said, *"the buffalo are our cattle"*. The Chickamauga fought hard and long to protect their hunting grounds, but eventually both the Chickamauga and buffalo were overcome by the white settlers moving in to take their lands.

The huge Bledsoe's Lick, caused by sulphur water springs that left deposits of salt and minerals, was used by great herds of buffalo, elk, and numerous whitetail deer. The lick was located some 30 miles east of Nashville between present-day Gallatin, Tennessee and Hartsville, Tennessee near highway 25 which connects the two cities in Sumner County, Tennessee. The north side Sumner County borders the south boundary of the State of Kentucky. Bledsoe's Lick is in Bledsoe Creek Valley not far north of the Cumberland River which flows west toward Nashville, Tennessee.

While Major William Hall was attending a Chickamauga conference in Nashville as requested by Colonel James Robertson, a party of fifteen Chickamauga Indians formed an ambush between his house and his neighbor Gibson. Major Hall's two sons, James and William, were going to the pasture to get their horses when they were attacked by the party. James was killed and scalped and William barely made his escape by out running his pursuers.

Major James Lynn from Bledsoe's Station and five other men started in pursuit and intersected the Indians at Goose Creek wounding two. Goose Creek runs into Shoals Creek in present-day Lauderdale County, Alabama, and Shoals Creek runs into the Tennessee River between Little Muscle Shoals and Big Muscle Shoals, the stronghold of Doublehead and his Chickamauga warriors.

Spring 1787—The Chickamauga also killed a man by the name of Prince, his wife, and children. The bodies were cut up and scattered. In addition, John Beard was killed with tomahawks and scalped.

Nashville

June 12, 1787—The Cumberland stretches through the northern portion of Middle Tennessee with Nashville being one of the largest cities on the Cumberland River. On June 12, 1787, Colonel James Robertson wrote Governor Caswell of North Carolina complaining that Chickamauga Indians living on the Tennessee River were stealing horses and killing white people in the Cumberland settlements. Doublehead's warriors loved to steal horses and inflict as much damage as possible to discourage additional settlers from entering their sacred hunting grounds of the buffalo.

Robertson requested permission for a military force to invade and remove the stealing and murdering raiders from the Town of Coldwater at the mouth of Coldwater Creek which had its beginning at Big Spring in present-day Tuscumbia, Alabama. The town reportedly consisted of 54 men who were made up of 35 Cherokees, ten Creeks, and nine Frenchmen, including some women and children.

June 13, 1787--The area around Nashville, Tennessee was another large buffalo, elk, and deer lick known as the French Lick, Big Lick, or Bluff. The great licks in middle

90

Tennessee were created by the numerous sulphur water springs located in the Cumberland River Valley, especially in Davidson and Sumner Counties. The French Lick or Big Lick was a favorite buffalo hunting area of the Chickamauga Indians and became a primary target for stealing horses, taking prisoners, and collecting scalps by Doublehead's raiders.

On June 13, 1787, some of Doublehead's warriors killed Mark Robertson, the younger brother of Colonel James Robertson near Nashville, Tennessee. Without waiting for permission from the Governor, Robertson with a force of 130 men began to pursue the enemy to the mouth of Blue Water Creek and then down the Tennessee River to Coldwater. Robertson's men were following a 100 mile Indian trail south that became Doublehead's Trace from Franklin, Tennessee to the mouth of Blue Water Creek in present-day Lauderdale County, Alabama.

When Robertson's forces reached Coldwater, the Chickamauga Indians were taken completely by surprise and made a run for their canoes. Robertson's men opened fire killing some fourteen Lower Cherokees and six Creeks along with some French traders who were instigating the raids in the Cumberland River Valley. Robertson's forces burned the town and returned to Nashville, Tennessee. With the assistance of Cumberland settlers who fought against the Chickamauga at the French trading post at Coldwater in present-day Tuscumbia, Alabama, Robertson's campaign failed to diminish raids on the Nashville, Tennessee area. Chickamauga warriors under Doublehead's command would continue their war against the Cumberland settlements into 1795.

Bledsoe's Fort

August 2, 1787—Major William Hall, another of his sons Richard Hall, and a man named Hickerson were killed in an attack by the Chickamauga. The Halls were in the process of moving their household goods and family to Bledsoe's Fort for safety. They were making their last trip hauling their possessions to the fort when they were attacked.

August 5, 1787—The Bledsoe brothers, Isaac and Anthony, were initially attracted to the Cumberland River Valley because of the huge herds of buffalo, elk, and deer that used the mineral licks in the area. They settled just north of the Cumberland River near Bledsoe Creek, a small tributary to the river. Shortly after the Bledsoes moved into the Cumberland area, the Chickamauga under the leadership of Doublehead began making raids on their settlement in order to force them from their sacred hunting grounds.

On August 5, 1787, Colonel Anthony Bledsoe wrote the following letter to Governor John Sevier, Governor of the State of Franklin to be forwarded to Governor Caswell of North Carolina.

Dear Sir:

When I last had the pleasure of seeing Your Excellency, I think you were kind enough to propose that in case the perfidious Chickamauga should infest this country, to notify Your Excellence, and you would send a campaign against them without delay. The period has arrived that they, as I have good reason to believe, in combination with the Creeks, have done this country very great spoil by murdering numbers of our peaceful inhabitants, stealing our horses, killing our cattle and hogs, and burning our buildings through wantonness, cutting down our corn, ect.

I am well assured that the distress of the Chickamauga Tribe is the only way this defenseless country will have quiet. The militia being very few, and the whole, as it were, a frontier, its inhabitants all shut up in stations, and they, in general, so weakly manned that in case of invasion, one is scarcely able to aid the other, and the enemy daily in our country committing ravages of one kind or another, and that of the most savage kind. Poor Major Hall and his eldest son fell a sacrifice to this savage cruelty, a few days ago, near Bledsoe's Lick. They have killed about twenty four persons in this country in a few months, besides numbers of others in the settlements near to it. Our dependence is much that Your Excellency will revenge the blood thus wantonly shed.

Anthony Bledsoe

Fall 1787—John Pervine, the father of Esquire John Morgan, Charles Morgan, and Jordan Gibson were killed by the Chickamauga near Bledsoe's Fort.

Year of 1788

Little River

May 1788--Although the military operation commanded by James Robertson was successful in destroying Coldwater, it did not stop the raids against the Cumberland and upper Tennessee River valley settlers that were orchestrated by the Chickamauga. Due to John Sevier's brutal attacks on the upper Tennessee River Cherokee towns, the Chickamauga made raids in retaliation. The raids were carried out against white settlers who were encroaching on Cherokee lands.

Little River flows from present-day Great Smoky Mountains National Park through the towns of Townsend, Maryville, Alcoa, and Rockford prior to empting into the Tennessee River. It was on one of these Chickamauga raids on Little River twelve miles southwest of Knoxville, Tennessee in May1788 that eleven members of the John Kirk family had been killed except for the father John and his son John, Jr. who had been away on a hunting trip. This act led directly to the revenge murders of Doublehead's brother, Old Tassel and other Cherokee Chiefs by John Kirk, Jr.

Chilhowee-Death of Old Tassel

June 1788--In June 1788, a peace meeting of Cherokee chiefs had been organized and arranged by one of John Sevier's soldiers under a flag of truce. The peace meeting was held at the home of Old Abram's at the Cherokee town of Chilhowee on the Little Tennessee River. After a series of peace talks, the unarmed Chief Old Tassel was escorted to a smokehouse where he was to spend the night. That night, with Lieutenant James Hubbard guarding the door, Kirk's oldest son, John, Jr. armed with a tomahawk entered the building and killed the old chief as he lay sleeping. This same blood thirsty murder would be repeated several times that night.

Another version of the murders states that Lieutenant James Hubbard assembled all the unarmed chiefs in attendance in the small home of Old Abram. Hubbard then had his soldiers to guard all the doors and windows. Hubbard then allowed John Kirk, Jr., who was armed with an ax, to kill all the Cherokee Indians present.

Governor John Sevier

Under the disguise of peace, Sevier allowed Lieutenant Hubbard to take Kirk's son on the murderous spree of peace seeking Cherokee chiefs. Hubbard encouraged John Kirk, Jr. to club to death with a hatchet seven chiefs as revenge for the killing of his family. Among those murdered were Old Tassel, Old Tassel's son, Old Abram, Longfellow, Fool Warrior, and two other sub chiefs.

Following the brutal murder of his beloved brother Old Tassel, Doublehead vowed a dark and bloody vengeance upon the white settlers invading Indian lands. With a murderous rage, Doublehead and his Chickamauga warriors would descend upon the settlers and try to force them from the Cherokee homelands and sacred hunting grounds in the upper Tennessee River Valley and the Cumberland River Valley.

Bledsoe's Station

July 20, 1788—Colonel Anthony Bledsoe was killed near Bledsoe's Lick by a party of Chickamauga under the leadership of Doublehead. Colonel Anthony Bledsoe was one of the early pioneer frontiersmen to establish a white settlement in the Cumberland River Valley in present-day Sumner County, Tennessee. He was a leader in the middle Tennessee area and a friend to General James Robertson. The killing of Colonel Bledsoe was a major blow to the Cumberland settlements and a rallying point for Doublehead's Chickamauga.

Year of 1789

Mayfield's Station

March 10, 1789—Mayfield's Station was built about 1785 by Southerland Mayfield near the head of Mill Creek a few miles east of Little Harpeth River in Williamson County, Tennessee. The log fort was built just south of the border of Davidson County, Tennessee.

On March 10, 1789, Southerland Mayfield, Andrew Martin, and William Mayfield (son of Southerland) were killed by Chickamauga. Southerland's other son George was taken prisoner and his fate is not known.

Year of 1790

Houston's Fort

1790—Houston's Fort was located about ten miles from Maryville which is located southwest of Knoxville in east Tennessee. The fort had in it several families, but only seven gunmen that were proficient marksmen. It consisted of a crudely constructed cabin, one story high, that was provided with the usual frontier defenses of port-holes for guns. A large party of two or three hundred Chickamauga Indians approached the fort, with the evident design to attack and destroy. The Chickamauga could have undoubtedly effected with suitable resolution, but were deterred by the method adopted for its defense. The besieged, including James Houston and others, reserved their fire until the assailants were near enough for very decisive and certain aim. The discharge at that moment of the seven

94

rifles was calculated to impress the enemy with the belief that a more formidable force was lodged within. The firing was repeated with great vigor. The Indians picked up their dead and wounded and retired. The fort did not lose a man. It is uncertain if this large Chickamauga force attacked other sites before leaving the area.

Greenfield Station

1790--Chickamauga killed Alexander Neely near Greenfield Station at the fort where Anthony Bledsoe had lived. Greenfield Station was part of the Cumberland settlements located in Sumner County, Tennessee on the east side of Bledsoe Creek Valley and north of the Avery Trace and Bledsoe's Lick. Greenfield was in the prime buffalo hunting area of the Chickamauga and was the focus of more attacks in the near future. In the year 1769, the first white long hunter was killed by the Indians protecting their hunting grounds near the area.

1790—Chickamauga killed a young woman of the name of Norris, near Brown's Station on Brown's Fork of the Red River, and wounded two other persons one of whom was named Blair. The river was one of the prime buffalo hunting areas of Doublehead's Chickamauga Cherokee who considered it their land.

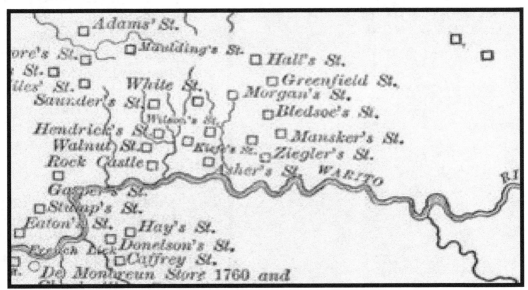

Stations on Cumberland River

The Red River begins in Sumner County, Tennessee and is 100 miles long. It is a major stream in the north-central portion of middle Tennessee and south-centralKentucky and a major tributary of the Cumberland River. The South Fork of the Red River runs south of the main river for several miles and drains the northern portion of middle Tennessee. Another important tributary of the Red River is the Sulphur Fork. The Red River and Sulphur Fork both form a small portion of the Robertson County-Montgomery County line and flows toward Clarksville, Tennessee. About one and a half (1.5) miles above its mouth, the Red River is joined by the West Fork of the Red River just before it joins the Cumberland. This area was one of the prime hunting areas of Doublehead and his followers and therefore subject to several attacks by the Chickamauga.

Brown's Station

1790—Chickamauga killed three persons at Brown's Station, eight miles from Nashville. They wounded John McRory, and caught and scalped three of Everett's children and killed John Everett. Not only horses, but also greatly prized by Doublehead's warriors were white scalps and white captives which could be exchanged for Indian prisoners.

Mayfield's Station

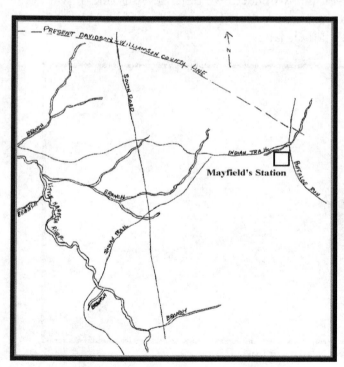

Mayfield's Station Map by Phil Norfleet

1790--Within a year of the first raid, Doublehead's Chickamauga attacked Mayfield's Station again and killed John Glen. John had married the widow Mayfield after the Indians had killed her first husband, Southerland Mayfield, on March 10, 1789. This was the second attack on the station near the head of Mill Creek and the second husband of the widow that had been killed by the by Doublehead's warriors.

A man by the name of Hague erected a cotton cleaning machine on Mill Creek near Mayfield's Station. At the site of the mill, some persons were killed by the Chickamauga but their names are forgotten or not known. Not all the white settlers killed by Doublehead's Chickamauga were known or recorded.

96

Gnatt's Station

1790--Francis Armstrong was fell upon by a party of Chickamauga Indians near Gnatt's Station. The Indians fled after being fired upon, and Armstrong was able to regain five horses. In addition, Colonel Weakly shot and killed one of the Indians who had come to the settlement near Gnatt's Station to steal and plunder. The Indians sometimes met with the fate of being killed by the white settlers, but more frequently escaped unhurt with their booty of prisoners, scalps, and horses.

Year of 1791

Nashville

February 27, 1791--A census, taken in 1791, shows a total white population of seven thousand and forty-two settlers in Nashville's Metro District. One thousand of these whites were males capable of bearing arms. The population of the Indian tribes surrounding the territory at that time is variously estimated at from twenty-five to fifty thousand (Albright, 1909).

In February of 1791, Colonel Robertson informed Governor Blount of aggressions by the Chickamauga Indians. On the evening of February 27, 1791, the Chickamauga killed a Mr. Thompson in his own yard, then jumped into his house and killed all the women and children except two. The exact total of the dead was not recorded.

Station Camp Creek

April 1791—Station Camp Creek is located about four miles south of present-day Gallatin in Sumner County, Tennessee close to the Cumberland River. Station Camp Creek was established in 1771 by early long hunter, Kasper Mansker, who used the site as a primary station or hunting camp for his men. The station was on the present-day Gallatin Road where it crosses the creek toward Nashville.

In April, 1791, a Negro man of Captain Caffrey's was killed at work in the field. A great number of horses were taken from the settlements, and particularly from Station Camp Creek in Sumner County. Some horses were taken from the neighborhood of Nashville in May, and some were stolen again in June. In addition, several horses were likewise taken from Red River and Sumner County in the same month. Horses were highly sought after by Doublehead's raiders and were utilized in raids made against the settlers. Doublehead owned many horses at his death.

Sumner County

May 3, 1791-- On May 3, 1791, George Wilson, a young man in Sumner County, was killed six miles from the courthouse, on the public road to Nashville. Sumner County is on the north side of the Cumberland River east of Nashville, Tennessee.

Rolling Fork

May 1791--In May 1791, John Farris was wounded, and Mr. Miller and five of his family killed, and his house robbed, on the Rolling Fork. John Farris of Kentucky escaped death this time but very soon he would not be so lucky. The Rolling Fork of the Salt River runs north out of central Kentucky and begins just north of the Cumberland River drainage. Again in May the Chickamauga attacked and this time killed John Farris and his brother, of Lincoln County, Kentucky near Nashville, Tennessee.

Moccasin Gap

May 1791--In Russell County, Virginia, near Moccasin Gap, Mrs. McDowell and Frances Pendleton were killed and scalped. Doublehead's nephew Bob Benge was very familiar with this area of Virginia where he and his party made numerous raids. Bob Benge was a quarter blood Chickamauga Cherokee and three-quarters Scots who rode with Doublehead on several raids.

Poor Valley

May 1791--James Patrick was killed in the Poor Valley, seventeen miles from Rogersville, early in September. Poor Valley is located northeast of Knoxville, Tennessee. This was another area of east Tennessee that was the target of attacks by Doublehead's nephew Bob Benge.

Nashville

June 2, 1791--The Chickamauga killed John Thompson in his own corn field, within five miles of Nashville. As noted already, the Cumberland settlements around Nashville, Tennessee were favorite targets of Doublehead's Chickamauga from the Muscle Shoals.

June 14, 1791--On June 14, 1791, the Chickamauga killed John Gibson and wounded McMoon, in Gibson's field, within eight miles of Nashville. The Chickamauga attacks around the Nashville area begin in the 1770's and continued through 1795.

Bledsoe's Station

June 1791—The Chickamauga killed Benjamin Kirkendall in his own house, within two miles of Colonel Winchester's, in Sumner County, Tennessee and plundered his house of everything the Indians could use. The area around Bledsoe's was attacked on many occasions by Doublehead and his warriors.

Natchez Trace

June 1791--In June, three travelers from Natchez to Nashville, were found dead on the trace near the mouth of Duck River. There were eight people in company and only two of those survived. This area of the Natchez Trace was within Doublehead's hunting grounds and subject to attack from his Chickamauga raiders.

Red River

July 3, 1791--On July 3, 1791, Thomas Fletcher and two other men, were killed on the north side of Cumberland, nea r the mouth of Red River. During the scalping of the two men, the Indians entirely skinned their heads. This area is close to Clarksville, Tennessee and one of the haunts of Doublehead and his warriors.

Nashville

July 1791--In July, a man was killed by Indians within a hundred and fifty yards of Major Wilson's on the public road as he was riding up to the house. The area around Nashville, Tennessee was subject to attack at any time during Doublehead's campaign against the white settlement of the Cumberland basin.

Faris (Ferris) Station

August 26, 1791—The Chickamauga led by Bob Benge attacked Faris Station and killed Elisha Faris, his wife, and two family members. The station was located about two miles east of Moccasin Gap, Virginia.

1791--In the Fall of 1791, Doublehead and a hunting party of some 28 warriors not including women and children made a hunting expedition near the mouth of the Cumberland River. In violation to the Treaty of Holston, Doublehead and seven of his warriors decided to go on a scalping excursion. Doublehead killed an operator of a salt boat on the Cumberland, took what he wanted, and continued his quest for scalps.

Year of 1792

Cumberland Trace

January 12, 1792--On the 12th, Thomas White was killed on the Cumberland Mountain and on the Cumberland trace. Chickamauga warriors were opportunistic in their attacks on white settlers and took every occasion to kill their enemy in order to make their presence known.

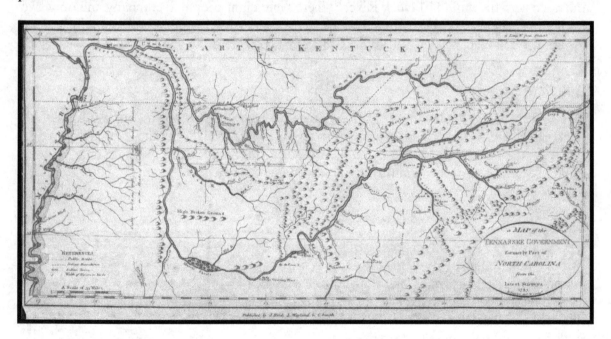

Cumberland and Tennessee Rivers John Reid Map 1795

Seven Mile Ferry

January 16, 1792--On January 16, 1792, Doublehead discovered a group of young men traveling up the Cumberland River toward Nashville by canoe. John Rice and three of Valentine Sevier's boys were killed by a party of Indians under Doublehead as he and some other young men were on their way from Sevier's Station on the Cumberland near

100

Clarksville to Nashville. They were answering a call from General James Robertson to help track down and kill Doublehead. In the group of seven to eight young men, three were the grown sons of Colonel Valentine Sevier's, Robert, William, and Valentine, Jr., who were the nephews of John Sevier. Doublehead set up an ambush near Seven Mile Ferry on the Cumberland and waited for the group to get at close range before opening fire. In the initial gunfire, five of the men were killed including Colonel Valentine Sevier's three sons, John Curtis, and John Rice. The men were scalped and their possessions and goods were taken. General James Robertson's expedition to kill Doublehead was unsuccessful.

Details of the raid near the mouth of the Cumberland River are given in the book *Tennessee, The Volunteer State* (1923). *Near the mouth of the river he* (Doublehead) *fell in with Conrad's salt boat, which he took after killing one man. He then proceeded up the river as far as Clarksville. It so happened that while he was skulking in the neighborhood, January 17, 1792, General Robertson called for Volunteers to act as spies and rangers, and John Rice, notable as the grantee and original proprietor of the tract of land on which the City of Memphis now stands, Robert, William and Valentine Sevier, the only grown sons of Colonel Valentine Sevier, and nephews of General John Sevier, John Curtis, and two or three other young men from Clarksville and Sevier's Station, set out to join him at Nashville. There being a scarcity of horses in the settlement they determined to go up the Cumberland in a canoe.*

Doublehead, who was watching for just such an opportunity, discovered their movement, and hastily crossing one of the numerous horseshoe bends in the Cumberland, secreted his party on the bank, at a place now known as Seven Mile Ferry. When the boat came round to where they were concealed, they fired a volley into it, killing the three Seviers, Curtis and Rice. Before the Indians could reload, the other members of the party pushed their canoe across the river, and commenced its descent back towards Clarksville, hugging the opposite shore. Doublehead then re-crossed the isthmus, intending to intercept them on their return, but this movement being anticipated, the canoe was hastily abandoned and turned adrift. The Indians found and boarded the derelict, scalped the five young men, and carried away their goods and provisions, even to their clothing; the hat, coat, and boots of Curtis being subsequently identified by a trader. A week later three of his warriors killed a man named Boyd in Clarksville, after which he returned to his camp, and was in the neighborhood of New Madrid, March 11, 1792. On the very day that Doublehead killed the young men on the Cumberland, a delegation of Cherokee chiefs headed by Bloody Fellow, concluded a treaty with Secretary Knox, at Philadelphia, by which their annuity under the treaty of Holston was increased from $1,000 to $1,500 (Moore and Foster, 1923).

January 19, 1792—Varying details of the death of Valentine Sevier's sons are given in <u>The Annals of Tennessee</u> by Ramsey (1853). *On Monday, the 19th of January, 1792, the Indians killed Robert Sevier and William Sevier, sons of Valentine Sevier, who lived at the mouth of Red River, near the present site of Clarkesville; they had gone to the relief of the distressed families on the Cumberland River, who had sent an express for assistance; the officers of Tennessee County could give none. A part of the crew was on shore getting provisions to be carried in boats to the sufferers; the boats were ahead of them when these young men discovered the enemy, whom they mistook for their own party, the Indians having been seen late in the evening at a considerable distance from that place. Robert Sevier hailed them, who answered they were friends, with which answer being satisfied, he sailed on, and the Indians carelessly began to chop with their hatchets, till the young men in the boats got very near them. Robert said to the man who was with him in the boats, ' these are not our friends, steer off.' The Indians then fired upon them; the man leaped out of the boat, and left them in it about three rods distant from the shore. Before the 25th, William was found and buried, but Robert met a party of twelve white men, pursued, but did not overtake the Indians. On the 10th of the same month, Valentine, a third son of this unfortunate parent, also fell by the hands of the savages; he was in a boat ascending the river, and was fired upon and killed dead in it; two others were wounded, one of them, John Rice, died, and both he and Valentine were buried about sixty miles below the mouth of Red River. Until Valentine fell, he and two others kept up so brisk a fire, that they intimidated the Indians and saved the crew. Deprived of all his sons who had come with him to Cumberland in so short a time, the afflicted parent wrote to his brother, General Sevier, to send to him his son John to come and see him; as, said he, in the moving language of suffering innocence, I have no other sons but small ones.*

Bledsoe's Station

January 28, 1792—Bledsoe's Station or Fort was built on the east side of Bledsoe's Creek on the Avery Trace. Avery's Trace was a 300 mile road built on old buffalo trails by Peter Avery in 1787 from South West Point (Kingston, Tennessee) to the French Lick (Nashville, Tennessee). Forts or stations were built along the route included South West Point, Fort Blount, Bledsoe's Fort, Mansker's Fort, and Fort Nashborough. These forts or stations were built for the protection of white settlers moving into the Cumberland River Valley.

On January 28, 1792, Oliver Williams and Jason Thompson were encamped at night on the road leading from Bledsoe's Station to the ford on Cumberland River. They were on the north side of the river, where they were fired upon by Indians, both were wounded, and their horses and other articles were taken from them. The area around Bledsoe's Lick and Bledsoe's Station was a favorite raiding site for Doublehead's Chickamauga warriors.

102

Nashville

March 1, 1792--About the beginning of March 1792, the Chickamauga Indians attacked the house of Mr. Thompson, within seven miles of Nashville, Tennessee. They killed and scalped the old man, his wife, his son and a daughter. The Indians made prisoners of a Mrs. Caffrey, her son, a small boy, and Miss Thompson. Doublehead, Bob Benge, and other Chickamauga warriors recognized that white prisoners were valuable for trade negotiations in the exchange for Indian captives.

March 5, 1792--On March 5, 1792, twenty-five Indians attacked Brown's Station, eight miles from Nashville, and killed four boys. Brown's Station was north of Nashville on the Red River that flows into the Cumberland at Clarksville, Tennessee.

March 6, 1792---On March 6, 1792, the Chickamauga burned Dunham's Station. It is not known if any people were killed or horses stolen.

Stones River

March 12, 1792--On March 12, 1792, Chickamauga Indians killed McMurray on his own plantation, at the mouth of Stone's River. Stones River enters the Cumberland River at Nashville, Tennessee. Stones River watershed includes the counties of Davidson, Cannon, Rutherford, and Wilson in middle Tennessee.

April 5, 1792--On April 5, 1792, the Chickamauga killed Mrs. Radcliff and three children near Stones River.

Cumberland Settlements

April 8, 1792--On April 8, 1792, the Chickamauga killed Benjamin Williams and party, consisting of eight men, in the heart of the Cumberland settlements.

Hind's Valley

April 1792--One of the guards came express to Campbell's Station with the news that the Indians had just killed two boys at Mr. Wells' in Hind's Valley. On this occasion the Indians came to Colonel Campbell's and fired at him and another man, plowing by his side. The report of their guns being heard by Mrs. Campbell, she very coolly barricaded the door of the house, took the rifles from the rack, and waited at the port-holes for the approach of the Indians. In that position she was found by the men escaping from the field. She handed out the rifles and the Indians were pursued, but were not overtaken.

Nashville

May 13, 1792---On Sunday, May 13, 1792, a man and two girls were fired on by the Indians within four miles of Nashville. The man and one girl escaped but the other girl was tomahawked and killed by the Indians.

Station Camp Creek

May 16 and 17, 1792--On Station Camp Creek a boy was wounded in three places and at the same place two boys, sons of Robert Desha, were killed in the field in the daytime, near their father's house. The Chickamauga also killed a Kirkendall, on May 16, 1792, and another man on May 17, 1792.

Robertson's Lick

May 24, 1792--On May 24, 1792, General Robertson and his son Jonathan Robertson were at or near Robertson's Lick half a mile from his station where they were fired upon by a party of Indians; the General was wounded in the arm and thrown by his horse amongst the Indians; his son was wounded through the hip, but seeing the dangerous situation in which his father was in, he dismounted, though badly wounded, and fired on them as they rushed towards his father; this checked them for a moment, and gave time to the General to get off, and both got safely into the station. On the 25th, a boy was wounded near the General's and died of his wounds on the 6th of June.

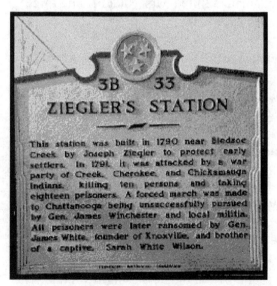

Zeigler's Station

June 26, 1792--Doublehead and the Chickamauga continued their attacks on the settlers invading their frontiers. On June 26, 1792, a large number of Chickamauga including Creeks attacked Zeigler's Station killing five and capturing eighteen other persons as seen in the following books:

Heiskell's Version-- Andrew Jackson and early Tennessee History (1918) - *It will bring conditions of pioneer life very close to General White's descendants in Knoxville to reflect that his sister, Mrs. Joseph Wilson, and her six children, were captured by the Indians in Sumner County, Tennessee, on the night of June 26, 1792, at Zeigler's Station. Hearing of the capture of Mrs. Wilson and her* *children, General White sent a message to the Cherokees and by paying a ransom procured the release of the mother and five of the children, and they were returned to their home. But one daughter had been taken to the Creek Nation where she was held for many years, but was ultimately restored to her people. We have no record of what was paid for the release either of Mrs. Wilson or the five children, or for the daughter who had been taken to the Creek Nation.*

The attack on Zeigler's Station was made by a large force of Creeks, Cherokees and Chickamauga, and the Station was burned and Jacob Zeigler was burned to death with it. Four persons were killed and Captain Joseph Wilson was wounded; two children of Jacob Zeigler and nine other persons were captured. Mrs. Zeigler escaped with one child in the darkness (Heiskell, 1918).

Ramsey's Version—<u>The Annals of Tennessee</u> (1853) - *On the 26th of June, 1792, Zeigler's Station, within two miles of Bledsoe's Lick, was attacked by a large party of Indians, first in the afternoon and again by night. This station was picketed and was defended by thirteen men, including the son of Mr. Joseph Wilson, a lad not fully grown. They killed five persons, burnt one in the station and wounded four others but escaped; three escaped unharmed, and 18 were made prisoners. Of the prisoners, nine were regained by purchase, made by their parents and friends. One, Miss Wilson, and four Negroes, were carried into captivity.*

Albright's Version—<u>Early History of Middle Tennessee</u> (1909) - *On the night of June 26, a force of several hundred Creeks, Cherokees and Chickamauga made an assault on Ziegler's' fort, in Sumner County, Tennessee. During the morning preceding some of their advance guard had killed Michael Shaffer while he was hoeing in a field adjoining the station. When the neighbors who had collected went out to bring the body into the fort, the Indians fired upon them from ambush, wounding Joel Eccles and Gabriel Black. The latter was a brother-in-law of Gen. James Winchester.*

The men were thus forced to leave the body of Shaffer and flee for safety into the fort. The enemy kept up the fire for some time, but finally dispersed. About sundown the occupants of the fort again ventured out and brought the dead body into the enclosure.

The alarm having been given, people for several miles around, including the occupants of the Walnut field station, came into the fort to spend the night. These numbered in all probably thirty persons.

For some unknown reason, they all retired at an early hour, leaving no sentinels on guard. About 10 o'clock the attacking party stole out from the neighboring thickets, surrounded the fort, broke down the doors of the cabins, and fell in merciless assault upon the sleeping settlers. The latter thus awakened, fought as best they could, but were able to make but poor defense against such overwhelming numbers. At length the savages fired the fort, thus forcing the inmates to face the tomahawk in an effort to escape the flames.

Jacob Ziegler, founder of the fort, ran up into the loft of his cabin and was burned to death. Archie Wilson, a fine young fellow, who had volunteered his services to defend the fort that night, fought bravely, but finally, when wounded and retreating, was brought to bay and clubbed to death. His body was found next morning about a hundred yards from the station. Beside these, three other persons were killed, one of them a Negro girl. Four were wounded, among them being Captain Joseph Wilson. The wife and six children of Captain Wilson, two children of Jacob Ziegler, and nine other persons were taken prisoners and spirited away into captivity.

Mrs. Ziegler escaped with one child by thrusting her handkerchief into its mouth, thus preventing the noise of its crying as she fled through the darkness. The destruction of the station was complete.

General White, of East Tennessee, hearing that his sister, Mrs. Wilson, and five of her children, had been carried into the Cherokee nation, sent a messenger to the chief and had them released by purchase. One of the Wilson children, a daughter, was captured by the Creeks and for many years remained among them a slave. After returning from captivity she long retained the manners and customs of her captors. On the morning after the destruction of the fort a party under command of General Winchester and Col. Edward Douglass went in pursuit of the Indians. Capt. John Carr, John Harpool and Peter Loony were sent forward as spies. They took the trail of the retreating party and followed them across Cumberland River. From thence they proceeded up Barton's Creek to within about three miles of where Lebanon now stands. Here they came upon twenty-one packs of the plunder from the station, all of which had been nicely tied up and hung on trees. The packs were carefully protected from the weather by strips of peeled bark which had been placed over each. Having but few horses, the Indians had thus disposed of a part of their luggage until a part of them could go back and steal horses enough to bring it forward. In the meantime the main body was hurrying on with the prisoners.

The pursuing party having now come up with their advance guard, some of them were sent back home with the captured plunder, and also that they might warn the settlers to be on the lookout for the horse thieves. The rest hastened on after the retreating enemy. At the big spring now on the public square at Lebanon they stopped to rest and drink. There Captain Carr and others cut their names on a cedar tree which stood by the spring for many years thereafter. Again on the chase the party came to a small stream of water which ran across the trail. On the banks of this they saw barefoot tracks of the children who had been captured. A little further on they found the smoldering embers of a fire from

106

which the Indians had lighted their pipes and around this were scattered scraps of dressed skins, from which it was supposed they had made moccasins for the children, the feet of the latter having become sore from hard traveling. This was confirmed when later on they saw in the mud the little moccasin footprints. This is at least one instance of savage kindness to those who were so unfortunate as to fall into their hands.

The whites camped that night at Martin's spring near the subsequent home of Esquire Doak. Next morning they came to the place where the Indians had camped the first night out. As the latter were already a day and a half ahead, General Winchester advised that the pursuit be abandoned, thinking it probable that the captives would be killed if the savages should be overtaken.

On the journey homeward it was found that the horse-stealing party had returned in the meantime to the camp on Barton's creek and there discovering the loss of their plunder had followed on to the big spring. Here they had cut on the surrounding trees signs of various characters in mock imitation of the names previously carved by Carr and his companions.

On her return from captivity Mrs. Wilson related that when the advance party of Indians having in charge the captives, came to Duck River on the journey south, they halted in waiting for the rest of their number, upon whom they relied to bring up the captured plunder. When the latter arrived empty-handed, there was almost a pitched battle. In the fray knives and tomahawks were drawn by members of each party against those of the other. Mrs. Wilson said she was much alarmed lest in their rage they should kill her and the rest of the captives.

Kentucky Road

July 15, 1792--Isaac Pennington and Milligen were killed, and McFarland was wounded, on the Kentucky Road.

Bledsoe's Lick

August 11, 1792-- Bledsoe's Lick was named after Isaac Bledsoe and his brother Anthony who first came to the place about 1772. Within ten years, the brothers had established a thriving community that had to be on constant alert for attacks by the Chickamauga who claimed it as their hunting grounds. The area contained large mineral licks that attracted animals from miles around and was one of the favorite hunting places of the Chickamauga Cherokee. When Dragging Canoe pointed toward Kentucky at the Treaty of Sycamore Shoals and said the buffalo are our cattle, this lick was one of the sites where he and other Cherokees hunted the buffalo; therefore, the area was well known to

Doublehead's band of warriors. Shortly before August 11, 1792, the Indians killed a boy and wounded a man near Bledsoe's Lick.

August 27, 1792--On the night of August 27, 1792, a party of fifteen Chickamauga put fire to Captain Morgan's house near the Bledsoe's Lick; the fire was extinguished and the party repulsed by the aid of Captain Lusk's company stationed for the protection of the frontiers. On the preceding night, the same party opened the stables of James Douglas and took his horses; the next day Samuel Wilson fell in with them, wounded one, but the party took flight and regained the horses, a gun and a bloody blanket.

August 31, 1792--At Greenfield's Station, a few miles north of Bledsoe's Lick, John Berkley, Jr. was killed and scalped by the Chickamauga. John Berkley, Sr. was wounded in the attack, but was able to kill the Indian that scalped John Berkley, Jr. The attack took place while the Berkleys were working in their peach orchard.

Pistol Creek

September 13, 1792--Mr. Cochrane lived on the farm afterwards occupied by Doctor McGee. As his son was returning from Pistol Creek, he was met by a white man, a stranger, who detained him a minute in conversation; Indians lying in ambush, fired on him, their bullets passing through his hat and clothes without inflicting a wound. He and his father's family escaped down the creek and alarmed the neighborhood, who began to build a fort.

September 16, 1792--A few days after, Gillespie and two boys went home after some corn. The Indians killed Gillespie and the eldest boy, but the youngest they took prisoner. A white man in the company of the Indians excused the murder of the oldest brother by stating that they had fired at and missed a pale-face, (Cochrane) and killed his brother for satisfaction for their lost powder.

Buchanan's Station

September 30, 1792--On September 30, 1792, the Chickamauga Cherokee were on the war path but went up against some tough Tennesseans at Buchanan's Station. Doublehead's nephew John Watts, Jr. was wounded and 14 other warriors involved in the attack were killed. The following account is given in Ted F. Belue (1996), *"Desperate, Indians took up the hatchet. In a burst of pan-Indian action, warriors stormed Buchanan's Station in September 1792. Tennesseans barely beat back four hundred to five hundred Chickamauga and Cherokee, two hundred Creeks, and a score of Shawnee. Fort defenders shot fifteen Indians dead and wounded John...(Watts, Jr.), leading man among the Cherokee."*

108

According to the "Chronicles of Oklahoma", Volume 16, Number 1, March 1938, not only Doublehead but also John Watts, Jr. was in a rage over the vicious murder of his uncle Old Tassel. *Watts was determined to prove that Indians could "fight in armies" as well as white men. His plan of campaign was well thought out. He proposed to throw the whole strength of the Nation against the Cumberland settlements, wipe them out, then turn eastward and repeat the process at Watauga. He himself marched against Nashville at the head of three hundred warriors. To block assistance or word of his coming,*

Doublehead was sent with a hundred men to lie in wait upon the Kentucky road. Middlestriker, with the same number, was sent to cover the new Cumberland road, a shorter route just opened from Knoxville to Nashville. Middlestriker intercepted and defeated a band of forty white militia on the way to Nashville, capturing the commander, Captain Samuel Handley. Doublehead found the Kentucky road almost deserted, took a couple of scalps, and departed post-haste for Nashville to assist in the attack.

Two days later he camped at Horseshoe Bend of Caney Fork River. His men scattered to hunt, leaving a single sentry at the camp. About noon, Captain William Snoddy in command of thirty-four militiamen, discovered and plundered the camp. The sentry escaped, and feeling sure that he would be attacked, Snoddy chose a strong position, protected on three sides by a high bluff, and went into camp for the night. It soon began to drizzle rain.

The men were kept at high tension throughout the night by Doublehead assembling his warriors. The howl of a wolf, answered by the scream of a panther, the hoot of an owl, or bark of a fox, culminated about daybreak with a terrific yell, followed by profound silence. Four of Snoddy's men bolted in terror, and were seen no more. At daylight, Doublehead attacked. A desperate hand to hand struggle, lasting an hour, ensued. Doublehead lost thirteen men, and Snoddy four. The Indians withdrew eventually, and proceeded toward Nashville. That day, Doublehead was met by two runners who informed him that Watts had failed, and was being carried, mortally wounded, to Wills town. Doublehead, scourge of the frontier wept. "Vengeance I will have for Watts!" he said.

The Indian campaign had indeed failed. Watts had with him numerous Creek allies under Talotiskee of Broken Arrow, and thirty Shawnees under Shawnee Warrior. About

109

dark on September 30, 1792, the Indians approached Buchanan's Station, five miles east of Nashville. Watts insisted they proceed to Nashville, which was the principal object of the campaign. His two allies objected to leaving white men in their rear. "Buchanan's must be taken first!" they argued. About midnight Watts consented. A furious assault, which lasted through the night, was made. No white men were killed, but the Indian loss was serious. Talotiskee and Shawnee Warrior were killed; as were Little Owl, Dragging Canoe's brother, and Kiachatalee, a brave young chief of Nickajack. Watts, desperately wounded, was placed upon a stretcher between two horses, and the Indian army retreated rapidly. Watts recovered. The following year, 1793, he led an army of a thousand warriors against the settlements around Knoxville.

Ramsey's Version—<u>The Annals of Tennessee</u> (1853) - *Two other men, however, were sent off to reconnoiter the country through which the Indians were necessarily to pass in coming to Nashville. These were Jonathan Gee and Seward Clayton, who went on the Indian trace leading through the place where Murfreesborough now stands, to Nashville, eight or ten miles from Buchanan's Station; as they travelled along the path talking loudly, they saw meeting them the advance of the Indian army, who called to them in English to know who they were, to which question, without disguise, they answered. Upon being asked in return, who they were, they said they were spies from General Robertson's Station, and were returning home; both parties advanced till they come within a few steps of each other, when the Indians fired and killed Gee dead in the road. They broke the arm of the other, who ran into the woods, but being pursued by a great number of them, they overtook and killed him also. Thence they marched rank and file, in three lines abreast, with quick step till they arrived at Buchanan's Station, where the people were wholly unapprised of their coming, and did not expect it. This was on Sunday next after the discharge of the troops, being the 30th of September.*

In addition to the account, as given in Governor Blount's letter to the Secretary of War, of the attack on Buchanan's Station, we extract further details of that invasion, and of the remarkable and successful defense by the brave men within the fort.

McRory rose and looked towards the place whence they ran, and saw sixty Indians not more than a few feet from the gate of the fort; he instantly fired through the port-hole, and killed the chief leader of the Indians, who on receiving the wound, immediately expired. He was a Shawnee, and had quarreled with Watts, who insisted upon deferring the attack until day, and until after the garrison had dispersed to their various avocations. The whole garrison, consisting of nineteen men, flew to arms, and fired upon the Indians through the port-holes; the Indians, in turn, fired upon the fort. Captain Rains was sent for; he and five other men went off in full gallop to Buchanan's Station, and arrived just in time to see the Indians leaving the plantation at the fort; they had lost some of their men; some were found on the ground near the outside wall of the fort; others were carried off and buried in different places, and were afterwards found by the white people. Of the wounded, were John Watts, with a ball through one thigh, which lodged in the other, supposed to be dangerous; the White Man Killer, the Dragging Canoe's brother, the Owl's son, a young man of the Lookout Mountain, a Creek warrior, who died, and a young warrior of the Running Water, who died.

There were also sundry young Cherokee warriors with Watts, besides those who lived in the five Lower Towns, particularly John Walker and George Fields, two young half-breeds who had been raised amongst the white people, and in whom, everyone who knew them, had the utmost confidence. The former was quite a stripling, and, apparently, the most food-natured youth the Governor ever saw; for so he thought him. he acted as the advanced spies of Watts's party, and decoyed and killed Gee and Clayton. The Cherokees said that many of the Creeks kept at such a distance from the station, that they could hardly shoot a bullet to it. With Watts, there were sixteen Cherokees from Hiwassee; one from Keuka; five from Connnsnuga, and one from Strington's. "When the Indians retired, General Robertson hastily collected what troops he could, and pursued them to Hart's big spring, near Stewart's Creek. It was discovered that they marched out as well as in, in three columns. The general's force, not being more than a hundred and eighty men, and that of the enemy being greatly superior, and they having got for ahead, he deemed it most advisable to return home, 'which he did."

Ramsey's version continues -- *On the 30th September 1792, about midnight, John Buchanan's Station, four miles south of Nashville, (at which sundry families had collected, and fifteen gun-men,) was attacked by a party of Creeks and Lower Cherokees, supposed to consist of three or four hundred. Their approach was suspected by the running of cattle, that had taken fright at them, and, upon examination, they were found rapidly advancing within ten yards of the gate; from this place and distance they received the first fire from the man who discovered them (John McRory). They immediately returned the fire, and continued a very heavy and constant firing upon the station, (block-houses, surrounded with a stockade,) for an hour, and were repulsed with considerable loss, without injuring man, woman, or child, in the station.*

During the whole time of attack, the Indians were not more distant than ten yards from the block-house, and often in large numbers round the lower walls, attempting to put fire to it. One ascended the roof with a torch, where he was shot, and, falling to the ground, renewed his attempts to fire the bottom logs, and was killed. The Indians fired thirty balls through a port-hole of the over jutting, which lodged in the roof in the circumference of a hat, and those sticking in the walls, on the outside, were very numerous.

Upon viewing the ground next morning, it appeared that the fellow who was shot on fort the roof, was a Cherokee half-breed of the Running Water, known by the whites by the name of Tom Tunbridge's step-son, the son of a French woman by an Indian, and there was much blood, and signs that many dead had been dragged off, and litters having been made to carry their wounded to their horses, which they had left a mile from the station. Near the block-house were found several swords, hatchets, pipes, kettles, and budgets of different Indian articles; one of the swords was a fine Spanish blade, and richly mounted in the Spanish fashion. In the morning previous to the attack, Jonathan Gee and Clayton were sent out as spies, and on the ground, among other articles left by the Indians, were found a handkerchief and a moccasin, known to belong to Gee, and the other to Clayton, hence it is supposed they are killed."

The repulse of so large a body of warriors by the small party of fifteen gun-men at Buchanan's, is a feat of bravery, which has scarcely been surpassed in all the annals of border warfare. The number of the assailants, Creeks, Cherokees and Shawnees, was afterwards ascertained to be above seven hundred, some of them well mounted, and all well-armed, and led by distinguished Braves of their several tribes. According to the Indian version of the affair, the assault was led by Kiachatalee, a daring half-breed warrior of Running Water Town. When it was found impracticable to carry the fort by other means, he "attempted to fire the blockhouse, and was actually blowing it into a flame, when he was mortally wounded. He continued, after receiving his mortal wound, to blow the fire and to cheer his followers to the assault, calling upon them to fight like brave men, and never give up till they had taken the fort."Amongst the numerous wounded, was the Cherokee chief, John Watts.

Black's Block House

October 3, 1792—According to the Knoxville Gazette printed on October 10, 1792, on October 3, 1792, Black's Block House on the head of Crooked Creek, a branch of Little River, in Blount County, Tennessee. There was a sergeant's command of Captain Crawford's company. It was attacked by surprise, about an hour and a half in to the night by a party of Indians commanded by a Cherokee of Will's Town, called the Tail, a brother of the Bench and Talohteske. The party consisted of three other Cherokees and five Creeks. The Tail was the nephew of Doublehead. James Paul was killed in the house and George Morse, John Shankland, and Robert Sharp were wounded at a fire on the outside. In addition, three horses were killed, and seven horses were taken off.

Nashville

October 8, 1792--On Monday October 8, 1792, William Stuart was killed about six miles from Nashville on the north side of Cumberland. On the night of the same day, the Indian's burnt Stump's distillery on White's Creek on the north side of Cumberland.

Sycamore Creek

October 9, 1792--On October 9, 1792, a party of Chickamauga Indians went to Sycamore Creek, eighteen miles from Nashville, and burnt the house of James Frazier, Mr. Riley and of Major Coffield, a large quantity of corn, and shot down a number of hogs.

Brushy Creek

October 10, 1792—The Chickamauga proceeded to Bushy Creek of Red River where they burnt the house of Obadiah Roberts, and took off a number of horses. They were followed by a party of whites, who killed one of the Indians and regained the horses.

Little River

October 1792—Little River is in east Tennessee southwest of Knoxville. On a Monday night, five Chickamauga of the Creek faction were headed by young Lashley, the son of a Scotchman in the Creek nation. They came to the settlements on the Little River in east Tennessee, about twenty miles from Knoxville. The group stole and carried off eight horses and were traced toward Chilhowee, the nearest Cherokee town. The same Lashley that headed the party killed and captured Gillespie's son on the 13th September. This gave reason to suspect the Chilhowee Indians of the theft, whereupon, as many as fifty-two of the neighboring people, including the sufferers, assembled together in arms and determined to go and destroy Chilhowee and Tallassee. They actually did march, but General Sevier received information of their intentions, and dispatched orders to them to disperse and return home. They obeyed, and thus the matter happily ended.

Crab Orchard

November 1792—Ramsey's Version (1853) *Captain Handley, when marching with his company of forty-two men, two hundred miles, for the protection of the stations on Cumberland, was attacked near the Crab-Orchard by a party of Indians, fifty-six in number, commanded by the Middle Striker. The party of Chickamauga consisted of Cherokees, Creeks and Shawnees. When the attack was made upon his company, a panic seized most of them, and they fell back. Handley labored in vain to rally them. He believed that if this could have been done, the Indians would have been defeated. He saw one of his men, named Leiper, in a most hazardous position, at a little distance from the Indians, and unhorsed. Handley conceived the design of rescuing him instantly, by seizing the horse's bridle and running him to the place where he was, to give the soldier an opportunity to re-mount. In doing this, he ran too near the enemy, and his own horse fell under him, pierced with wounds. Handley was immediately surrounded by Indians, furiously brandishing their uplifted tomahawks, the signal of death or submission. He jumped behind a tree, and was* met by a warrior, who held over him a tomahawk, in the act of striking. He arrested the stroke, by seizing the weapon, with the cry " Canawlla"—friendship. " Canawlla" was responded by the Indian, who instantly began to seek his rescue. This he at length effected, by hurrying the captain around, till he brought him to the principal chief, where, for a short time, he was free from danger. While the Indian was thus drawing him off, Handley received numerous licks from other Indians, some of which seemed to be inoffensive, being made with the flat side of the hatchet. One was made by his own sword, from which he narrowly escaped. In another instance, a gun was fired at him, the muzzle not ten feet distant, which was only escaped, by some other Indians striking the gun upwards at the moment of its discharge. The efforts of Handley to rally his men, and in laboring for the escape of Leiper, seem to have drawn off the attention of the enemy from his men, and to have concentrated it nearly on him. Only three of them were killed. The rest all escaped. Poor Leiper was seen by Handley lying scalped and lacerated with wounds. He exclaimed, " dear captain," to one who could no longer command nor protect, who was hurried away by his Indian captor, and never saw him more.

Captain McClelland was, at this time, at South West Point and with his company of light horsemen was dispatched to the scene of the discomfiture, to bury the dead, and to rescue the survivors from their captivity, and cut off the enemies' retreat. The first report was that Captain Handley was killed because the last time he was seen by his men, he was fighting hand to hand and surrounded by a crowd of warriors. The light horse followed the Indian trail and found that wherever they had camped was the fixtures used by the Indians in securing a prisoner. Along the trail at different places, they found slips of torn paper which were parts of Handley's muster-roll, which he had considerately torn and dropped along the path, hoping thereby to furnish those who might attempt his rescue the means of ascertaining the route his captors had taken. The pursuit was unsuccessful, and the light horse returned to South-West Point.

Captain Handley was taken to Wills Town. On his way, he was confined carefully at night, and watched closely by his captors through the day. Arriving at the end of their journey, the Indians debated three days whether he should be killed or permitted to live. At length, he was adopted into the Wolf Clan of the Cherokees, and treated like one of them, from November till March. Before his adoption into the tribe, he received repeated insults and injuries. He was made to run the gauntlet. Another mode of torture, was that of tying his hands and feet fast, and then hurling him over their heads, at the imminent hazard of dashing his nose and face against the ground. During his captivity, the Cherokees became tired of war, and requested their prisoner to write a letter for them to Governor Blount, at Knoxville, proposing conditions or preliminaries of peace. He obtained liberty, at the same time, to write a letter in his own behalf, to his brother-in-law, Colonel James Scott, which is preserved and is here given:

114

Wills Town, December 10, 1792

Dear Sir:—I am a captive in this town, in great distress, and the bearer hereof is a runner from the Upper Towns, from the Hanging Maw, and is now going up with a Talk from Colonel John Watts, with the Governor, on terms of peace. These people are much for peace, and if Governor Blount sends a good answer back to the Talk they have sent up by the runner, I am confident their Talk is true and sincere; and, upon the whole, we are not ripe for war with these people, for they are properly fixed for war; but Watts is entirely for peace, at this time, and wishes for a good answer to their Talks. Dear Sir, I have been much abused, and am in great distress. I beg that you and John Cowan, and every good friend, would go to the Governor, and try all you can to get him to send a good answer, so that I can get away—for if an army comes before, I am sure to die. Send word to my wife, and send me a horse down by the Hanging Maw's runner, for I am not able to come without. Dear friends, do what you can, for I am in a distressed way. No more, but—
Samuel Handley

John Watts sends to the Hanging Maw to send Calaka, the Hanging Maw's nephew, and another young fellow, down with the Governor's Talk and the horse for me, for he is a safe fellow, and if they come I am sure to get home, but if not, I expect never to get home; and I once more beg you to do your possible for me, and do them soon as you can.

To James Scott, Nine Mile, Henry's Station
The letter was favorably received by Governor Blount, and though the Cherokees did not come to an adjustment till after another bloody struggle and ruinous defeat at Etowah, they commissioned eight of their braves to escort Captain Handley in safety to his friends, in Blount County, with no other ransom than a keg of whiskey given them as a present.

When a Captain Samuel Handley was debriefed by Governor William Blount in 1793 following his captivity by the Cherokee faction of the Chickamauga, the first question he was asked was, *"During your captivity with the Cherokees, in the Lower Towns, did you become acquainted with John McDonald?"* The captain said that he had. *"Did you experience any civilities and friendship"* from either McDonald or Alexander Campbell, another former British agent? *"Yes, very great from both – all their situation admitted of,"* the captain replied.

Governor Blount – Do you suppose they wish peace with the United States?
Captain Handley – I am confident they both wish it.
Governor Blount – Did you hear both, or either of them, say whether or not the Spanish officers had encouraged the Indians to go to war, or whether they gave them ammunition?
Captain Handley – They at first denied both; but afterwards, in conversation, they acknowledged they had learned that the Spanish governor told them, that he did not bid

115

them go to war; but, if they were imposed upon, then he would furnish them with arms, ammunition, and men, to recover their country to the old line – the line made by the British.

Governor Blount – What do you suppose to be the numbers of the five Lower Towns?

Captain Handley – Messengers McDonald, Campbell, and Adair compute them to seven hundred, exclusive of old men; that Watts had a list drawn, and that appeared to be the number.

Governor Blount – Did they appear to be well armed?

Captain Handley – Yes; taking them collectively, better than I ever saw the same number of militia men.

Governor Blount – Have they any powder and lead in store?

Captain Handley – Plenty.

Governor Blount – From whence do you suppose they obtained their ammunition?

Captain Handley – From the Spaniards, so they say.

Governor Blount – Did you understand that the Indians had formed any companies of cavalry?

Captain Handley – Yes; three companies.

Governor Blount – Who commands them?

Captain Handley – John Taylor and Will Shory command two, the third I do not know.

Governor Blount – Did you see any swords and pistols among them?

Captain Handley – Yes; I saw some. The pistols and holsters were new, the swords were of the British dragoon kind.

Governor Blount – During your captivity did you see or hear of any parties of Creeks passing through the nation, for war against Cumberland?

Captain Handley – Yes; I heard of several, particularly one of 150 lately.

Governor Blount – Was it understood in the Lower Towns that the Creeks were at peace with the United States?

Captain Handley – No; it was understood the Upper were at war with the United States.

Governor Blount – Do you think Watts is sincere in his overtures for peace?

Captain Handley – Yes; except as to Cumberland. It is my opinion that small parties of Creeks and Cherokees will continue to infest that district.

Captain Handley resided sometime after near Tellico Block house, where the Indians frequently came for the purpose of trading. When any of his Indian acquaintances from Wills Town came there, they crossed over to see him, share his hospitality, and repose upon his premises, as with a genuine brother of their own order. He afterwards moved to Winchester, Tennessee where he died (Ramsey, 1853).

Nashville

December 7, 1792--On December 7, 1792, a party of cavalry, in service for the protection of the District of Mero, about eight miles from Nashville, was fired upon by about twenty Indians, who put them to flight. They killed John Hankins, who was scalped and his body much mangled. The Indians stole horses in this district without intermission through all the month of December, 1792.

December 29, 1792--On December 29, 1792, John Haggard was killed and scalped about six miles from Nashville; twelve balls were shot into him. His wife was killed by the Indians in the summer, and he left five small children in poverty and wretchedness.

Year of 1793

Knoxville

January 22, 1793--On Tuesday, January 22, the Indians killed and scalped John Pates on Crooked Creek about sixteen miles from Knoxville.

Little River

January 29, 1793--On the 29th, the Cherokees stole three of William Davidson's horses from Gamble's Station on Little River.

February 26, 1793--On February 26, they stole ten horses from Cozby's Creek. These aggressions prompted the spontaneous assemblage of the militia at Gamble's Station for the purpose of marching to the nearest Indian towns and retaliating upon them the injuries they were suffering.

Little Pigeon

March 1793--In March, a party of Indians led by Towakka formed an ambuscade near the house of Mr. Nelson living on Little Pigeon about twenty-five miles from Knoxville. Two of his sons, James and Thomas, were killed and scalped.

Knoxville

March 16, 1793--On the 16th, fourteen horses were stolen from Flat Creek within sixteen miles from Knoxville.

Little Laurel

March17, 1793--In March, Joseph Brown, whose capture in 1788 has already been mentioned, accompanied Thomas Ross, the mail carrier, and Colonel Caleb Friley, from the Holston settlements by the way of Kentucky to Cumberland. They were fired upon the third evening after they started on the east side of Little Laurel but sustained no damage. They went in full speed, crossed the river, and in about a quarter of a mile ran into a large body of Indians. Ross was killed but Brown and Friley escaped severely wounded.

Knoxville

March 18, 1793--On March 18, two young men named Clements were killed and scalped sixteen miles below Knoxville.

Powell's Mountain Gap

March 20, 1793--On March 20, a party of Indians killed and scalped William Massey and Adam Greene at the gap of Powell's Mountain on Clinch about twenty miles from Rogersville.

Holston River

April 8, 1793—On April 8, a party of Creeks, led by young Lashley, burned the house of Mr. Gallaher on the south side of Holston and within twenty miles of Knoxville. A detachment of mounted infantry pursued, but did not overtake them. The same party hovered about the settlements till the 15th when a party of Lieutenant Tedford's rangers fired upon and killed one of the Indians who proved to be a Cherokee—Noon-Day of Toquo.

Bledsoe's Station

April 9, 1793—Colonel Isaac Bledsoe was killed by the Chickamauga on April 9, 1793, at Bledsoe's Fort. Isaac Bledsoe was a long hunter who first entered the area of Bledsoe's Lick in 1769 and eventually with the help of his brother, Anthony, established the settlement on Bledsoe's Creek in present-day Sumner County, Tennessee.

Greenfield Station

April 27, 1793- Ramsey's version (1853) - *An opportunity was soon found by the Indians to attack the station near Greenfield in Sumner County, Tennessee. This was a position of some strength, and guarded by a few men. A number of Negroes had left the*

118

station early in the morning of April 27, to work in the adjoining fields. As was the general custom, a sentinel, John Jarvis, accompanied them. About two hundred and sixty Indians had the previous night formed an ambush, not far from the field. When the horses were attached to the ploughs by the negroes, and their attention was directed to their work, they were suddenly fired upon by the Indians. The Indians formed a line between them and the fort across a field, so as to cut off their retreat, and intercept them, should they attempt it in the direction of the station

As soon as the firing and the war whoop reached the men in the fort, four of the men William Hall, William Neely, William Wilson and another snatched up their guns and ran to the gate of the station, from which point they could see over the entire field, where the enemy was pursuing the sentinel and the Negroes. It was evident that without a bold and immediate rescue, their comrades would all be killed. Hall and the other soldiers dashed forward, and met the advancing Indian column at a cross fence in the field. They received their fire and took the fence from them, killing three or four of the warriors. They kept the whole bunch of them in check, until all but one of the unarmed negroes reached the fort. One was shot on his retreat, and after he had got fifty yards within the fence, from which the whites were firing. Poor Jarvis was unfortunately killed. It is remarkable, that though nearly a hundred guns were fired at the gallant men who were bravely repulsing the Indians at a distant not more than thirty yards, not one of them was seriously hurt. Mr. Hall was without his hat and a ball passed through his hair, cutting it off close to the skin, and abrading it about three or four inches long but doing slight damage. The little party gained the fort, under a heavy fire from the Indians. This they kept up for a considerable time, but at such a distance that the guns from the station could not reach the enemy. During their firing, the Indians caught all the horses and took them off, carrying upon them a number of their dead and wounded and raising the war whoop as they marched off.

This repulse, at Greenfield, of two hundred and sixty warriors who well-armed and flushed with late successes, made by four men exposed to the constant fire of the Indians during the whole attack is almost without a parallel. One of the brave men who participated in it, General William Hall, of Sumner County still survives and esteemed by his countrymen for his gallantry, his patriotism and private worth. He has since occupied the highest stations in the civil and military service of his state and presents a proud specimen of the heroic age and of the early times of Tennessee. The three comrades of Hall exhibited also signal bravery of which Neely and Hall were stimulated by the spirit of revenge each of them felt for the loss by the savages of a father and two brothers. Because of such bravery, the assailants did not make further attempts upon the station and withdrew from the place.

Dripping Spring

April 28, 1793--But, upon the next day, Francis Ransom was killed on the Kentucky Trace, near the Dripping Spring.

Nashville

May 9, 1793- At Johnson's Station near Nashville, a party of Chickamauga fired upon and wounded three boys, one of whom they scalped. A fourth boy was caught by the jacket, but he stripped it off and escaped unhurt.

May 10, 1793- *Ramsey's version (1853) Early in May, Nathaniel Teal, the carrier of the mail, had arrived in Nashville from Natchez. After delivering the mail, he went out in the evening and spent the night with General Robertson, five miles from town. Next morning within a mile of the General's house, the Indians fired upon and killed him. Two companies of horsemen were instantly paraded—one, commanded by old Captain John Rains; the other, by Captain John Gordon, the same who afterwards, in 1813, commanded the spy company in the Creek war. To the latter, Joseph Brown attached himself. He was still suffering from the wound he had received in the ambuscade on Laurel River, in March, but he had made the heroic resolve, to obtain redress for the injuries inflicted on his family, and was among the first to volunteer on this occasion. The force of the two companies united, was one hundred. They were instructed by General Robertson, to scour the woods, and paths and crossing places, of creeks and rivers, and to discover the trails of the enemy coming against Cumberland. They set out on the 12th of May. Teal was killed by a party of Indians who had made a hunt on Cathey's Creek, about twenty miles west of where Columbia now stands. Needing horses to carry the results of their hunt home, they had come into the settlements and stole a number, and killed Teal. The horsemen soon found their trail, and on the fifth day overtook them, on the Second Creek that runs into Tennessee, below the mouth of Elk River. The Indians had stopped at noon, and twenty men were sent forward to fire upon them. The hills were open woods, but the creek bottom was a close cane-brake. Rains' men advanced on the right of the Indians, while Gordon's went to their left. When the advance of twenty fired, the two companies dashed forward with all speed. Gordon's Company came to a high bluff of the creek, which horses could not descend. When the Captain and Joseph Brown dismounted, and took down the precipice each of them killed an Indian. The horsemen had to ride around the bluff, and the most of the Indians escaped into the cane-brake before they were seen. Six of them were killed and a boy captured. The companies then returned home.*

120

Drake's Creek

May 20, 1793 -The Chickamauga Indians continued to prowl around and be seen near the settlements. On May 20, 1793, they killed John Hacker on Drake's Creek.

Raccoon Valley

May 25, 1793—On May 25, 1793, Thomas Gillam and his son James, were killed and scalped by the Chickamauga Indians in the Raccoon Valley some eighteen miles from Knoxville. Captain Beard with fifty mounted infantry made immediate pursuit.

Nashville

June 4, 1793--On June 4, 1793, Adam Fleener, Richard Robertson, and William Bartlett, were also killed, and Abraham Young and John Mayfield were wounded.

Coyatee

June 13, 1793--General John Sevier was at this time at Jonesboro, and Captain John D. Chisholm wrote a letter forwarded from Knoxville informing him as follows.

"That on yesterday morning, Captain John Beard, with a party of forty men, attacked the Indians at the Hanging Maw's, and killed twelve or fifteen on the spot, among whom were a number of the principal chiefs, called there by the express order of the President. Major Robert King, Daniel Carmichael, Joseph Sevier and James Ore, were acting for the United States. This will bring on inevitable war, the Indians are making vigorous preparation for an assault on us. The frontier is in a most lamentable situation.

Pray, sir, let us have your immediate presence, for our all depends upon your exertion.

The Hanging Maw and his wife were wounded. Killed in the action were Scantee, a Chickasaw chie, that was at the Maw's, Kittigeskie's daughter and other principal Indians. Two hundred Indians were in arms in thirty minutes. Beard and his party have fled, leaving the frontier unprotected. My dear sir, much depends on you—for your presence itself will be a balm to the suffering frontier."

John D. Chisholm

At this time Governor William Blount was absent during Bread's raid on Coyatee. His secretary General Smith, was on duty and wrote immediately to the Hanging Maw and other chiefs, in explanation of the atrocious conduct of Beard's party, and begged them not to retaliate the outrage.

"Be not rash and inconsiderate," said he; *"hear what your and our Great Father, the President, will say. Go and see him as he has requested. I assure you, I believe he will give you satisfaction, if you forbear to take it yourselves."*

Daniel Smith

The Secretary, communicating the state of things to the War Department, adds, *"to my great pain, I find, to punish Beard by law, just now, is out of the question."* The affair was deemed of such consequence that it demanded the arrest and trial of that officer. The court martial, before which he was arraigned, inflicted no punishment.

Greenfield Station

June 20, 1793--On June 20, 1793, James Steele and his daughter were killed and his son wounded. On this summer day, James Steel, his daughter, son and his brother, Robert, left Greenfield to go to Morgan's Station. William Hall and seven others of the light horse were eating dinner when the Steeles announced they were leaving. Hall attempted to persuade the Steeles to wait until the soldiers could finish eating so they could serve as an escort. James Steele insisted that there was no danger and left.

The men were still at dinner when gunshots were heard. Rushing down the road they found James Steel lying dead, shot through the heart, and scalped. His beautiful seventeen-year-old daughter Betsy was lying on the ground mortally wounded and scalped. Her brother was wounded in the shoulders but escaped with his Uncle Robert. Betsy apparently fought her attackers with her bare hands as they were found cut and bleeding and clutching wisps of Indian hair.

Hay's Station

July 1, 1793--July 1, 1793, the Chickamauga Indians attacked Hay's Station and killed Jacob and Joseph Castleman, and wounded Hans Castleman.

Joslin's Station

July 15, 1793--On July 15, 1793, Mr. Joslin was wounded at his own house by a group of Chickamauga Indians.

Nashville

July 18, 1793---On July 18, 1793, William Campbell was wounded near Nashville.

Johnson's Lick

July 19, 1793---On July 19, 1793, Mr. Smith was killed at Johnson's Lick.

Joslin's Station

August 5, 1793--On August 5, 1793, Captains Rains and Gordon pursued a party of Chickamauga Indians who had killed Samuel Miller, near Joslin's Station. After they crossed the Duck River, they found Indian signs were very fresh and on following the Indians seven miles further, they were overtaken. The pursuers killed some of them on the ground, and took prisoner a boy of twelve years of age. One of them called out that he was a Chickasaw, and by this finesse made his escape. On examining the prisoner, they found the Indians to be members of the Creek faction of the Chickamauga.

Henry's Station

August 29, 1793—At daylight on August 29, 1793, a large party of Indians attacked Henry's Station. Lieutenant Tedford was taken prisoner and horribly butchered.

McGaughey's Station

August 29, 1793--Andrew Creswell was living in the neighborhood of McGaughey's Station and two other men constituted the force in his house. William Cunningham passing near was waylaid by the Indians and shot. He escaped to Creswell's house. One of the men proposed to Creswell to go to the station. The latter replied that from his knowledge of the Indian character he believed they would not strike a second blow in the same place. Mr. Creswell then enquired from his wife, whether she would rather go to the station than to stay at home? She replied, it seemed like death at either place, and she would rather risk her life there, than any place else. *"That's my sort,"* said Creswell; *" I will keep this house till the Indians take me out of it."* The house was a new log cabin with a single door fastened by a shutter of hewed puncheons too thick to be penetrated by a bullet. His stable was immediately in rear of his house that Mr. Creswell himself could not open the door of it without first entering his dwelling-house. Then he would go to the head of his bed and raising a large bolt with a long lever. Near this lever was a porthole through which he defended his stable. On each side of his house, were other holes through which he defended his family. The Indians came in sight, but never attacked him. Mr. Cunningham recovered but he died a few years since in Monroe County.

Hutter House

August 30, 1793—On August 30, 1793, two Indians came to the house of Philip Hutter in Washington County, about eleven o'clock, and tomahawked and scalped his wife and left her for dead. They cut the head off his daughter and carried it away with them, and plundered the house.

Cavet's Station

September 30, 1793--As Sevier's army continued attacks on the Cherokee, a deterioration of peaceful relations with Sevier's settlers in east Tennessee reached a boiling point with the Lower Cherokee. In addition, John Beard attacked and killed nine Cherokees at Hanging Maw's home and subsequent acquittal caused the Cherokees to elevate their attacks on white settlements. Chickamauga Chief John Watts, Jr., Doublehead, and other prominent Lower Cherokee leaders planned a large raid on Knoxville, Tennessee.

Home of James Vann

Chief John Watts and Doublehead called for warriors to gather into the largest Chickamauga war party in history. Robert Benge was one of the first among them to volunteer. Also joining were Shawnees from Running Water in southern Tennessee and a large group of Creeks enlisted by Chief Doublehead. As the war party moved north, Nettle Carrier and Doublehead's brother, Pumpkin Boy went ahead to scout. The scouts approached the blockhouse at Ish's Station which was commanded by John Sevier. The two were spotted by sentries and Pumpkin Boy was shot and killed. Doublehead became enraged and wanted blood; however, because of dissension in their ranks and the firing of a cannon on the morning of their planned attack on James White's Fort at Knoxville plans were changed.

The following is the account leading to the raid on Cavet's Station given in The Annals of Tennessee by James Gettys McGready Ramsey: *Captain Michael Harrison,*

124

with his company of eighty light-horsemen from Washington County, was in service (early in September, and visited the several stations on Pigeon, before coming to Sevier's headquarters at Ish's Station, south of Holston. From this point, scouts were sent out to guard the approaches to Knoxville, which it was apprehended would be the object of Indian attack, on account of the public stores that were known to be there. On the 24th September, Captain Harrison's light-horse had scoured the country in every direction, but made no discovery of the enemy. But the same evening, a body of a thousand warriors, under the lead of John Watts and Doublehead, crossed the Tennessee River, below the mouth of Holston, and marched all night in the direction of Knoxville. Of this large force, seven hundred were Creeks—the rest were Cherokees. Of the former, were one hundred well mounted horsemen. The Indians had expected to reach Knoxville before day, on the morning of the twenty-fifth, but some detention at the river had prevented. The horsemen had out-marched the main body, and some altercation between the leaders occurred, and produced confusion. Knoxville being the principal object of attack and plunder, orders were given by some of the Creeks to press forward at once, and not delay their march, by stopping to disturb and plunder the smaller settlements. Doublehead advised a different policy, and insisted on taking every cabin as they passed. A further cause of delay was the rivalry between this chief and Van, each of whom aspired to the leadership of the expedition. Upon the question, "shall we massacre all the inhabitants of Knoxville, or the men only?" these savage warriors differed in opinion; Van advising lenity to the women and children. Before the plan of procedure was adjusted, the night was so far spent as not to allow the invaders time to reach Knoxville before daylight. That town was, however, in the opinion of all, the primary object of attack, and, with that purpose in view, Campbell's Station—one of the chief forts of the country, and in which, at that time, twenty families were there stationed for mutual protection—was carefully passed, undisturbed. At daylight they had reached the head of Sinking Creek, in the Grassy Valley, and were in a rapid march for Knoxville. The United States troops at that place, as usual, fired off a cannon at sunrise, which the Indians heard, and understood to be an evidence that their attack was expected. This dis. concerted their plans, and led to the abandonment of their meditated assault. The Indian force was halted immediately. In sight of them, was the house or station of Alexander Cavet, in which were only three gun-men and his family, thirteen in number. This house stood on the plantation now owned by Mr. Walker, about eight miles west of Knoxville, and about six hundred yards north of the present stage-road, where its foundation can yet be seen.

Disappointed in their hopes of plunder, and too cowardly to run the risk of obtaining it by attacking Knoxville, the Indians determined to wreak their vengeance upon a defenseless family, and marched at once to and invested Cavet's house. It was put in the best state of defense which three men could do against a thousand savage assailants. The fire from the house killed one Creek, one Cherokee, and wounded three more. This held back the Indians for a time, and they sent in Bob Benge, a half Creek, who spoke English, proposing that if the station were surrendered, the lives of the besieged should be spared, and that they should be exchanged for a like number of Indian prisoners. These terms were accepted, and the house surrendered. It's unfortunate inmates had scarcely left the door, when Doublehead and his party fell upon the prisoners and put them to death, mutilating and abusing the bodies of the women and children especially, in the most barbarous and indelicate manner possible. Cavet himself was found in the garden barbarously murdered, and having seven bullets in his mouth, put there by himself, for the greater convenience of speedily loading his rifle. John Watts interposed, and saved the life of Alexander Cavet, Junior, a lad. Benge also interceded for the prisoners, who had capitulated with him, but Doublehead was inexorable, and all efforts were unavailing to save the poor victims. The house and stables were plundered and burnt, and the Indians went off, carrying with them into captivity the only survivor of a large family. He was afterwards killed in the Indian towns (Ramsey, 1853).

During the raid, members of the Cavet Family were promised safe passage and surrendered to Robert Benge, who negotiated a promised freedom for the family. Even though Benge was his nephew, Doublehead refused to recognize the agreement that had been negotiated. Doublehead and his friends attacked and killed the Cavet Family while Benge, Watts, and Vann tried in vain to stop the slaughter.

The Bench (Robert Benge) acting as an interpreter had convinced the people to surrender. Soon as they had surrendered, Doublehead killed every one. The Bench wept because he had given his word and felt that his honor had been betrayed by his uncle Doublehead. The relationship between The Bench and Doublehead would never be the same.

Probably in a state of rage over the recent death of his beloved brother Pumpkin Boy, Doublehead refused to allow any white people at Cavett's Station escape death. James Vann had hoisted a young white boy to his saddle in order to protect him; however, Doublehead was intent on killing all the white people at Cavett's Station. Doublehead rode up and killed the child with his tomahawk while he was mounted behind Vann. From that day forward, Vann called Doublehead "Baby Killer" or "Kill Baby" and became his lifelong enemy. Later, James Vann would be most instrumental in the death of Doublehead. Vann, Ridge, and Charles Hicks formed an alliance to eventually assassinate Doublehead.

Dandridge

October 1793--While Sevier was absent with so many men on the Etowah campaign, the Indians came in suddenly and killed a lad and woman on the south of the river above Dandridge. They were found stuck in the throat like hogs, their skin taken entirely off their heads, and the bodies left naked. A party of friends accompanied their remains to a burying ground three miles off. Two of the party were Cunningham and Jacob Jenkins, who went on some distance before the rest. A body of fifty Indians fired upon them. Cunningham was killed, scalped, and bruised with war-clubs. He was found by the company, carried to the burial place, and interred with the other two in the same grave. Jenkins received several bullets shot through his clothes, and a blow from a war-club, but his horse being struck with a ball, dashed down a precipice, and escaped.

McGaughey's Station

October 1793--Hearing of this massacre of his friends, W. H. Cunningham went from his home on Boyd's Creek for the purpose of advising them to remove to the stronger station at McGaughey's. He was to bring home his son Jesse, (then a little boy,) who was staying at the Buffalo Lick. He carried his little son before him for some thirty miles and left the main road to follow by-paths. He escaped the attack of the Indians till he got within about half a mile of the fort when he passed through a party of thirty in number. It was night, and he escaped unhurt. The Indians prowled around the station, but found it too well defended to justify an assault. They broke open the stable doors, stole the horses of the besieged, and withdrew. The condition of the country did not allow a pursuit.

Two weeks after, Mr. Cunningham was going out from the fort alone. At the distance of two hundred yards from the fort gate, he was fired upon by a party of ten Indians lying in ambush fifteen steps from him. He escaped every ball, but the Indians having intercepted his return to the gate, chased him in the opposite direction. The fire from one of their guns proved effectual and wounded him. He turned the corner of a fence and would have been soon overtaken, but the men in the fort came out and made pursuit of the Indians. When the Indians saw the men from the fort, they withdrew to their retreats in the mountains.

Croft's Mill

November 9, 1793—Some horses were stolen from Croft's Mill by a party of Indians and a number of them were seen in the area.

Sumner County

1793--In this year, 1793, the Indians fired on Thomas Sharpe Spencer near where Major David Wilson since lived in Sumner County. Mrs. Anthony Bledsoe was thrown from her horse, but Spencer bravely rescued her from the hands of the Indians and conducted her to a place of safety. About this time several persons were killed in the County of Sumner, whose names were not known.

Hay's Station

1793--In this year James McCuoe was killed by the Indians at Hay's Station on Stone's River. One of the Castleman's was also killed and another wounded.

Caney Fork

December 1, 1793--About December 1, 1793, James Randal Robertson, son of General Robertson, and John Grimes were killed by the Cherokees of the Lower towns on the waters of the Caney Fork where they had gone to trap for beavers.

Dripping Springs

1793--In 1793 at Dripping Springs, Kentucky, Doublehead, Robert Benge, and other Lower Cherokees set up an ambush on the Kentucky Road. They attacked and killed Captain William Overall and a Burnett man who were carrying whiskey and numerous supplies. After getting drunk with the whiskey they had taken, Doublehead scalped the men. He then cut off pieces of their flesh, roasted the meat, and ate their flesh. Doublehead was later to say, *"We, the Cherokees, had eaten a great quantity of the white men's flesh, but have had so much of it we are tired of it, and think it too salty."* Later, Doublehead carried the scalps to the Tennessee River Towns using them in scalp dances and putting them on public display.

Year of 1794

Nashville

February 20, 1794--On February 20, 1794, numerous small divisions of Indians appeared in all parts of the frontiers of Mero District marking every path and plantation with the fatal signs of their visitation. They stole nearly all the horses that belonged to the district and butchered a number of the citizens. In many instances they left the divided limbs of the slain scattered over the ground. Jonathan Robertson was with three lads of the name of Cowan and was fired upon by five Indians. One of the lads was slightly wounded and a ball passed through Robertson's hat. He and the lads returned the fire, drove off the Indians and wounded two of them mortally. On the death of Helen, Captain Murray followed the Indians and at the distance of one hundred and twenty miles came up with them on the banks of the Tennessee. He and his company destroyed the party of eleven Chickamauga. Two women of the party were captured and treated with humanity.

Middleton's Station

March 12, 1794--In March 1794, Doublehead and his warriors set an ambush on the road from Kentucky to Hawkins' Courthouse near Middleton's Station and killed four including two Baptist preachers. From this time forward, circuit riding preachers were very cautious when entering territory controlled by Doublehead and his warriors.

The following details are given in the book <u>Tennessee, The Volunteer State</u> (1923): After Colonel Watts' forces had been dispersed by General Sevier, and the Upper towns of the Cherokees had declared themselves for peace, Doublehead recruited a party of about one hundred warriors and again moved to his favorite field on the frontiers of Cumberland and Kentucky, and was responsible for all the mischief done in those quarters during the spring of 1794-5. On the 12th of March he formed an ambuscade near Middleton's Station, on the road from Kentucky to Hawkins' Courthouse, and firing upon the post rider and twelve travelers who were in his company, killed four men, two of them Elders Haggard and Shelton being Baptist preachers. And for some years after peace was permanently established the Methodist circuit rider crossed the Wilderness with fear and trembling, rumors still being current that Doublehead was under a curse to be avenged on the white people (Moore, 1923).

March 1794--Also in March 1794, Doublehead killed the Wilson family which consisted of eight women and children and took one of their young sons as his prisoner. *"In the same month, Doublehead killed the Wilson family, consisting of eight women and children, except one boy whom he took into his possession"* (Moore, 1923).

Nashville

March 20, 1794--On March 20, 1794, James Bryan was fired upon by the Chickamauga Indians from an ambush near a path within four miles of Nashville.

Bledsoe's Lick

March 20, 1794--On March 20, 1794, Charles Bratton was killed and scalped by the Chickamauga near the house of Major White in Sumner County.

March 21, 1794—On March 21, 1794, Anthony Bledsoe, son of Colonel Anthony Bledsoe, and Anthony Bledsoe, son of Colonel Isaac Bledsoe, were killed and scalped by Indians at a stone quarry near the house of Searcy Smith in Sumner County, Tennessee. The two young Bledsoe sons both of whom were named Anthony Bledsoe, were killed and scalped by Doublehead's Chickamauga. They were killed while returning to Rock Castle, General Smith's home where they were boarding while attending a nearby school on

Drakes Creek. In addition, Smith's black slave was captured by same party and two horses were taken from Mr. Smith's wagon.

Calvin's Blockhouse

April 1, 1794—On April 1, 1794, a party of 30 to 40 Chickamauga Indians, ambuscaded a path near Calvin's Blockhouse on Crooked Creek and fired upon Samuel Wear, his two sons and William McMurray. They escaped unhurt.

Spencer's Hill

April 1, 1794--A more tragically attack was made by a party of forty Chickamauga near the Crab-Orchard upon a company of travelers. Thomas Sharp Spencer was killed and James Walker was wounded. The rest of the party escaped to the South West Point Block-house. The hill down which the whites were descending and on which Spencer was killed is still known as Spencer's Hill.

Doublehead set the ambush near Crab Orchard on the Knoxville to Nashville Road.

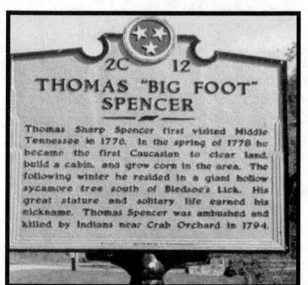

Thomas Sharpe Spencer and four other traveling companions had passed Knoxville and stopped at South West Point. From there they were traveling across the wilderness on Avery's Trace toward Nashville when they were ambushed by Doublehead. Spencer, who was a giant of a man, and James Walker were riding in front of the party when they were surprised by the attack. Spencer was killed in the first volley of shots and fell dead. His horse ran off but threw the saddle bags in which Spencer was carrying over $1,000.00 in gold and other valuables.

The details of Spencer's death is given in the book <u>Tennessee, The Volunteer State</u> (1923): *The first day of April, 1794, found Doublehead near Crab Orchard, on the road from Knoxville to Nashville, at a point since called Spencer's Hill, where he secreted his party and lay in wait for the unhappy traveler who might find it necessary to venture across the Wilderness. At this point let us pause long enough to notice a few incidents in the career of the earliest and most picturesque pioneer of the Cumberland, Thomas Sharpe Spencer. He was a man of giant proportions and herculean strength. A hunter left by Timothy Demonbreun in charge of his camp on the Cumberland, in the fall of 1777,*

130

discovered Spencer's tracks, and was so alarmed by their uncommon size that he fled and did not rest until he had joined Demoubreun at Vincennes on the banks of the Wabash. A few years later, at a general muster two boys became involved in a fight. Old Bob Shaw, who considered himself a mighty man, insisted on letting them fight it out. Spencer, however, was of a different opinion, and parting the crowd right and left he seized one of the belligerents in either hand, pulled them apart with scarcely an effort, and bade them clear themselves. This Shaw took as a fighting offense and struck Spencer in the face with his fist. Spencer instantly caught him by the collar and waistband of his trousers, and running a few steps to a ten-rail fence, tossed him over it. This much is on the authority of General William Hall. He, George Espey, Andrew Lucas, and a man named Johnson were out hunting on the headwaters of Drake's Creek. As they stopped to let their horses drink, the Indians made their attack. Lucas was shot through the neck and mouth. He dismounted, however, with the rest, but in attempting to fire, the blood gushed out of his mouth and wet his priming. Perceiving this he desisted and crawled into a bunch of briers. Espey, as he, alighted, received a shot which broke his thigh, but still fought heroically. Johnson and Spencer acquitted themselves with incomparable gallantry. Spencer received a shot, but the ball split on the bone of his arm and saved his life. They were finally obliged to give way, and leave Espey, whom the Indians scalped; but they did not find Lucas, who shortly afterwards reached the fort, and recovered from his wound.

In the fall of 1793, Spencer made a journey to Virginia to settle an estate, and receive a legacy that had fallen to him. Having completed his business, in the following spring, be started back to the West, having in his saddle bags $1,000 in gold, besides other valuables. His route carried him by way of Knoxville and Southwest Point. He left the latter place in company with four other travelers and started across the Wilderness, April 1, 1794. Spencer and James Walker were riding together in advance, and when they reached the point at which Doublehead had formed his ambuscade, they received a volley which brought Spencer dead from his horse and wounded Walker. When Spencer fell his horse fled, and made his escape with the travelers in the rear, but his saddlebags coming off, his money and other valuables fell into the hands of the enemy (Moore and Foster, 1923).

Town Creek Blockhouse

April 2, 1794--Twenty-five Indians secreted themselves at night near the Blockhouse at the mouth of Town Creek. The next morning of April 3, the party of Indians fired upon and killed William Green. Attempting to storm the block-house, the Indians were repulsed and several of their warriors wounded.

April 15, 1794--On April 15, 1794, the Indians stole ten horses from Mr. Gibbs. More than fifty horses had been stolen in that neighborhood within a few days.

Greenfield Station

April 21, 1794--A month after the young Anthony Bledsoe was killed, Thomas, another son of Colonel Anthony Bledsoe was surprised and mortally wounded near his deceased father's station at Greenfield. The Bledsoes had received vast grants of land for their services in opening the frontier but had paid a far greater price for it in blood.

Casteel's Cabin

April 22, 1794-*Ramsey's version (1853)-Among other acts of Indian hostility perpetrated in Knox County was one which occurred on April 22, 1794. William Casteel lived south of French Broad, about nine miles above Knoxville, and two miles from the then residence of Doctor Cozby. The latter had been an old Indian fighter, from the first settlement of the country, and was, of course, held in deadly hatred by the Indians, and had often been selected as the victim of their vengeance. He had his house always well prepared for defense, and never allowed himself to be taken by surprise. At evening, of the 22nd, his domestic animals gave the usual tokens of the presence of Indians, when, observing from his house, he could discern, obscurely, the stealthy march, in Indian file, of twenty warriors passing across the end of a short lane, and concealing themselves in the fence corners and the adjoining woods. The door was at once barricaded, the fire extinguished, two guns primed afresh, and with these he prepared to defend his castle and his family, consisting of his wife and several children, one of whom only could shoot. A space of more than one hundred yards had been cleared around his building, and there was light enough to see the approach of an assailant within that distance. From the port-holes, in each angle of the house, a constant watch was kept, and orders were given by Cozby, in a loud voice, to the members of his family, as if commanding a platoon of soldiers. The stratagem succeeded.*

An hour before day the Indians withdrew, and went off in the direction of Casteel's cabin. Early next morning Anthony Ragan came to Casteel's, and found him dead, from a lick received on his head from a war club; he was scalped, and lying near the fire, dressed, and with leggings on, having arose early for the purpose, as was supposed, of accompanying Reagan to a hunt, which had been agreed on the preceding day. Mrs. Casteel was found on the floor, scalped in two places—a proof that it required two warriors to conquer her—her nightcap with several holes cut through it, a butcher knife stuck into her side, one arm broken, and a part of the hand of the other arm cut off. She seemed to have made resistance with an axe, found near her, stained with blood. One of the daughters received a stab, which, piercing through the body, went into the bed-clothes. She and two brothers were scalped. The youngest child, two years old, having the cranium entirely denuded of the scalp, was thrown into the chimney corner. Elizabeth, the oldest daughter, ten years old, now Mrs. Dunlap, still living near the scene of the horrid massacre of her father's whole family, was found weltering in her blood, flowing from six wounds inflicted with a tomahawk. Besides these, she was also scalped. Reagan gave the alarm to the settlement; urgent pursuit was immediately made, but the savages escaped. While preparations were made for the interment of the massacred family, Elizabeth showed signs of life, moaning when an attempt was made, by Colonel Ramsey, who was present, to close one of the gashes upon her head. She was taken to Mr. Shook's, who then owned Major Swan's mills, where Doctor Cozby dressed her wounds. She did not recover for, two years. The rest of the family, six in number, were buried in one grave, under a black-oak tree, still standing. Mr. Casteel was a soldier of the Revolution, from Green Brier County, Va., and had never received any thing for his services. Of the heroic wife and mother, nothing more is known. An effort has been made to procure a pension for the surviving daughter but was fruitless (Ramsey,1853).

Station Camp Creek

May 26, 1794—On May 26, 1794, one of the guards on duty was wounded by Chickamauga Indians on Bledsoe's Creek. On the same day on Station Camp Creek in midst of a thick settlement, a party of Indians fired on Mr. Strawder and his son, at work within one hundred yards of his house. They killed and scalped the son and pursued the father to his house, and wounded his wife as she opened the door to let him in.

Nashville

June 11, 1794--On June 11, 1794, the Chickamauga killed Mrs. Gear within four miles of Nashville. Captain Gordon followed the Indians on their retreat upwards of ninety miles, killed one of them and lost one of his party Robert McRory. He overtook them at the foot of Cumberland Mountain near the place where Caldwell's bridge was located.

Muscle Shoals

June 1794--In June, Scott's boat left Knoxville for Natchez. On board were William Scott, John Pettegrew, William Pettegrew, Mr. Tate, Mr. Young, John Harkins, three women, four children, and twenty black slaves. As this boat passed down the Tennessee, it was fired upon by the Chickamauga of the Running Water and at the Long Island village without receiving any injury. On the other hand, the fire was returned and two Indians were wounded. A large party of a hundred and fifty Indians then collected, headed by Unacala, the same who was wounded at the attack upon Buchanan's Station in September, 1792, and they pursued the boat to the Muscle Shoals where they overtook it. They killed all the white people who were in it, made prisoners of the blackss, and plundered the boat of its lading. The white people killed three Indians and wounded a fourth.

Nashville

July 6, 1794--On July 6, 1794, Isaac Mayfield was killed by Chickamauga within five miles of Nashville. He was standing sentinel for his son-in-law while he hoed his corn and got the first fire on twelve to fifteen of the Indians. The Indians were to near for him, to escape. Eight balls penetrated his body, he was scalped, a new English bayonet was thrust through his face, and two bloody tomahawks left near his mangled body. He was the sixth person of his name who had been killed or captured by the Chickamauga. Major George Winchester was killed and scalped by the Indians near Major Wilson's in the District of Mero, on the public road leading from his own house to Sumner Court House. He was a Justice of the Peace and was on his way to Court. He was a valuable citizen and a good civil and military officer.

Bledsoe's Lick

July 9, 1794--In separate attacks in Sumner County, the son of Hugh Strother was killed on Station Camp Creek. Hugh Webb and a frontier spy along Bledsoe Creek were also killed by Chickamauga.

On the morning of July 9, 1794, Major George Winchester, commander of the local Militia and brother to General James Winchester of Cragfont, was on his way from Bledsoe's Lick to a meeting of the Sumner County Quarterly Court where he was a member. As he neared Gallatin, at the junction of present day Hartsville and Scottsville Pikes, he was ambushed, killed and scalped.

Ish's Blockhouse

July 24, 1794-Ramsey (1853)- *On July 24, 1794, a party of Chickamauga killed John Ish at his plough in his field, within one hundred and eighty yards of his own block-house and scalped him. Ish lived eighteen miles below Knoxville. He left a wife and eleven children, the eldest not more than eleven years of age. Major King, Lieutenant Cunningham, John Boggs and ten other Cherokees, sent by the Hanging Maw, went in pursuit of the offenders. They returned a few days afterwards with a Creek fellow, whom the Hanging Maw wished to scalp, but was dissuaded from his purpose and took only the war-lock with which they danced the scalp dance all night. The Cherokees apprehended for this act the resentment of the Creek Nation. Major King in the pursuit came upon the trail of the murderers leading into the path that was travelled from Coyatee to Hiwassee within two miles of Hiwassee. He there received information that those he was in pursuit* *of passed with a fresh scalp about the middle of the afternoon and would tarry all night at Wococee, eight miles ahead. The pursuers went to Wococee and finding the murderers still ahead, they continued the pursuit. They were overtaken by a runner from Hiwassee with information that one of Ish's murderers was behind ad stopped at a little village two miles from Hiwassee. Failing to overtake the main body, they turned back and found the Creek as the runner had reported, in the house of a Cherokee. After some consultation whether the Cherokees or white people should kill or take him, the Maw's son Willioe, with three others, seized and tied him. Having tied him, four warriors took him in charge and were particularly careful that he should not escape until he was delivered to the agent of the United States, Mr. McKee, at the Tellico Blockhouse on the evening of July 28, 1794. The Governor issued a commission of Oyer and Terminer for the trial of this Indian pursuant to the stipulations contained in the treaty of New York. A court was held by Judge Anderson, and an indictment was found by the grand jury against Obongpohego, of Toocaucaugee, on Oakfuskee. When charged, he confessed the fact. But the court permitted him to withdraw his plea and to plead not guilty; which being done. The trial proceeded and the petit jury found him guilty of the murder of John Ish, as charged in the bill of indictment.*

Crab Orchard

July 13, 1794--On July 13, 1794, Lieutenant McClelland, who had with him thirty-seven of Captain Evans's company, was attacked on the Cumberland Path, near the Crab-Orchard, eighteen miles from South-West Point, by a body of Creeks, consisting of upwards of one hundred warriors. He made a brave and soldierly defense, twice repelling the Creeks, but was finally compelled to retreat with the loss of four men killed, one wounded, four missing, thirty-one horses, thirty-eight saddles and bridles, blankets, great-coats and provisions. On the side of the Creeks the loss was not ascertained, but from the obstinacy and bravery of the defense, and the report of Lieutenant McClelland and others, there was reason to believe they lost from twelve to sixteen. The Creek commander was conspicuously bold, and was numbered amongst the slain. The white men killed, were Paul Cunningham, Daniel Hitchcock, William Flennegan, Stephen Renfroe. Abraham Byrd was wounded and the four men who were missing from the detachment after the action, but later reached South-West Point. William Lea, one of that number, arrived on the 18th, and reported that he had been made prisoner by the Indians and had escaped from them.

Red River

September 12 and 16, 1794--On September 12, 1794, in Tennessee County, Miss Roberta was killed on Red River, forty miles from Nashville. On September 14, 1794, Thomas Reasons and wife were killed, and their house plundered, near the same place, by the Chickamauga Indians. On September 16, 1794, a third party of Indians killed a woman on Red River, near Major Sharp's about forty miles northeast of Nashville and carried off several horses.

John Donnelson's Station

September 16, 1794--On September 16, 1794, in Davidson County twelve miles above Nashville, a party of Chickamauga killed a Chambers and wounded John Bosley and Joseph Davis. They burned John Donnelson's Station and carried off a bunch of horses.

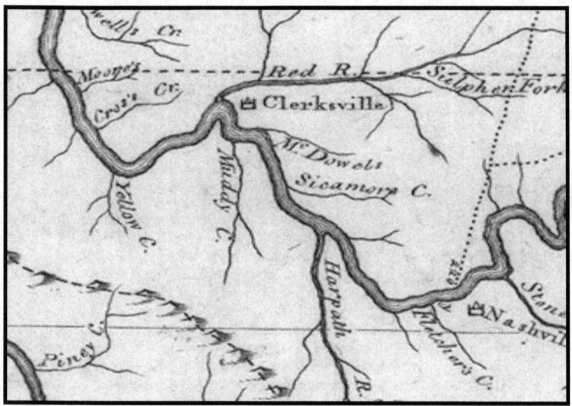

Red River, Tennessee 1795 John Reid Map

Kentucky

September 1794--Previous to the march of Major Ore from Nashville, Colonel Whitley with about one hundred men arrived from Kentucky. They had followed a party of Indians who had committed depredations on the southern frontier of that country. Whitley was in the pursuit and had a man killed by the Indians. The Indians had taken several horses and Whitley was determined to pursue them to the Lower Towns.

Red River

October 24, 1794--On October 24, 1794, a party of Indians fired upon John Leiper and another man, near the house of the former, on the east fork of Red River, in Tennessee County.

November 5, 1794--On November 5, 1794, a party of fifty Indians, on the waters of Red River, in Tennessee County, fell upon the families of Colonel Isaac Titsworth and of his brother, John Titsworth. They killed and scalped seven white persons, wounded a black woman, and took prisoners including white man, three children and a black fellow, and also a daughter of Colonel Titsworth. Pursuit was made by the neighboring militia. After the Indians, discovered the approach of the militia, they tomahawked the three children and scalped them, taking off the whole skins of their heads. The white man and the black fellow they either killed or carried off with the daughter. These murders were said to be the Creek Saction of the Chickamauga.

Sevier's Station

November 11, 1794—During this attack, Doublehead was actually in a hunting party of some 40 Chickamauga which included several creeks. They first passed Sevier's station but later after becoming intoxicated, they decided to make a raid. The description of the attack is from Old Frontiers by John P. Brown 1938: *The family of Valentine Sevier, like his brother, John, was a prominent settler on the Tennessee frontier. During the Indian wars he lost four sons, two daughters, two sons-in-law, and several grandchildren. In March 1781, during John Sevier's campaign against the Middle Cherokee settlements, he swam the Little Tennessee River to burn their cabins and narrowly escaped an ambush. He accompanied his brother's campaign against the Chickamauga Indians. In 1785 he attempted to settle the Great Bend of the Tennessee, descending the river with 90 frontiersmen in boats, but Indians kept them in a state of siege until they abandoned the undertaking in 1786.*

Valentine's Station near Clarksville, Tennessee, was attacked by Chief Doublehead on November 11, 1794. The old frontiersman stood off the Chickamauga, but his daughter and her husband, Charles Snyder, and his son, Joseph Sevier, were killed in Snyder's cabin. His daughter Rebecca was wounded and scalped, but she eventually recovered. A frontiersman, who came to their assistance from Clarksville, reported that "there were twelve or fifteen Indians. The Colonel prevented the savage band from entering his house, but they cruelly slaughtered all around him," (Brown, 1938).

The following concerning the raid on Sevier's Station is from Tennessee, The Volunteer State 1769-1923: *Colonel Valentine Sevier was one of the early settlers of Tennessee County. His father was a Virginian of French extraction, from whom he inherited something of the cavalier spirit, so prominent in the character of his brother, Governor John Sevier. Spare of flesh, with an erect, commanding, soldierly presence, a bright blue eye, and a quick ear, he was at once ardent, brave, generous, and affectionate. He had served his country faithfully, both in the Indian wars, and the War of Independence; had been prominent in the civil affairs of Washington County; took an active interest in the establishment of the State of Franklin, soon after the fall of which in 1788, he emigrated to Cumberland, and erected a station on the north side of Red River, near its mouth, and about a mile from Clarksville. In 1792 Doublehead and his party killed three of his sons, Robert, William, and Valentine, while on their way to Nashville to join General Robertson in the defense of the settlements. He now had a still more severe trial to endure.*

About eleven o'clock on the morning of November 11, 1794, when the men were all away from the station except Colonel Sevier and his son-in-law, Charles Snyder, the Indians surprised and made a furious assault on Sevier's Station. The scene was wild and tragic. The screams of the women and the crying of the children were mingled with the roaring of the guns and the yelling of the Indians, while they killed and scalped, robbed and plundered, in frantic confusion. Colonel Sevier, assisted by his wife, successfully defended their own house, but the Indians were in nearly every other building before they were discovered. Snyder, his wife, Betsy, their son, John and Colonel Sevier's son, Joseph, were all killed in Snyder's house, but the colonel prevented the Indians from getting Snyder's scalp. Mrs. Ann King and her son, James, were also killed, and Colonel Sevier's daughter, Rebecca, was scalped and left for dead, but revived and finally recovered. The people of Clarksville heard the firing of the guns, and John Easten, Anthony Crutcher, and two or three other men, who happened to be in the town, ran over to the relief of Colonel Sevier, when the Indians hastily disappeared, having looted the houses and killed the stock. Colonel Sevier abandoned his station and moved over to Clarksville, which place was itself upon the eve of being evacuated, when General Robertson ordered Captain Evans, with a part of his command, to scout on the frontiers of Tennessee County.

After the massacre of Sevier's Station, the Indians retired to the country around Eddyville, Kentucky, where they waylaid a hunting party, and killed Colonel John Montgomery, who has appeared more than once in this history (Moore, 1923).

According to Ramsey (1853), Colonel Valentine Sevier had removed west of Cumberland Mountain, and built a station near Clarkesville. This the Indians attacked. An account of the assault is copied from his letter to his brother, General Sevier, dated—

Clarkesville, December 18, 1794.
Dear Brother:—The news from this place is desperate with me. On Tuesday, 11th of November last, about twelve o'clock, my station was attacked by about forty Indians. On

138

so sudden a surprise, they were in almost every house before they were discovered. All the men belonging to the station were out, only Mr. Snider and me. Mr. Snider, Betsy his wife, his son John and my son Joseph, were killed in Snider's house. I saved Snider, so the Indians did not get his scalp, but shot and tomahawked him in a barbarous manner. They also killed Ann King and her son James, and scalped my daughter Rebecca. I hope she will still recover. The Indians have killed whole families about here this fall. You may hear the cries of some persons for their friends daily.

The engagement, commenced by the Indians at my house, continued about an hour, as the neighbors say. Such a scene no man ever witnessed before. Nothing but screams and roaring of guns, and no man to assist me for some time. The Indians have robbed all the goods out of every house, and have destroyed all my stock. You will write our ancient father this horrid news ; also my son Johnny. My health is much impaired. The remains of my family are in good health. I am so distressed in my mind, that I can scarcely write.
Your affectionate brother, till death.
Valentine Sevier

Tennessee County

November 27, 1794--On November 27, 1794, a party of Indians killed and scalped Colonel John Montgomery, and wounded Julius Saunders and Charles Beatty on the northwestern frontier of Tennessee County.

Sumner County

November 29, 1794--On November 29, 1794, another party of Indians on the northern frontiers of Sumner County killed and scalped John Lawrence, William Hains, and Michael Hampton, and wounded a fourth whose name was not reported.

Cowan Cabin

December 20, 1794--On December 20, 1794, a party of Indians, about two hours after dark, secreted themselves within twenty feet of the door of Thomas Cowan. They fired upon his wife and son as they stepped into the yard and pierced the clothes of the latter with eight balls. He escaped under cover of the night into the woods and Mrs. Cowan returned into the house unhurt. The firing alarmed the neighborhood, and Captain Baird was at Cowan's with twenty men. Within an hour and a half, they patrolled the woods the whole night in search of the Indians, hoping they would strike up a fire by which he could discover them. On the next day, by order of Governor Blount, he went in pursuit of them.

December 20, 1794--On December 20, 1794, Hugh Tenin of Sumner County who was Colonel of Orange County, North Carolina, John Brown, and William Grimes were killed and scalped by the Chickamauga Indians on the Harpeth River south of Nashville.

Year of 1795

Nashville

January 5, 1795—On January 5, 1795, Elijah Walker was one of the mounted infantry on duty for the defense of Mero District. He was acting as a spy on the frontiers and was killed by the Chickamauga Indians twelve miles south of Nashville.

March 5, 1795--On March 5, 1795, a party of Chickamauga of the Creek faction, seven miles from Nashville, fired upon Thomas Fletcher, Ezekiel Balding, and his brother, who were at work in their field. They wounded two with balls through their bodies, knocked down the third with a war club, broke his skull bone, and skinned his whole head during the scalping.

March14, 1795--On March 14, 1795, a man was killed by the Indians, within five miles of Nashville.

Bledsoe's Lick

June 5, 1795--On June 5, 1795, old Mr. Peyton was killed, and a black slave belonging to Mr. Parker was wounded in a field of Mrs. Bledsoe, near Bledsoe's Lick, by the Chickamauga Indians.

Doublehead's Hostilities End

By 1795 Doublehead was said to have shed more blood by his own hands than anyone in America, but his terror on the Appalachian frontier suddenly came to a halt in June 1795, a year after his meeting with President George Washington in June 1794. It was on April 9, 1794, that his great nephew Robert Benge was ambushed and killed by Lieutenant Vinson Hobbs. Benge's long red-headed scalp was taken and delivered to Governor Henry Lee III of Virginia. On April 29, 1794, the senior militia officer Colonel Arthur Campbell sent Robert Benge's scalp to the governor along with a letter quoted in L. P. Summers, *History of Southwest Virginia 1746-1786, Washington County, 1777-1870*, Richmond, Virginia, 1903, page 443:

"The scalp of Captain Benge, I have been requested to forward to your excellency, as a proof that he is no more, and of the activity and good conduct of Lieutenant Hobbs, in killing him and relieving the prisoners. Could it be spared from our treasury, I would beg leave to hint that a present of a neat rifle to Mr. Hobbs would be accepted, as a reward for his late services, and the Executive may rest assured that it would serve as a stimulus for future exertions against the enemy."

The General Assembly of Virginia sent Mr. Hobbs a silver-mounted rifle. Robert Benge's red headed scalp was sent to President George Washington. Benge's scalp eventually wound up in the Smithsonian. Benge rode with Doublehead on many of his raids on the settlers. Doublehead probably thought it was time for him to make a change before he wound up like his nephew; therefore, he agreed to a meeting with the President of the United States and signed a peace treaty with Secretary of War Knox on June 26, 1794, in Philadelphia; however, his hostilities did not cease until June 1795. Finally, Doublehead's 25 year war came to an end.

Political Leader

Doublehead was selected for negotiations by United States government officials because he was the last of the Cherokee chiefs to seek peace. He had carried on his private war along with his nephew Robert Benge into the Spring of 1795. Both Doublehead and Benge were engaged in separate attacks on white settlers through the first week of April 1794 just some two months before Doublehead's scheduled meeting with President George Washington.

One year prior to Doublehead and the Cherokee delegation meeting with President George Washington, trouble was brewing in Indian country because of white raiding parties attacking peaceful Cherokee people while meeting with government officials. The incident that instigated letters from Hanging Maw, Upper Cherokee Chief, and Doublehead, Chief Speaker in the National Council, occurred at a gathering of Chiefs and delegates sent by Governor William Blount.

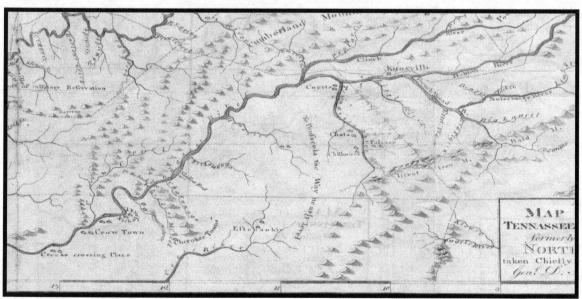

Note: Coyatee at the mouth of the Little Tennessee River 1792 Tennessee

Attack at Coyatee

On June 12, 1793, a party of whites under the leadership of Captain John Beard attacked the town of Chief Hanging Maw at Coyatee, Sacred Old Place, near the mouth of the Little Tennessee River in present-day Loudon County, Tennessee. During the raid, a total of nine Cherokees were killed, including Scantee, Fool Charlie, and Betty, a daughter of Kiegusta. In addition, old chief Hanging Maw and his wife were wounded during the attack. Also wounded in the attack was Doublehead, who thought they were trying to kill him.

The meeting at Hanging Maw's Town was actually attended by United States government officials who were trying to arrange a peace conference with President George Washington. The commissioners for the territorial governor William Blount were headed by Major Thomas King, Daniel Carmicheal, and James Ore. The peaceful meeting of the white delegation and Cherokees erupted into chaos when the mounted militia under Beard's command raced their horses through the town shooting into houses at random. Major King, who was sleeping with Hanging Maw's daughter, escaped the carnage by jumping out the back window. Carmicheal and Ore were also fired upon as they raced for cover. Beard was eventually tried and acquitted.

Claim of Hanging Maw's Widow

The following is a claim from the widow of Hanging Maw (Betsy) communicated to the House of Representatives, January 17, 1797. The claim was made by Mr. Dwight Foster, from the Committee of Claims, who petitioned for the widow: *"That she complains against the conduct of one John Beard, and a number of armed men, who, she states, in the year 1793; contrary to law and the good faith of Government, attacked the dwelling house of the petitioner and her husband; killed and wounded a number of well-disposed Indians; burnt and destroyed and carried away their property, and wounded the petitioner. She now prays, that some provision may be made for her...*

Previous to the attack on the Hanging Maw, the frontier settlers of Tennessee, and the Indians in that quarter, had been guilty of mutual acts of aggression and hostility. A party of the Indians had killed some settlers; their trail was discovered, conducting across the Tennessee; this circumstance induced a belief in their pursuers, that the Hanging Maw had been concerned in that business, and occasioned his being wounded, and the misfortunes complained by his widow. The general opinion, however, represents the Hanging Maw as having been uniformly friendly to the settlers, as vigilant to apprize them of the approach of banditti, and constant in his exertion, on all occasions, to compose differences between them and his nation, and, withal, as possessing considerable influence over the Indians. The same disposition is also attributed to his widow, the present petitioner, who, instead of exciting her people to acts of retaliation, has abated nothing in her friendship to the white people."

Letter from Hanging Maw

Evidently, Hanging Maw, who was considered Chief of the Upper Cherokees, and Governor Willie Blount had been on friendly terms, but for the time being Daniel Smith was representing the governor; therefore, Hanging Maw addressed his letter to Smith. He complained that Smith was not holding up their previous agreement and that Smith was afraid of the attackers.

Letter from the Hanging Maw (Scolacuttaw) to Secretary Smith, Coyatee, June 13, 1793

Friend and Brother:
It is but a few days since you were left in the place of Governor Blount. While he was in place, nothing happened. Surely they are making their fun of you. Surely you are neither head-man nor warrior. I am just informed you will take satisfaction for me, and I shall reckon it just the same as if I had taken it myself. I reckon you are afraid of these thieves, when you talk of sending to Congress. If you are left in the place of Governor, you ought to take satisfaction yourself. It was but a few days since I was at your house, and you told me that nothing should happen to me or any people at my house; but since that, blood has been spilt at both our houses. I reckon that the white people are just making their fun of you. Governor Blount always told me that nothing should happen to me as long as I did live, but he had hardly got out of sight until I was invaded by them, and like to have got killed. I think you are afraid of these bad men. They first killed the Chickasaws at your house, and this is the second time of their doing mischief. I think you are afraid of them. When is the day that a white man was killed at my house? I think the white men make fun of you. Now, blood is spilt at both of our houses by your people. I think they are making fun of you, and won't listen to your talks.

Letter from Doublehead

Two days later Doublehead responded to the incident and indicated that the invitation to meet with President George Washington had been put on hold until he was assured satisfaction from Smith. He also indicated that the head-man is at the Lower towns, referring to John Watts, Jr. or Little Turkey. John Watts, Jr. became Chief of the Cherokee after the death of Dragging Canoe on March 1, 1792, and held that position for a few years. Little Turkey resided at Little Turkey's Town (Turkey Town) on the Coosa River in Alabama and became a leader of great influence. In the Grand Cherokee National Council of 1792, Little Turkey was referred to as the great beloved man of the whole nation. After the death of Hanging Maw in 1795, Little Turkey moved to the position as Principal Chief of the Cherokee Nation.

144

Doublehead was at Hanging Maw's town at the time of the attack and when he wrote his letter to Daniel Smith, since it was addressed from Coyatee. Hanging Maw was the brother-in-law of Doublehead's brother Old Tassel. Doublehead was demanding satisfaction for the deaths of nine of his people before he went to the Lower towns to confer with Chief Little Turkey and Chief John Watts, Jr. In his letter Doublehead was letting the government officials know that he had survived the attack and was still living in gores of blood.

Letter from Doublehead to Secretary Daniel Smith, dated Coyatee, June 15th, 1793

Friend and Brother:
I am still among my people, living in gores of blood. When is the day that I shall get a full answer from you? Be strong, and don't be afraid, but get satisfaction for me. I am still waiting to get a satisfaction talk from you. Why do you talk of sending to the President to ask advice? These people did not ask any advice when they came and killed our people: for the head-men can't give out any peace talk concerning going to Philadelphia until you give us satisfaction for what is done. The head-man is at the Lower towns. I am but a boy, although I am giving out this talk. I can't think of going to the Lower towns until I get a fuller answer. If you will give me satisfaction for my people, I shall think you our friend, and think you mean to do justice to our land. We have lost nine of our people that we must have satisfaction for. My heart is much troubled about what has passed, and I shall not go from this place until I get a full answer from you and as soon as I get a full answer, shall start down to the head-men, and let them know the truth of everything. There is some of the first and principal head-men of our nation fell here, and they are not without friends, and the head-men of their land is their friends. This is the third time that we have been served so when we were talking peace, that they fell on us and killed us.
Your Friend and Brother,
Doublehead

Letter from Daniel Smith

In order to avoid further bloodshed, Secretary Smith wrote to Doublehead condemning the killing of Cherokees at the home of Hanging Maw. He insisted that the President would keep his word so that peace would be restored between the Cherokee and white settlers. Smith wanted to prevent the old Cherokee blood law which required the same number of the enemy to be killed. He also wanted to make sure that the meeting with Doublehead and President George Washington would take place as had been planned.

Letter from Secretary Smith to Doublehead dated Knoxville, June 17, 1793

Friend and Brother:

I am in much sorrow and trouble on account of the blood which has lately been shed in your land in so disgraceful a manner. I want to redress your wrongs, and doubt not of doing it, if you forbear to take satisfaction yourselves. The Hanging Maw has written to our beloved father the President. I will have his letter conveyed with one which I will write myself, to him and Governor Blount. I beg you to wait till you hear from them. The innocent ought not to die for the guilty, which would be the case if you take satisfaction yourselves. The President has waited long, and forborne to take satisfaction of those who have killed and robbed his people, because he knows the innocent would then be punished with the guilty, which would make him sorry. You know it was agreed, in the treaty at this place, that if any white men of the United States should go into your land and commit crimes there, against your people, they shall be punished for it in the same manner as if the crime had been committed against white people. You know that it was also agreed that, in case of violence being committed on the personal property of the individuals of either party, neither retaliation nor reprisal should be made by the other, until satisfaction should have been demanded of the offending party, and refused.

The President is a great and good man, and will keep his word, and I beg of you not to take satisfaction yourselves, but wait, and let us punish them for you. Thus may peace be restored to the land.
Daniel Smith

Doublehead's Presidential Meeting

In June 1794, Doublehead led the Cherokee delegation to Philadelphia to meet with President George Washington. Doublehead became the center of attention for the President and other dignitaries. On June 26, 1794, Doublehead negotiated for and signed a treaty giving the Cherokees an annuity of $5,000.00 per year plus a trading post on a large land reserve on the Tennessee River in the area along Blue Water Creek, in present-day Lauderdale County, Alabama.

The trading post was to be located at the mouth of Blue Water Creek where it empties into the Tennessee River. This area along the great bend of the Tennessee at the mouths of Path Killer (Big Nance) Creek, Shoal Town Creek, and Blue Water Creek was the largest Cherokee town in northwest Alabama. The town was known as Shoal Town and was accessible by the South River Road (corridor of the present Alabama highway 20), Doublehead's Trace (corridor of the present Alabama highway 101), and North River Road (corridor of the present Alabama highway 72). This large Indian town was under the leadership of Doublehead's nephew, Taluntuskee Benge, the half-brother of Sequoyah, and located in the present Alabama counties of Colbert, Lauderdale, and Lawrence.

The Shoal Town village actually lay on both sides of Hogohegee (Tennessee) River about six miles from the eastern upstream end of Big Muscle Shoals. At this point, the Blue Water Ferry crossed the river from the mouth of Blue Water Creek on its eastern bank to the west bank of the mouth of Path Killer (Big Nance) Creek. Path Killer Creek was originally named after Path Killer who was Chief of the Cherokee Nation

General James Robertson

from 1811 until 1826 and was renamed Big Nance after Doublehead's sister Nancy settled near the creek's mouth.

After the meeting with President George Washington, Doublehead took his time returning to his home at Doublehead's Town near Browns Ferry in present-day Lawrence County, Alabama. He traveled down the east coast and stopped at Charleston, South Carolina, and did not reach home until October 29, 1794.

Peace with United States

At this time, John Watts, Jr. (Doublehead's nephew) was principal Chief of the Cherokee Nation; and, therefore, was notified in the following letter from General James Robertson that he was aware of the meeting and peace agreement with the President. Robertson letter was also a warning to the Cherokee of the consequences of not maintaining peace agreements and is given in the following:

Letter from General James Robertson

The following letter is from General Robertson addressed to John Watts, Chief of the Cherokee Nation, from Nashville, Tennessee, dated September 20, 1794.

Dear Friend:

I am glad to hear you talk as you did in old times, "that peace is good;" this I hear from your people, (prisoners). They say that Nickajack and Running Water were just listening to good talks; but, that we did not know; for our people were killed every day; the trails came and went towards them towns; and, one thing we do know, we found property that was taken from our people when killed, and letters that people had who were killed on the Kentucky road; so them towns cannot plead innocence; and we have long known them to be our enemies; but, if they are about to be good, we are sorry we did not know it in time; but what is past cannot be recalled; so, if friendship is to be between us, we must take care, on both sides, for the future. We will not listen to half-way peace that we are tired of; our ears are shut to such talks; but our eyes are open, and, if we see no white people killed, we shall not kill or distress the Cherokees.

Our people were strong enough to have gone to Look-out Mountain, or Will's Town; but they heard Dick Justice was head of Look-out Mountain, and is known to be a good man, and that the Middle Striker did live at Will's Town, and you were now giving good talks; so they returned, to see if enemies come again from that way, and, if they do, our people will soon return the visit. This I do not tell you as a threat, but you may depend on the truth of it; so let your people not blame us for the future, if the innocent should suffer with the guilty: for, when our people go to the towns, they cannot distinguish the innocent from the guilty; so, it will lay on your head-men to send a flag, which can, at all times, come safe, and let us know who are enemies; so that the innocent can be spared. We have borne with your injuries a long time; but you will find our people as dreadful, when forced to take arms, as they are peaceable when you do not injure them. There are so many of them who have seen their near relations lying cut to pieces, by your people; that, when they find their enemies, they will have no mercy on them. Your nation sent men to make a treaty with the President; and, in the meantime, while they were talking, you killed his people. These are the talks we are done listening to. I do not hear that one of you talk of punishing those that murdered the people in the boats, taken this summer, neither have I heard of your sending in the negroes; but it is as well to say no more; we want peace, and love it, and, if you do the same, take steps to bring it about. Do not let the Creeks pass through your country to war against us. There is a new town settling below; if that is to flourish, let them be peaceable, or their towns will be spoiled. We have got seventeen of your people prisoners, who will be well treated till we hear from you.

Our people will not go to war against your towns any more, if you come in and make peace. We shall wait long enough for you to come with a flag; but, if you do not come, our people will be sure to come again to war; and we have men enough to fight, and destroy you all, and burn your towns. Four of your prisoners are taken to Kentucky, by some of their men who went with us to war, and they will keep them till you send in four

148

negroes you have taken from General Logan, who lives in that country, and will come after his negroes if peace is not soon made. The prisoners we have will be returned, if you will come in with a flag, and good assurances of a peace, and bring in a girl you took prisoner, and killed her father and mother, on the Tennessee, on their way from the Chickasaw nation; whose name was Collins; when I say you, I mean your nation.

I am your old friend

James Robertson

Letter from Doublehead

During the next month, Doublehead sent a letter to Governor Blount in Knoxville, Tennessee, assuring him that the Cherokee intended to keep the peace agreements made to the President and General Knox. General James Robertson had told John Watts that while the Cherokee delegation was in peace talks with President Washington that his people had been killed by Cherokees; however, Doublehead blamed the Creeks for the killings that made the white people retaliate and kill some Cherokee. Notice in the following letter, Doublehead tells Governor Blount that the Creeks have created the anger between the Cherokees and whites, but he intends to hold fast to peaceful relations:

The following letter is from Doublehead to Governor Blount from Coosawatee dated October 20, 1794.

Friend and Brother:

I send you this talk from this town, on my way home, just returned from our father the President, and our beloved brother General Knox. Now, my brother Governor Blount, you know very well, and the rest of the white people, when I and some of our people went to Congress, we were sent by our head-men of our land to go to that place. Now we have returned back, the head-men and warriors, and young men also, are satisfied with what we have done, and are determined to hold the United States fast by the hand, and keep peace. Now, this is the talk of them all, and I am glad to inform you so, my friend, and it is pleasing to me that I did not spend my breath for nothing. But, it appears now we shall have a lasting peace between us, which the old head-men strove a long time for. We shall now live in peace like brothers.

My people are now wanting to go out a hunting, which you know is high time to be out; for you all know very well where our hunting ground is, on the other side of the Big river, and on the mountain, and on the waters of Cumberland, though you know very well where we hunt, and we hope you will keep the white people from coming to hurt the hunters, as we all want to live in peace now with you all. Now, if some of our mad young men should go and steal a horse from some of your people, you must not get in a passion

149

for that with us, but wait till the horse or horses shall be returned to you again. This is what the great beloved men told us, to return all such horses, and keep our young men from doing any bad thing to the white people.

When I was at Oconee Mountain, we sent all the head-men at it to the Big river (the Tennessee) to come down there and hear all the talk we had brought with us. But, however, they did not all come, on the account of some people having come in and killed some of them; that it was not our people's doings that made the white people come in and kill our people, but it was the Creeks doings that caused all this. And when we gave them the talk, they all received it, and have taken hold to it fast; and we all mean to hold the talks that are given us by the President and General Knox, and we hope the white people will not let our hands go, but hold us by the hand as we mean to do.

What mischief has been done by the Creek Indians' doings; and if the white people hold us by the hand, we may still stand our ground with them: for, it is they who have made us angry with one another. We hope you have now found them out, and our foolish young men who used to be set on by them. We send the Quadroon and his friend to carry this talk to you, and we hope you will receive them kindly, and treat them well, that they may have a good talk to tell their friends when they come home, and we hope you will send us the truth about our people's going a hunting: for they will all be wanting to hear the news from you, whether they may hunt in peace or not.

I am your friend and brother,

Doublehead, his X mark

Letters from Governor Blount

In Governor William Blount's reply to Doublehead and also in the follow up letters of November 1, 1794, sent to Brigadier General James Robertson, Colonel Whitley, and General Benjamin Logan, it is obvious that the governor wants peace with the Cherokee. He tells the military leaders to desist from unauthorized invasions of Lower Cherokee towns in order to maintain peace and security to the frontier inhabitants. Based on his letters to military leaders, it appears a large invasion of the Lower Cherokee towns was already planned. Governor Blount states to his military leaders, *"The newspaper you will receive herewith, contains copies of a letter of the 26th ultimo, to me, from Double Head, a principal chief of those towns, and my answer to him of the 29th, by which you will understand these towns, as well as every other part of the Cherokee nation, are considered in the peace of the United States....Therefore, I command you, as well as the men with you, or under your command, forthwith , to desist from the attempt of invading the Lower Cherokee towns, who are in the peace of the United States. And, I further command you, respectively, not to enter, in a hostile manner, the country or lands guaranteed to the*

150

Cherokee nation, by the treaty between the United States and the said Cherokees, commonly called the treaty of Holston, warning you and them, that, in case of a violation of this order, which is issued by virtue of the authority in me vested, you and they will answer the same at your peril."

Governor William Blount takes on the role of mediator between the Cherokees and the military leaders under his command. It is obvious that he considers Doublehead as a Principal Chief of the Lower Cherokee towns and seeks peaceful relations with his people. As evidenced in his letter, Governor Blount takes the first steps in convincing Doublehead and the Cherokees that they may be forced into war with the Creeks in order to maintain peace with the United States. Later during the Creek Indian war, his statements were prophetic when the Cherokees helped Andrew Jackson defeat the red stick Creeks at the Battle of Horseshoe Bend in 1814. The following is Blount's reply to Doublehead's letter:

Letter from Governor William Blount, Knoxville, Tennessee, to Double-Head, a Chief of the Cherokees, dated October 29, 1794

My Friend and Brother:

Your letter of the 20th instant, was delivered to Mr. John Mckee, the agent at Tellico block house, and by him forwarded to me express by Andrew Miller. The Quadroon, the Turkey's Son, and the other two messengers, wait there for my answer, which I hasten to give you. Mr. Mckee, I am sure, will treat them well. That you and other deputies of the Cherokees have been to visit the President of the United States, and your beloved brother General Knox, there made a peace, and that you and your people, now you are returned, are well pleased, and determined to keep the peace you have made, is truly pleasing to me. It is hardly necessary for me to repeat to you and to your nation, that ever since I have acted in the character of superintendent of it, I have always wished and exerted myself to keep peace between your nation and the citizens of the United States, and now, with your exertions for peace on the part of your nation, and the continuance of mine on the part of the United States, I hope we shall have no more war. In your letter, you say, "now, if some of our mad young men should go and steal a horse or horses, from some of your people, you must not be in a passion or mad with us, but wait, and the horse or horses so stolen, shall be returned to you again." To this proposal I agree, and whenever a horse is stolen, I will give your nation notice, and allow thirty days to return the horse or horses stolen, to John Mckee, at Tellico block house; but, if the horse or horses stolen are injured, damage must be paid, as well as the horses returned.

You next ask, "if your hunters may go out to their hunting grounds in safety?" My answer to that question is, that though the white people have lost a great deal of blood, and many horses, they wish peace, and will not hurt your people, if all red people cease to injure them. I say the white people will not hurt your people, if all red people cease to injure them, and by all red people, I mean Creeks as well as Cherokees: for, if Creeks hurt them, they will not be able to distinguish them from Cherokees, and may hurt your hunters in retaliation.

Governor William Blount

It is true, I have long found out that the Creeks kill citizens of the United States, and I fear they will continue so to do, and if they do, your people will surely be blamed for it; and if you earnestly wish peace, you and your people must stop them, and turn them back from annoying our frontiers. Or if you see or hear of their returning with hair or horses, you must apprehend them, and bring them to Tellico block house, as the Maw's people served one last summer: for it is better you have war with the Creeks, who, you say, have already brought great mischief upon your people, than with your friends, the citizens of the United States, who sincerely wish peace with your nation, and the world at large. And if you, for the sake of peace with the United States, are forced into a war with the Creeks, you may be sure of friends enough: for, besides the white people, who must be your friends, the Upper Cherokees, the Chickasaws, and Choctaws, neither love the Creeks.

It now appears, that you, and myself, and our people wish peace; and, for fear it should be disturbed or broken, while some or both sides can't quite forget their relations and friends, I would advise your hunters for this winter, not to cross the ridge that divides the waters of Duck river and Cumberland nor Kentucky traces, nor near the frontiers of this country; there is ground enough besides to hunt on this winter; and this winter passing off in entire peace, people will be more good humored next summer, and will more firmly believe that there is really a peace taken place between us. My friend Colonel Watts, who has received a letter from General Robertson, respecting the destruction of the Running Water and Nickajack, will inform you the reasons the general gave for its being done. The Quadroon, the Turkey's son, and your other runners, will report to you the good understanding and peace that subsists between the United States and the good old Maw, and all the Upper towns. John Mckee resides at Tellico block house, in the character of a temporary agent, to cherish and keep up this friendship, and all times, when you wish to write me, or send me a runner, let it be done by way of that place. Peace is my wish, but, by peace I mean that not one more white person is to be killed.

I am your friend and brother,

W. M. Blount

Doublehead's Associates

Doublehead had several friends and acquaintances that were influential in his life. These individuals were people that Doublehead trusted and some of their actions inadvertently contributed to his demise. Doublehead made himself a target by some of his vicious actions and acceptance of misguided favors that brought him death threats and tremendous individual wealth. He did not seek handouts that put his life in jeopardy but did accept the bribes that he was offered; therefore, he was as much at fault as his friends who made the offers. Even the friends, who unknowingly became guilty of placing Doublehead on the chopping block, sought favor from Doublehead to promote their own agenda, but they did not pay the ultimate sacrifice as did Doublehead.

Black Fox

Black Fox (Inali, Enoli, or Eunolee) was the Principal Chief of the Cherokee Nation from 1801 to his death in 1811. He lived in Lawrence County, Alabama in a Cherokee village known as Mouse Town or Monee Town near the mouth of Fox's Creek on the Tennessee River some five miles upstream from Doublehead's Town. Fox's Creek in the northeastern corner of the county still bears his name. Black Fox and Doublehead were friends who tried to honor each other in treaties with the United States Government. In treaty negotiations, they said good things about each other and had benefits inserted that promoted that friendship.

Black Fox's People

Black Fox was associated with many important Indian people and leaders in the Muscle Shoals area during his reign as chief: Doublehead; George Colbert and his brother Levi Colbert; John Melton and his half-blood Cherokee sons; Cuttyatoy; Pathkiller; Kattygisky; Charles Hicks; John Brown and his son Richard Brown; George Fields and his son Richard Fields; and others had their names associated with the area of northwest Alabama. However, after the Turkey Town Treaty of September 1816, the historical records of Indian people became somewhat clouded for the Cherokee territory of northwest Alabama. Nevertheless, very influential Indian people made their reputations, homes, and lifestyles in Franklin, Colbert, Lauderdale, Lawrence, Limestone, and Morgan Counties of the Tennessee Valley from 1770 through 1816. These people, their exploits, and historic significance became intertwined with the life of the old Chief Black Fox.

During Black Fox's reign as chief, eight Cherokee Indian towns flourished along the Big Bend of the Tennessee River. These Indian towns included Mouse Town or

Monee Town, Fox's Stand, Doublehead's Town at Brown's Ferry, Melton's Bluff, Cuttyatoy's Village, Gourd's Settlement (Courtland), and Shoal Town. The towns were located adjacent to the Elk River Shoals and Big Muscle Shoals at major Indian trail crossings of the river. These Indian towns benefited from the shoals that provided isolation from white settlements that were claiming and taking Cherokee lands to the east and north.

Black Fox and Doublehead

Black Fox and Doublehead lived in Lawrence County, Alabama a few miles from each other on the old Brown's Ferry Road. Black Fox lived for a while at Mouse Town on the Tennessee River at the mouth of the creek that became his namesake (Fox's Creek) before moving a few miles to the road junction that became his stand. Later his son who was also called Black Fox ran the store. In early 1802, Doublehead moved down the river to Shoal Town, which was located some seven miles from the eastern end of the Big Muscle Shoals between the mouths of Big Nance Creek, Shoal Town Creek and Blue Water Creek. Shoal Town was controlled by Doublehead's nephew and Bench's brother, Taluntuskee Benge.

Black Fox and Doublehead signed numerous treaties with the United States Government. Doublehead would sign treaties benefiting Black Fox and Black Fox would sign treaties that benefited Doublehead. John Watts, Doublehead, Black Fox and others signed the Treaty with the Cherokee on July 2, 1791. On October 20, 1803, Black Fox places his (X) between his name and Principal Chief; however, this treaty refers to *"our beloved Chief Doublehead"*. Both Black Fox and Doublehead signed Cherokee treaties of October 25, 1805, and October 27, 1805. Also Doublehead signs the Cotton Gin Treaty of January 7, 1806, that gives the Cherokees a machine for cleaning cotton and places the gin at Melton's Bluff. The treaty also gives the old Cherokee Chief Black Fox $100.00 annually for the rest of his life. The final payment recorded for Chief Black Fox is found as follows: *"Abstract of Disbursements made by Return J. Meigs, Agent of war in Tennessee on account of the Indian Department between the 30th June & the 1st of October 1810...date of payments. July 11th, number of payments. 4. to who made, Black Fox Cherokee King, Nature of Disbursements. Being the amount of Annual Stipend for the current year received by his proxy, Amount. $100.00."* It is probable that Black Fox was getting in bad health because he had some of his people to pick up the money and died the next year.

Cherokee Chiefs

Doublehead's nephew, John Watts, Jr. (Chief from 1792-1794) was elected Chief of the Chickamauga over him after the death of Chickamauga Chief Dragging Canoe (Chief from 1775-1792) on March 1, 1792. Chief Watts was wounded at Buchanan's Station near Nashville in September 1792 but recovered and led his army the next year against Cavett's Station near Knoxville, Tennessee. John Watts, Junior died at Wills Town in 1808. Little Turkey (Chief from1794-1801) preceded Black Fox (Chief from1801-1811) as the Principal Chief of the Cherokee Nation. Pathkiller (Chief from 1811-1827) succeeded Black Fox as chief of the Cherokee Nation. Doublehead was assassinated on August 9, 1807. Black Fox died in 1811. Path Killer died in 1828. Thus, as the great Cherokee leaders of the lower or southern faction of Cherokees died, the tribal control and leadership shifted to the upper or northern faction.

After Black Fox was elected chief in 1801, he had to deal with a lot of differences between the Upper and Lower Cherokees. With the lower towns in the north Alabama area having secured control of the tribal leadership, they were assured favorable distribution of annuity funds. A delegation of Upper Cherokees complained to President Thomas Jefferson that the Lower Cherokees divide all funds from annuities and land sales among those of their own neighborhood. President Jefferson explained that once the funds were turned over to the authorized representatives of the tribe that it was purely a Cherokee affair. Alexander Saunders proposed that the funds be split between the Lower and Upper Cherokees. Both Black Fox and Doublehead, who were Lower Cherokees, had serious conflicts with Major Ridge and Saunders, Cherokees of the upper towns. After Doublehead signed the Cotton Gin Treaty of 1806, giving up Cherokee claims to lands on the north side of the Tennessee River except for Doublehead's Reserve between Elk River and Cypress Creek, he was assassinated by Major Ridge, Alexander Saunders, and John Rogers on August 9, 1807.

Fox's Land Exchange Proposal

In early 1808, Colonel Return J. Meigs had convinced Black Fox and Taluntuskee to seek the Cherokee council approval for exchanging their lands for territory west of the Mississippi. At the fall council meeting of the Cherokee Nation, Black Fox made the proposal as follows, *"Tell our Great Father, the President (Thomas Jefferson), that our game has disappeared, and we wish to follow it to the West. We are his friends, and we hope he will grant our petition, which is to remove our people towards the setting sun. But we shall give up fine country, fertile in soil, abounding in water-courses, and well adapted for the residence of white people. For all this we must have a good price".*

The Ridge was very upset and spoke against Black Fox in such an eloquent manner that the tribal council rejected both Fox and his proposal. Black Fox was reinstated at a later council meeting, but felt disgraced for the rest of his life. However, in the summer of 1808, Taluntuskee took the offer from President Thomas Jefferson and in 1809 some 1,131 Cherokees left the Shoal Town area to lands west of the Mississippi River. Taluntuskee told President Thomas Jefferson that his reason for leaving was the fear of assassination as his uncle Doublehead. Jefferson was the first president to strongly advocate Indian removal west of the Mississippi River.

Creeks and Black Fox

On December 20, 1807, John Sevier, Governor of Tennessee, writes to Black Fox concerning a report from Colonel Return J. Meigs about the Creek Indians settling on the Tennessee near Elk River. Sevier writes, *"I am informed that the Creeks have built Huts, and is living on the banks of the Tennessee; what business have they there? They have none only to be convenient to kill come of our people, and plunder our Boats as they are going down the River –You know the Creek people are Rogues, and you say steal from and rob your own people; if it be true, why don't you drive them from out of your Country? For a people who both murder & steals, ought not to be Suffered to live in any place – You are Surely able to drive away the few that comes to do Mischief, and disturb the peace of your people and ours; If their nation means to protect them in their murdering and plundering excursions, you then know where you can resort to for protection and Strength enough to do yourselves Justice – I state these circumstances to inform You how you ought to conduct towards the white people, who are your Fathers, Brothers, friends, and your good neighbors."* It should be noted that Meigs and Sevier confirm that the old Chief Black Fox was still living near the Elk River Shoals some four months after the death of his friend and cohort Doublehead.

Black Fox II

The old Principal Chief Black Fox evidently had a son also known as Black Fox that also lived in Lawrence County, Alabama and his name appears on numerous Cherokee documents after the death of his father in 1811. John Coffee put the following note in his diary, *"26th July, 1816. Borrowed Capt. Hammond's large tent- left my old one – breakfasted with the Captain. Started on and got to Wilders where I dined, Bought corn to carry with me – bill $1.50. Went to the river – crossed at Brown's Ferry – paid ferriage & c $1.25. Hired young Wilder to go on to Col. Barnett & c. This night went to **Black Foxe's** and lay all night; bought _ bushels of corn to carry with me. Hired ____ Lancaster to carry six bushels to Major Russell's, for which I am to pay three and half dollars – bought some salt from **Fox**, hired him and McClure to carry the corn to the wagon road* *about two miles – paid bill at* **Fox's** *$6.75."* Coffee continued on to Major William Russell's (Russellville) to survey Indian boundary and begin his return.

Coffee's notes continue, "**1st August 1816**. This morning we start in towards Madison County – lay all night at the Path Killer's creek near Jones'. **2d August.** This morning we hired Vanpelt to carry letters to Col. Brown inviting him to meet us as Campbell's Ferry on the 12th. Come to the **Black Fox'es** – bought 2 1/2 bushels corn – paid the bill $1.75 –Same day came on – crossed the Tennessee River at Brown's Ferry and came to Wilders where we lay all night."

After the Turkey Town Treaty of September1816 took the Cherokee lands in the north central area of Alabama, the young Black Fox II moved east into the Cherokee Nation. Other historical references indicate there may have been other Cherokee men with the name Black Fox after the original died 1811. Also another important note is that Colonel Richard Brown was a Cherokee leader during the Creek Indian War and negotiated the Turkey Town Treaty of September 1816 for the Cherokee Nation.

Death of Black Fox

Black Fox, Principal Chief of the Cherokee Nation, died July 22, 1811. Black Fox's death was reported in the <u>Columbia Centinel</u>, Boston, Massachusetts on August 31, 1811. His obituary stated, *"In the Cherokee country, Black Fox, a worthy chief of the Cherokee Tribe of Indians, and a great friend of the U.S."*

According to <u>Chronicles of Oklahoma</u>, volume 16, number 1, March 1938, by John P. Brown, "Black Fox died in 1811. He was succeeded by Pathkiller, Nunna-dihi, a very honorable man who was to guide the destinies of the Cherokee through sixteen years."

According to an article titled <u>A Description and History of Blount County</u> from the Transactions of the Alabama Historical Society on July 9 and 10, 1855, "Most of the first settlers of Blount as well as those of the adjoining counties, believe that lead mines existed in Blount and Jefferson Counties, and that the Indians knew their location and obtained lead from them. Perhaps, this general belief originated from the following circumstances, which occurred in 1810: An old Cherokee Chief, named Black Fox, died in the north of our county, and was buried in an old mound; and in digging his grave, the Indians found some pieces of lead ore. This trivial discovery was magnified and circulated in Madison County, and many intelligent persons in the county believed a lead mine really existed, at, or near the grave of the old Chief. This opinion became so strong, that Alexander Gilbreath, who then resided in Huntsville, was induced to visit the grave of Black Fox. His searching there, proving unsuccessful….Mr. George Fields, at that time fifty or sixty years

158

old, informed him that the Indians knew of no lead mines nearer than those of Missouri and Illinois, and gave it as his opinion, that the lead found in the grave of Black Fox, had been brought from one of those States." George Fields was a Cherokee Indian who lived near Camp Coffee on the south side of the Tennessee River west of Ditto's south of present-day Huntsville, Alabama.

It is important to note that Blount County at one time included this area of north Alabama. According to a proclamation by David Holmes, Governor of Mississippi Territory, *"All that tract of country lying south of the River Tennessee, east of the Chickasaw boundary line, north of the high-lands that divide the waters of the Tennessee from the water of the Mobile Bay and west of the Cherokee boundary line shall form one other County to be called and known by the name of Blount, the courts of justice whereof will be held at Melton's Bluff."* Melton's Bluff is in Lawrence County some six miles northwest of Black Fox's Stand.

Black Fox was probably buried near home which was the custom of the Cherokees at that time. For example, Doublehead was killed in east Tennessee and transported back to his home overlooking Blue Water Creek where he was buried. Since Black Fox's family resided at his stand for several years after his death, they probably had his body interned nearby.

Black Fox Conclusion

Today, Fox's Creek is the name of a small tributary to the Tennessee River that flows into the river at the north border of Morgan and Lawrence Counties at an old Cherokee town site of Mouse Town or Monee Town. Black Fox moved from Mouse Town to Fox's Stand (trading post or store) located between the drainages of Fox and Mallard Creeks some three miles west of Doublehead's Town at Browns Ferry. Fox's Stand was near the junctions of three Indian trails-Browns Ferry Road, South River Road, and Black Warriors' Path.

Black Warriors' Path continued six miles northwest to Melton's Bluff which was established by Irishman John Melton, who had married Doublehead's sister, Ocuma. From Melton's Bluff, Black Warriors' Path (Mitchell Trace) crossed the river and went by Fort Hampton in present-day Limestone County, Alabama, then continued toward Nashville. From Fox's Stand, the Brown's Ferry Road continued west some eight miles to Gourd's Settlement where it joined Gaines Trace to Cotton Gin Port on the Tombigbee River in Mississippi. Gourd was a Cherokee Indian who fought with Andrew Jackson at Horseshoe Bend and established his village at present-day Courtland, Alabama on Path Killer's Creek (present-day Big Nance Creek). The South River Road continued west along the south bank of the Tennessee River passing Shoal Town at the present-day county line of Lawrence and Colbert at the mouth of Town Creek, then continued to the mouth of Bear Creek and into Mississippi.

Within a few years, Doublehead, Black Fox, Path Killer, and several magnanimous and powerful leaders of the Lower Chickamauga people of north Alabama were dead. Along with their demise, the colorful lives and exploits of these great chiefs faded as the sunsets disappear on the rolling hills and roaring shoals of the Great Bend of the Hogohegee (Tennessee) River. Today, near the old home sites of Doublehead and Black Fox, even the great shoals that could be heard for miles are buried under the waters of the impoundments of Wilson and Wheeler Dams.

John Melton

Doublehead thought enough of his white Irish brother-in-law John Melton that in the Cotton Gin Treaty of 1806, he negotiated for a cotton cleaning machine to be placed at Melton's Bluff by the United States Government. The following is stipulations of the Treaty of January 7, 1806: *The United States agree to pay in consideration for the foregoing cession, $2,000.00 in money upon ratification; $8,000.00 in four equal annual installments; to erect a grist-mill within one year in the Cherokee country; to furnish a machine for cleaning cotton; and to pay the Cherokee Chief, Black Fox, $100.00 annually for the rest of his life.*

Melton's Family

John Melton was married to one of Doublehead's sisters, Ocuma; and therefore, he was a member of Doublehead's extended family. The Cherokee village at Melton's Bluff was located in present-day Lawrence, County, Alabama between Mallard Creek and Spring Creek on the Tennessee River. The high flat land above the river bluff was the home of old Irishman John Melton, his Cherokee wife, and his half-blood Cherokee children. Their home was described as a large mansion by Anne Royall with an impressive courtyard that fronted the house. The house was a large two-storied home that was the central building with many outlying slave quarters, a cotton gin, stables, visitors' cabins that lined the bluff, and an inn for travelers. One guest said he never fared better in any part of the United States, but their bill was excessively high. By the time Ms. Royall described the village in 1818, it contained two large houses of entertainment, several doctors, one hatters shop, one warehouse, and several mechanics. From the front of the house, one could see east upriver eight miles to Brown's Ferry where Doublehead's home was located from 1790 until 1802.

Melton owned large farms and a great number of slaves. Cotton was a very important Cherokee product and the use of black slaves in the early 1800s was common among the Cherokee. Melton's Bluff was located about eight miles west of Brown's Ferry somewhat near the middle of Elk River Shoals on the Tennessee River in Lawrence County, Alabama. Melton had several children by his Indian wife, most married white people. According to William Lindsey McDonald's book, *Lore of The River*, third edition (2007) *"John Melton and his Cherokee wife had a number of children; the names of some of them are believed to have been Moses, James, Charles, David, Thomas, and Merida."* Moses Melton is listed in microfilm archives as the son of Lewis.

It should be pointed out that General John Coffee's diary specifically mentioned Charles Melton who moved east after the Turkey Town Treaty of 1816 and established the Cherokee Indian town known as Meltonsville. James Melton became a keel boat guide for Malcolm Gilchrist and some of his family remains in Lawrence County, Alabama today. David Melton sold Andrew Jackson all the land at Melton's Bluff and some 60 slaves. Lewis' son Moses Melton and Charles Hicks were given by treaty a tract of land on the south side of the Tennessee River near Melton's Bluff. Elick Melton was one of the signers of a letter from The Gourd.

General John Coffee's Dairy

In February of 1816, General John Coffee travels down the Tennessee River and stops at Melton's Bluff to pick up supplies and whiskey. He was in the process of surveying land for the Turkey Town Treaty that was approved on September 16 and 18, 1816, that ceded the Cherokee and Chickasaw claims that make up the present-day Alabama counties of Franklin, Colbert, Lawrence, and Morgan.

The following excerpt identifies Charles Melton one of John Melton's sons. According to *General John Coffee's Diary -1816* is the following: *"21st Feb'y 1816. This morning Maj. Hutchings left us to go to meet Gen. Jackson – Mr. Bright surveys and we pass on down the river. When at Huntsville I did not pay my bill – neither did I pay it at Mr. Austin's – I paid Mrs. Austin for buiskit, candles and washing $2.00 – paid Charles Melton 3 bushels corn $1.50 – fodder, $1.00 – whiskey 75¢. Paid to Charles for Reed $2.00. Encamped all night on Big Nance Creek."*

From Big Nance Creek, John Coffee continues down the Tennessee River to the mouth of Caney Creek in present-day Colbert County, Alabama and run a boundary line up Caney Creek and crossed Gaines Trace. Coffee continued the line to Cotton Gin Port before starting back to Melton's Bluff on March 2, 1816. The line Coffee was surveying became the Chickasaw boundary in the Turkey Town Treaty of September 1816.

Coffee's diary continues, "**6th March, 1816.** This day we reached Melton's Bluff about one o'clock. Bought sundry supplies &c Viz; whiskey $1.00-whiskey, $1.371/2- 3 dinners, 75¢ - 20 lbs. Bacon 9¢ $2.50 Paid for corn and fodder to Charley Melton $5.00"

Mouse Town Cherokees Killed

Charles Melton and Elick Melton signed a letter along with The Gourd requesting Negro Fox to be returned after two Cherokees were killed. It is important to note that this was the last recorded Cherokees attacked and killed at Muscle Shoals. The killings occurred at Mouse Town on Fox's Creek as a result of leases of Cherokee lands started by Doublehead. In microcopy 208, roll 7, and number 3533, is a letter from The Gourd (Goard), the two Melton brothers, and others giving account of two Cherokee Indians killed at Mouse Town which is just east of Elk River Shoals dated August 15, 1816.

James Burleson and seven other white men killed two Cherokees. Hope you will cause whites to give up Negro Fox as he is considered one of our people and we wish to try him by our law.

Signed by Goard X; Charles Melton (x) William Rains, Issac Wade, Breton Wider, Joseph Slauter, John Lambe, Nelson Bonds, Walter Eavens, Elick Melton, and William Phillips.

In microcopy 208, roll 7, and number 3534, is a continuation of the actions: *The Indians were killed by James Burleson, John Burleson, Robert Thrasher, Martin Tailer, Charles Tailer, John Bird, Edward Burleson, Joseph Burleson. They have left and gone to Madison County.*
Signed: Thomas Lovell, David Danault, William Fears, Don White, Lemuel Lovell, William Cosby, Rudolph McDaniel, George Cosby, Sam Cosby, Robert W. Woods, Sam B. McClure.

The incident was recorded on August 15, 1816, when two Indians were killed by white people near the head of Muscle Shoals on August 12, 1816. The settlers in the area sent the following letter from Mississippi Territory to the chiefs of the Cherokees in order for the innocent to avoid punishment.

To any of the Chiefs or hed men of the Chirokee Nation. Wee feel it our Duty to let you know who commited that offence against your subjects so that the inesant may not suffer. The offence was committed on the twelveth Inst by these under named: James

Burleston, John Burleson, Robt. Thrasher, Martin Tailer, Charle Tailer, John Bird, Edward Burleson, and Joseph Burleson.

These are all wee have any knowledg of they have left the settlement and gone in to Madison County where they will be delt with acording to law as soon as it can be put in force against them and as for old fox he has went of with those men that committed this offene therfore wee subscribe our names on the other side.

August the 15, 1816

Thomas Lovell	George Cozby	Saml B. McClure
David Devault	Samuel Cozby	William Cozby
William Fears	Robert W. Woods	Randolph McDaniel
David White	Samuel Lovell	

Additional information is given in microcopy 208, roll 7, and number 3544, dated August 25, 1816, in a letter to Louis Winston. The letter is, *"requesting him (Winston) to have apprehended certain men who murdered two Cherokees. Two Indians were killed August 12, a few miles above Melton's at head of Shoals by white men having with them Negro Black Fox who belonged to Cherokee Nation.*

Letter from Mississippi Territory signed by: Thomas Lovell, David Davolt, William Fears, David White, Lemuel Lovell, William Cosby, Rudolph McDaniel, George Cosby, Sam Cosby, Robert W. Woods, Sam B. McClure informing me that James Burleson, John Burleson, Robert Thrasher, Martin Taylor, Charles Taylor, John Bird, Edward Burleson, and Joseph Burleson were of the number who committed the deed and there were others in party whose names we do not know. All have gone to Madison County."

In microcopy 208, roll 7, and number 3546, a letter from Louis Winston on August 29, 1816, concerning the Burlesons: *"All the Burlisons have absconder others in this country but not this county."*

Negro Black Fox was probably the slave of the young Black Fox II who was thought to be the son of Chief Black Fox that died in 1811. The criminals, James, Edward, and other Burlesons, eventually moved to Missouri and by 1820 he was back in Lawrence County, Alabama. Later after authorities got after them again, James, Edward and other Burleson family members moved to Texas and owned a huge tract of land. Burleson, Texas was named after him. General Edward Burleson fought in the Revolution of Texas and wrote Moulton Democrat in 1887 mentioning Mouse Town and the last Indian fight that occurred there.

John Melton's Death

John Melton was one of the early Irish people in Lawrence County, Alabama who came during the 1780's with the Cherokee Indians and stayed until his death. Melton, an Irishman by birth, married a Cherokee woman who was the sister of the most powerful Chickamauga Cherokee of the Great Bend. He died at a large farm on the north side of the Tennessee River about June 7, 1815. According to Anne Royall, John Melton built a fine house on the north side of the river and died rich in a good old age.

Melton was quoted as moving to the north side of the river in present-day Limestone County, Alabama a few years before he died for fear of Creek raids from the south. In addition, some speculate that the assassination of his brother-in-law Doublehead was the reason John Melton moved. Melton and his family had personally benefitted from the Cotton Gin Treaty of January 7, 1806, negotiated by Doublehead. Melton was also accused by some of participating in piracy of folks stranded on the shoals and stealing their slaves and property.

Shortly after his death, John Melton's wife wrote a letter to Colonel Return J. Meigs voicing her concerns about her husband's brother getting all the property they had accumulated as found in microcopy 208, roll 7, and number 3229, and dated June 30, 1815. Mrs. Ocuma (Obema) Melton's letter to Colonel Meigs is as follows:

"My husband John Melton died at his residence below Ft. Hampton 7 instant. He became a resident of Cherokee Nation 35 years ago and married me not long afterward according to established custom of my nation. He died of considerable property which I am told me and my children will be deprived of by his brother, a citizen of the United States who resides on Duck River in Tennessee.
Please advise me what to do."

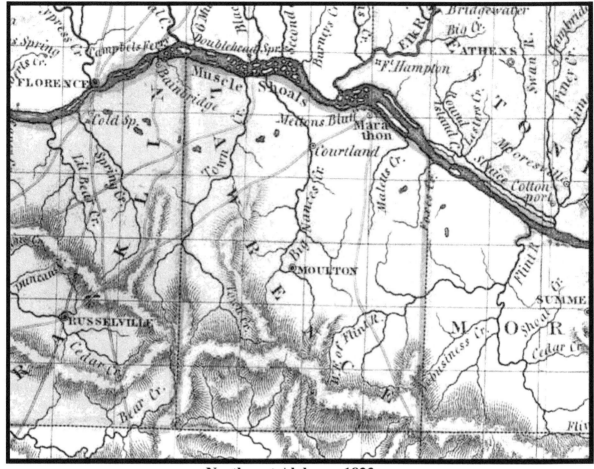

Northwest Alabama 1823

Notice on the map above the locations of Ft. Hampton, Melton's Bluff, and Doublehead's Spring at Shoal Town on the Tennessee River. The two roads from Melton's Bluff are the Gaines Trace which goes southwest to Cotton Gin Port, Mississippi on the Tombigbee River and Black Warriors' Path which goes southeast to St. Augustine, Florida on the Atlantic coast.

It appears that the Melton family was still residing at their place south of Fort Hampton in what is now present-day Limestone County after the death of John Melton and at least through June 1815. Some historical writers suggest that Colonel Return J. Meigs forced the Cherokees out of the Muscle Shoals area shortly after the death of Doublehead; however, Anne Royall and Ocuma Melton help establish that the second home built by John Melton was on the north side of the river and south of Fort Hampton, and that the Melton's were still occupying their home at the time of John Melton's death.

General Andrew Jackson Owns Melton's Bluff

It is uncertain what happened to Ocuma Melton's request to Colonel Meigs regarding John Melton's possessions, but it is clear that his property and some 60 slaves were deeded to General Andrew Jackson. General Jackson in partnership with his wife's nephew, Colonel John Hutchings, purchased Melton's Bluff from David Melton in 1816. David, a son of John Melton, signed the deed to Melton's Bluff on November 22, 1816, and described the property as follows:

"I David Melton of the Cherokee Nation do by these presents bargain and sell ... unto General Andrew Jackson and Captain John Hutchings all my right title and interest to the tract of land where I now live, and agree to give them possession of all the improvements laying north and east of the spring, including said spring, on said tract where I live and adjoining where I live, and the houses and ... land southeast of the spring. Possession to be given of as many Negro houses as will house the Negroes of the said Andrew and the said John ... and possession of the other houses on or before the first day of February ... For which I acknowledge to have received the consideration of sixty dollars in cash and in full of the above sale."

Jackson and Hutchings were owners of Melton Bluff at the time Anne Royall wrote her interesting letters from there in 1818. According to <u>Letters from Alabama 1817-1822</u>, Anne Royall wrote: *"Here is a very large plantation of cotton and maize, worked by about sixty slaves, and owned by General Jackson, who bought the interest of old Melton."*

In another letter written two days later Anne Royall described a visit by Jackson to his Melton's Bluff plantation: *"... I was devouring Phillip's Speeches ... in a corner, when a loud cry, 'General Jackson, General Jackson comes!' and, running to my window, I saw him walking slowly up the hill, between two gentlemen, his aids."*

There is no accounting for the number of trips Jackson made to his Alabama plantation over the period of ownership from 1816 until 1827. However, as many as they may have been, these infrequent inspections of his holdings were not enough to insure stability in matters of management. One noted historian concluded that Old Hickory *"... had trouble with over seers and fugitive slaves and was a rather anxious absentee landlord."*

A biographer, Marquis James, listed a number of the General's trips to Alabama. One such journey occurred following the emptying of Jackson's cotton warehouses at his Hermitage plantation and his Melton's Bluff plantation in March of 1822. This occasion

166

came about following the swelling of the Cumberland and Tennessee Rivers which allowed his boats, loaded with cotton, to commence their journeys to New Orleans. Three months later, General Jackson rode his horse from Nashville to Alabama to inspect his plantation. This same biographer, in relating the events of the 1824 national presidential election, wrote:

"During the last weeks before the balloting began, General Jackson visited Melton's Bluff to make arrangements for the marketing of his Alabama cotton - an important detail, as the winter in Washington had been costly and the absentee planter was pressed for funds."

General Andrew Jackson's political life and running for president was the major cause for his extended absences from his cotton plantations and by 1827 he was in financial trouble. His biographer noted:

"The General's cotton seemed to have suffered from inattention, however, the 1827 crop being no better than average in quality. A plague decimated the stables leaving Jackson without a team to take him to Alabama to straighten out an overseer tangle."

Soon after the 1827 harvest, General Jackson sold the Melton's Bluff plantation which he had named Marathon. Jackson started his run for President of the United States to which he was elected in 1828 and did not have the time to run two cotton plantations. Another problem with the Melton's Bluff Plantation was due to Jackson's extreme loyalty to his black servant, David Hutchings Smith. For this reason, General Jackson placed Smith, who had served him through many conflicts and had been his camp man during the Creek Indian War, as overseer of the Melton's Bluff Plantation.

David Hutchings Smith, known as "Old Pap", was as loyal to his master as Jackson was to him. Yet, Smith was probably to kind to Jackson's other slaves and not the man for the job of plantation overseer. After General Jackson sold Melton's Bluff, he gave Old Pap to Andrew Jackson Hutchings. David Hutchings Smith lived until he was 108 years old. During his last days, Smith lived in a small log cabin at the Ardoyne Plantation near Florence where he is buried. Many stories about Old Pap's service to General Andrew Jackson were handed down through John Coffee's family about the wars and when he was overseer of *"Marsa Jackson's Plantation"* at Melton's Bluff.

Moses Melton and Charles Hicks Reserve

After Andrew Jackson acquired John Melton's Plantation, Moses Melton and Charles Hicks tried to get a deed to their reserve a few miles west of Melton's Bluff near

Spring Creek. According to microcopy 208, roll 7, and number 3740, Captain Charles Hicks sends a letter dated January 15, 1817, about his and Moses Melton's Reserve.

"About reserve made to me and Moses Melton on Spring Creek near the mouth of Elk River by the Treaty of General Jackson with the Chickasaws. To whom I pay taxes and get deed." Moses Melton, the son of Lewis Melton, and Charles Hicks wanted a deed to their reserve, but it appears they were unable to secure title because of efforts to eliminate reserves.

About two months later in a letter to Major William Lovely, Colonel Meigs tries to extinguish all reserves according to microcopy 208, roll 7, and number 3760. Major William Lovely was given the appointment to administer Reserves at Muscle Shoals on March 9, 1817. According to microfilm archives, Major Lovely died on June 2, 1817. The letter from Meigs to Major William Lovely follows:

General Andrew Jackson appointed to obtain from Cherokees a formal extinguishment to the title of the reservations at the Shoals. Jackson deserves to have all original Reserves present on [ ] by proxy at Cherokee agency the 1st day of May.
Return J. Meigs

In microcopy 208, roll 7, number 3800, Captain Charles Hicks sends a note on March 10, 1817. It is not clear why Hicks sent this note, but he does identify some people who are still on the reserves and two of those are Doublehead's children.

Muscle Shoals Reservation – yourself and Bird, Doublehead's son, and his daughter Elcey are all in this country except the heirs of Moses Melton.

Charles Hicks realizes that the reserve he and Moses Melton had at Spring Creek in present-day Lawrence County, Alabama is to be sold to General Jackson as evidenced in microcopy 208, roll 7, and number 3675. The letter from Charles Hicks, dated May 31, 1817, says he was told that John D. Chisholm, who was a friend and legal advisor to Doublehead, will sell the reserves at Muscle Shoals to General Jackson.

"I am informed that John D. Chisholm has gone to Nashville to sell to General Andrew Jackson reserves at Muscle Shoals. Request you stop it." It appears that Charles Hicks was unable to hold on to his and Moses Melton's reserve.

168

Conclusion of John Melton

Even though Doublehead had the first cotton gin in north Alabama placed on the plantation of his friend and brother-in-law John Melton, time has removed all remnants of the Cherokee people who lived in the area. To the east side of Melton's Bluff and on the west side of Jackson's (Jack's) Slough, an ancient Woodland ceremonial mound indicating aboriginal occupation stands between a cotton field and the Tennessee River. The mound is the only visible reminder that the area was once occupied by Native American people from long ago to the time the Cherokees under the leadership of Doublehead.

Today, the only sign of Melton's Bluff is a historic marker that stands along a lonely stretch of a narrow black topped road that at one time was the South River Road used by the Chickamauga Cherokees under Doublehead's leadership. The largest portion of land that once made up Melton's Bluff became part of the vast General Joseph (Fighting Joe) Wheeler Plantation and today remains a part of his estate. A narrow fringe of Melton's Bluff that runs along the backwaters of Wheeler Lake is owned by the Tennessee Valley Authority and still contains the old stone hearths of the cabin chimneys that once lined the river bluff.

John D. Chisholm

John D. Chisholm and Doublehead were friends for several years and probably first met in 1791 at the signing of the Treaty of Holston. Both of their names are on the treaty as members of the signing party ratifying the terms of the agreement between the Cherokees and United States. As an agent for the Cherokees under the direction of Governor William Blount, John D. Chisholm and Doublehead established a friendship that lasted until Doublehead's death in 1807. Chisholm acted as Doublehead's attorney in his business affairs and wrote numerous letters for Doublehead. Chisholm eventually helped him establish Doublehead's Company and Reserve that leased land to many white settlers along the Muscle Shoals.

John Chisholm Early Life

John D. Chisholm was born in Scotland between 1737 and 1742 and migrated from Drum, Scotland to America in 1777. He was a large man with a fair complexion and had very red hair which is characteristic of Celtic people. He was married at least three times to the following women: Elizabeth Sims; Martha Holmes; and Patsy Brown, a Cherokee woman. John and his wives had several children.

John moved to General James White's Fort (Knoxville) with Governor William Blount in 1790. He built Chisholm Tavern on the same block as the William Blount Mansion and completed it about 1792. He became involved in the Blount Conspiracy that plotted to conquer Florida from the Spanish and make a new colony. In the Spring of 1792, he worked for Governor Blount as an Indian agent and messenger to the Creek Chief Alexander McGillivray.

Patsy Brown

The crossing of the Tennessee River at Doublehead's Town was known as Brown's Ferry from the Cherokee Indian family of John Brown. Captain John D. Chisholm, who served as a legal advisor to Doublehead, married Patsy Brown, one of John Brown's Cherokee daughters. Patsy was the sister of Colonel Richard Brown who fought with General Andrew Jackson at the Battle of Horse Shoe Bend during the Creek Indian War. John D. Chisholm and Patsy got a divorce in 1799 as follows:

His wife and seemed to be much attached. This deponent believes they lived together as man and wife and that he, John Chisholm, said he never would live with his wife Patsy Chisholm again and further did not.

M. Miller

Sworn before Joseph Greer, Justice of Peace, Knox County, Territory, October 4, 1799. After Patsy Chisholm obtained her divorce, she married William Brent.

James Chisholm, the Cherokee mixed-blood son of Patsy and John D. Chisholm, had several scrapes with the legal authorities who tried to remove him from Indian Territory. John D. Chisholm's son Ignatius married the daughter of Old Tassel, Doublehead's brother. Ignatius's son, Jesse Chisholm, became important in history working with western tribes and for his namesake the Chisholm Trail.

Chisholm Moves West

After Doublehead's death, John D. Chisholm continued to act as an advisor to Doublehead's nephew Tahlonteskee Benge in Arkansas. He went west with the Cherokees in 1809 under the authority of President Thomas Jefferson. The Chickasaws wanted the United States Government, not only to remove all the white settlers and intruders on Doublehead's Reserve, but also remove John D. Chisholm from their country. Their formal request for Chisholm's removal is found in microcopy 208, roll 4, and number 2130. The letter from King Henderson of the Chickasaw Nation is dated August 25, 1808, and is addressed to Henry Dearborn, Secretary of War.

"We are informed that the Cherokees in 1805 sold part of our country north of the Tennessee River opposite to Muscle Shoals to the United States. We went to Muscle Shoals to meet Doublehead and his friends but they were not there as Colonel Meigs had summoned Doublehead, John D. Chisholm, and all his friends to Highwassee.

Since Doublehead's death, Chisholm acts as [agent] for Doublehead-Meigs too. When Major Thomas Lewis was agent to Cherokees, John D. Chisholm was banished from the country and went to the Creeks, Colonel Hawkins moved him from thence and he come back to the Cherokees, he then found a friend in Doublehead and he supported him till his death.

"We request as a particular favor, that you will be so good as to remove John D. Chisholm out of the Indian country. We have no doubt but government has been informed of Chisholm's character. If the government does not choose to make Chisholm quit the red peoples land, please to give us leave and we will take him out of it.

Relying on the Government of United States to remove bad white men from the red peoples country, we have not attempted to remove Chisholm , depending on the government to have done it for us – otherwise we should have done it long since."

Signed By
Chinnabbe King et, George, William, James Colbert, and 28 others

Evidently, John D. Chisholm got the message from the Chickasaws and planned his move along with Taluntuskee and some 1,130 Cherokees. His letter to Colonel Return J. Meigs, Chisholm indicates that he will visit when his wound gets well. It is not certain how he was wounded and if it had an impact on his decision to move. In his letter on March 18, 1809, Chisholm requests from Meigs the laws of the United States as found in microcopy 208, roll 4, and number 2246 as follows:

"I hope you will write me by the bearer what prospects from your late travel to the Federal City. I also beg the favor of the Colonel to send me the 4th volume of the laws of the United States also the volume that contains the treaties of Hopewell – I will bring them back with great care. I am preparing to move over the Mississippi this summer – All the Indians are preparing in this quarter for the same purpose – nothing will be done until I see you and have your council, pray sir, let me hear by the return of Joel Walker the prospects. Let know how the European Business is like to terminate – Don't fail to lend

me Laws. They will be used to no bad purpose I will bring them up with me which will be as soon as Walker [the messenger] returns and my wound gets well."

    John D. Chisholm

Within a week Meigs replies to Chisholm letting him know that some of the Cherokees in the lower towns have requested to move west of the Mississippi River as found in microcopy 208, roll 4, and number 2074. The following statement is from Colonel Return J. Meigs to John D. Chisholm and dated March 24, 1809.

    "Cherokees of the lower towns requests permission to remove West of Mississippi."

Some seven months later, Meigs notifies the Secretary of War Henry Dearborn of the number of Cherokees willing to move west of the Mississippi River. According to microcopy 208, roll 4, and number 2371, Colonel Return J. Meigs writes to the Secretary War and addresses the Chiefs of Cherokees assembled at Wills Town on November 2, 1809.

    "On 20 day July, Taluntuskee brought me the names of 386 men and 637 women and children who wished move over the Mississippi after that 107 more wanted to go making a total of 1130. Cherokees now own no land west of Mississippi those there are there by counting on the government."

Chisholm's Legal Problems

    After John D. Chisholm removed West, he got into a legal confrontation of his own. The court case confirms that even though Chisholm's ancestry was Scots, he was a prominent member of the Western Cherokees. Other important information concerning his life is found in the court case published by the University of Arkansas at Little Rock, William H. Bowen School of Law, Territorial Briefs and Records:

    Robert Clary vs. John D. Chisholm
    Abstract
    23 January 1811
    Robert Clary acting through his attorney...filed suit against Dennis Chisholm, he also sued Dennis' father John D. Chisholm for a debt of $207.33 for whiskey, corn, pork, bacon, and flour...John D. Chisholm was born in Scotland and emigrated to America in the 1700's. He had several wives, and at one time married to a Cherokee woman...He lived for a while in Tennessee, where he and the Indian Chief Doublehead swindled settlers in fraudulent land deals in the Muscle Shoals area. He was a prominent member

of the Western Cherokees, who migrated to and settled western Arkansas in the early 1800's. He would later represent the Cherokees at the Treaty of Cherokee Agency in 1817...Ignatius Chisholm was John D.'s son, and father to Jesse Chisholm, of Chisholm Trail fame...Robert Clary...complains...said John D. Chisholm on 13th day of September 1810 was justly indebted...in sum of two hundred and seven Dollars & 33 cents.

Executed 8th March 1811

Death of John D. Chisholm

Prior to his death, John D. Chisholm supported Doublehead's nephew Talunskee and became one of the prominent leaders of the Cherokees West or Old Settlers. John D. Chisholm died at Hot Springs, Arkansas in September 1818. He had gone to the springs for their medicinal benefits and died there. Today, in Lauderdale County, Alabama, the Chisholm Road in the Florence area still bears his family name. In addition, the Chisholm Trail in the West is named in honor of his grandson Jesse Chisholm.

Return Jonathan Meigs

In May 1801, Colonel Return Jonathan Meigs, Jr., at the age of 61, was appointed Southern Indian Agent of the United States War Department and his subsidiary agent was Major William Lovely. Meigs accepted the dual appointment as Cherokee Indian Agent and Agent of the War Department in Tennessee.

Meigs' Cherokee Relationship

His reputation among the Cherokee Indians varied according to whether they were from the Upper Towns or Lower Towns. In general, the Lower Town Cherokees admired Meigs and were sympathetic to his actions especially those living in the Great Bend of the Tennessee River who were friends and relatives of Doublehead; however, many of the Upper Town Cherokees resented Meigs as much as they did Doublehead. To make matters worse for the Upper Cherokees, Meigs and Doublehead quickly developed a friendship and bond that lasted to the death of Doublehead on August 9, 1807.

It is important to note that Meigs worked with John McDonald Daniel Ross, grandfather and father of John Ross, who became principal chief of the Cherokee Nation during the removal period. John Ross's grandfather John McDonald in 1785 saved the life of a young man by the name of Daniel Ross that was a captive of Bloody Fellow. Since McDonald's mother was Barbara Ross, he may have been a cousin to Daniel Ross. Daniel Ross would marry McDonald's daughter Mollie and become the father John Ross. Daniel

Daniel Ross, father of John Ross

became McDonald's business partner and ran a trading post at Stecoe or Lookout Mountain Town. The Ross faction, who fought removal against the wishes of the Ridge/Watie faction that signed the Treaty of New Echota, was friends of Doublehead's relatives. Doublehead's assassination and other factors culminated in a blood bath when both factions came together in the west.

According to Henry Thompson Malone's Cherokees of the Old South (1956), the assignment of Colonel Return J. Meigs, Jr., was a godsend to the Cherokees. Malone writes, *"Fate smiled on the Cherokees in 1801 with the appointment of Return Jonathan Meigs as Indian Agent. A seasoned frontiersman, Meigs had a thorough knowledge of the Indians and a deep sympathy for their problems. Sensible, just, firm, and above desire for personal gain, the new agent devoted himself to promoting the well-being of the Cherokees. Diplomatic in spite of his rough background, he ably served his government, successfully dealt with state authorities, and generally gained the confidence of Indians. After the confusion of frontier crises Colonel Meigs was a stabilizing force in a crucial period of Cherokee history."*

From his appointment in 1801 and to his death on January 28, 1823, Return J. Meigs confirmed that he was a true friend to the Cherokee, but he was intent on opening the Cherokee lands to white settlement. *Colonel Return J. Meigs, Jr., known as White Path among the Cherokee, was born on December 17, 1740, in Middletown, Connecticut...and received several commissions making him instrumental in the treaties between the Indians and white man that eventually led to the settlement and development of the area North of the Tennessee River in Alabama.* (McDonald, 2007).

Meigs and Doublehead

Doublehead trusted Meigs so much that he requested that Meigs look after his young children should he die or get killed. Even though Meigs was skillful in getting Doublehead and other Cherokees to sign treaties giving up their lands, he also wanted to gain their lasting trust and friendship by making sure the United States Government up

174

held agreements that benefitted the Cherokee Indian people he represented. It appears that Doublehead knew that he could count on Meigs to keep his word and follow through with the commitments he had made.

However in his letters, Colonel Meigs sends mixed impressions and feelings in regards toward Doublehead. Colonel Meigs writes to William Lovely on July 20, 1802, bragging on Doublehead and calling him a friend with intelligence:

Colonel Return Jonathan Meigs

"Our Friend Double Head talks like a man of Sense and reflection on the subject of mechanics and of mills being erected ect. In the present situation of things I cannot say anything more than has been said, that our Government will continue to do them Justice, 'that when they become more liberal, they may expect liberality of the Government..."

On February 13, 1805, Colonel Return J. Meigs sends a letter to Benjamin Hawkins describing Doublehead in a very derogatory fashion by referring to him as a bloody minded savage. Meigs also states that Doublehead sets his foot on the neck of anything that may be in opposition:

"This man [Doublehead], it is true, from the force of his discernment estimates useful improvements and is exerting himself to live in a stile of some degree of taste; at the same time he is a vindictive, bloody minded Savage and his exertions to raise himself do no appear to arise from any refinement of disposition but to place himself in such a situation as that he may set his foot on the neck of anything that may oppose itself to his ill founded pride."

Then in another letter Colonel Meigs seems complimentary toward Doublehead in resolving grave issues as found in microcopy 208, roll 3, and number1850, and dated May 1, 1807. Colonel Return J. Meigs explains in this letter to Secretary of War Henry Dearborn the conditions respecting the murder of Stinson, a white man killed by Creeks.

"Letter from Doublehead informs me that last March some white men descended the Tennessee River and sold whiskey to some Creeks living at mouth of Elk River. As a compromise the Creeks quarreled with a white man named Stinson who lived and settled in that part of the country, stabbed him in the throat and killed him. The Cherokees in

Doublehead's Village upon knowing of the murder seized the Creeks and shot them both. This murder was due to smuggling of whiskey – 2,000 men could not prevent it."

> *Sincerely,*
> *Return Jonathan Meigs*

Numerous letters from Doublehead and other Cherokee people indicate that they looked to Colonel Meigs for help in resolving their problems. Whether it was a bad corn crop for the Cherokee or a problem with the personal property of an individual Cherokee, Meigs was sought out and asked to provide assistance and corrective measures. In most cases, Meigs was able to get United States government officials to provide support in alleviating problems faced by the Cherokee people under his jurisdiction. At the same time, Meigs was manipulating Cherokees through treaty deals in order to get possession of their property.

Meigs' Cherokee Agency

Recorded December 1816--A list of agents, subagents, interpreters and other persons employed in the Cherokee Agency specifying the amount of compensation, and pay allowed to each and the state or country where born.

Name	Office	State	Amount
Return J. Meigs	Agent	Conn	1920.00
Wm Lewis Lovely	Subagent	Ireland	1100.00
Samuel Riley	Interpreter	Maryland	109.50
Richard Taylor	Interpreter	Cherokee N	109.50
John Hildebrand	Miller	Penn	204.78
John McCarty	Clerk	Virginia	500.00

Meigs' Death

The final act of his life was in service to those whom he, in turn, loved and respected. The story goes that on a cold winter night at the Hiwassee Garrison, Colonel Meigs learned that a visiting chief, who was aged and not well, had no place to sleep. Meigs gave him his bed, and moved into a tent. As a result of this exposure to the elements, Meigs, then 82 years of age, contracted pneumonia and died January 28, 1823 (McDonald, 2007).

On February 14, 1765, Colonel Return J. Meigs married Joanna Winborn, and she died on October 30, 1773. After her death, Meigs then married Grace Starr also known as

Rising Fawn, an American Indian probably from the Cherokee Starr family, on December 22, 1774. Rising Fawn died in east Tennessee on October 10, 1807, and she was buried in the Old Garrison Cemetery near the Hiwassee Garrison overlooking the junction of the Tennessee River and Hiwassee River. Colonel Return Jonathan Meigs, Jr. (White Path) was buried beside his beloved Indian wife and son Timothy in a small country graveyard located in Rhea County, Tennessee some five miles east of Dayton, Tennessee.

Conclusion of Meigs

Of all his friends, Colonel Meigs' actions did more to contribute to Doublehead's assassination than all the others together. Meigs's bribes and so called secret agreements were tough for Doublehead to refuse. Meigs accompanied Doublehead and James Vann to Washington, D. C. to meet with President Thomas Jefferson of the United States and got them to sign the treaty of January 7, 1806. The treaty gave up Cherokee claims from the Tennessee River, except for Doublehead's Reserve, north to the Duck River and placed a cotton gin at Melton's Bluff. This treaty sealed the fate of Doublehead because he gave up sacred hunting grounds of the Cherokee.

In addition, Doublehead had agreed with his other friends to give the wedge shaped parcel of Cherokee land in the upper Elk River drainage, but before this deal was completed Doublehead was murdered. The land transaction was completed after Doublehead's assassination by friend or foe Return J. Meigs. In microcopy 208, roll 3, and number 1914 and found in the American States Papers (1832), Colonel Return J. Meigs writes to Secretary of War on September 28, 1807, stating: *"Sometime before Doublehead's death I met with him and 3 others and we agreed that the convention line should be extended to comprehend all the waters of Elk River."*

In the end whether a true friend or not, Doublehead's deals with Colonel Return J. Meigs was the primary catalyst that led to his assassination by his own people. Even after Doublehead's death, Meigs used his relationship with Doublehead to acquire the upper drainage of Elk River by getting his Chickamauga friends to sign their approval to the land deal that Doublehead had earlier agreed.

Doublehead: Businessman

Chief Doublehead, a Chickamaugan who became a successful businessman,... established a land agency called the Doublehead Company, which leased thousands of acres between the Elk River and Cypress Creek to more than fifty white settlers. The land Doublehead leased was in Cherokee territory, and as such, was not supposed to be available for this type of settlement. After Doublehead's death in the summer of 1807, the lease holders ran into legal problems which resulted in their eviction in 1811.

Doublehead was also the father-in-law of the prominent Chickasaw chief, George Colbert, who operated the ferry on the Tennessee River at the Natchez Trace. Through land speculation and by controlling transportation routes, Doublehead and his followers controlled the Mussel Shoals (later changed to Muscle Shoals) area for many years. Doublehead's prosperous business interests made him an influential leader in northwest Alabama" (Rozeman, 1995).

Farming Interests

Doublehead owned some 40 slaves and raised cotton, corn, horses, hogs, and beef cattle. His brother-in-law, John Melton, had some 60 slaves and was also heavily involved in farming cotton, corn, and other agricultural activities. Doublehead had a cotton gin placed at Melton's Bluff for cleaning their cotton. After moving to Shoal Town in early 1802, Doublehead continues his farming operations and wants transportation capability to send his cotton to the New Orleans market. According to a letter from Doublehead to Return Jonathan Meigs dated November 20, 1802, and found in Henry Thompson Malone's book, "*Cherokees of the Old South: A People in Transition*" (1956), Doublehead is requests a keel boat for transporting his produce.

Sir:

When I saw you at the Green Corn Dance...you Desired me to come and see you and get some goods from you—My intention is to come and trade with you. But I am so Engaged Hunting and Gathering my beef cattle that I expect it will be a moone or two before I can come---I...have now one Request to ask of you---that is to have me a boat Built---I want a good Keal Boat some 30 to 35 feet in length and 7 feet wide---I want her for the purpose of Descending the River to Orlians & back I want her to be lite & well calculated to stem the Streem I am Determined to by the Produce of this place & the Return back by Water...I shall want two of your big guns to mount on the Boat---I am

Determined for to see up the White & Red Rivers in my Route & open a trade with the western wild Indians---Let me here from you soon.

> *I am Sir Your Reale*
> *Friend & Brother*
> *Doublehead*

Wrote by
J. D. Chisholm
> *Who presents his Compliments*

Doublehead wants to expand his farm business and trade his produce with people in New Orleans and the western wild Indians by keel boat. He offers a description for the boat he wants and expects the government to construct the boat. Later, Doublehead was promised the boat for signing the treaty that authorized the Federal Road through Georgia. It is not certain what kind of response he gets from Meigs and whether he ever gets his boat, but it is for certain he has a market with the government for his beef cattle as observed by Reverend Patrick Wilson in 1803.

Wilson mentions that Tal Tsuske (Doublehead) supplied beef to a garrison on the Tennessee River below the Muscle Shoals. Wilson is again impressed with the Cherokee "advances in civilization" citing their ability to make and repair "accurately and strongly" laid fences. He draws particular attention to a cooperative work endeavor, which he compares to an American "frolic" or barn raising.

Because Tal Tsuske's (Doublehead) house was located on the north side of the Shoals, the expedition party stayed with another Chickamauga chief, Skiowska. Wilson's description of this Cherokee home is the most detailed in the narrative: not only were Skiowska's wife's "kitchen and household furniture in good order," but she also used "plates, bowls, tea cups and saucers, a tea kettle and coffee pot, and churned butter in a churn with a proper dasher and lid" to provide for her visitors. Wilson documents her use of "the large Indian spoon," an artifact that even today has communal significance among southeastern tribes (Hathorn and Sabino, 2001).

Reverend Patrick Wilson made the journey through Doublehead's territory in 1803; however, by that time, Doublehead had moved from Doublehead's Town at the Brown's Ferry crossing to Shoal Town on the north side of the Tennessee River near the mouth of Blue Water Creek where he operated his large trading post and store/stand. According to historical documents, it appears that Doublehead made his move from the south side of the river in present-day Lawrence County, Alabama to Shoal Town on the north side of the river in present-day Lauderdale County, Alabama in early 1802.

While living at Shoal Town, Doublehead requested help from the U.S. Government; however, he was no stranger to the government when asking for help, money, or handouts. This particular incident is also recorded in Malone's (1956) book:

"A scarcity of corn caused by a drought in the Cherokee Nation during the year 1804 was a crisis which Meigs faced in his typical fashion. The first request for food came from **Doublehead** *and other Cherokees in the Muscle Shoals area on the Lower Tennessee River. The Agent immediately sent them three hundred bushels of corn, for which the Indians paid $110. Meigs, however, requested and received permission from the War Department to return the money; he thought it his duty 'to give the necessary relief — believing that humanity and interest combine to make it proper especially when interesting negotiations with them are now soon to be opened.' Meigs' policy pleased his government. Henry Dearborn sent him the President's congratulations, urging Meigs to continue helping needy Indians: 'You will embrace so favorable an opportunity for impressing the minds of the Cherokees with the fatherly concern and attention of the President to the distresses of his red children.'"*

Business Interests

Doublehead quickly adopts the ways of the white people when it came to his business activities. According to McDonald (2007), *after being associated with Captain John D. Chisholm, Doublehead began to walk as a gentleman, speak as a friend, and do business as if he had been educated at Harvard. In 1802, he bought 100 barrels of flour for $2.00 a barrel from the operator of a boat that ran aground at the Muscle Shoals. He paid $20.00 and not a cent more and then when the owners offered to buy it back, he demanded no less than $8.00 a barrel. He was learning the white man's ways fast.*

Stands

As a businessman Doublehead tried to influence decisions that would be to his benefit. His attorney William Tharpe, was recommended by his friend and applied for the job operating the public store for the Cherokees; however, Meigs had his own recommendation. From South West Point on October 6, 1804, Meigs writes to Henry Dearborn, Secretary of War concerning a new factor at the public store at Tellico since the death of John W. Hooker. Meigs recommends Nicholas Byers instead of William Tharpe who was contracted by Doublehead to operate his stand as seen in the following letter:

Sir:

On the 22 ulto I wrote announcing to you the death of John W. Hooker the Factor at the Public Store at Tellico. At the same time I took the liberty to recommend Mr. Nicholas Byers as a proper person to take charge of the Factory. Since I wrote have heard that Charles Wright (&) William Tharp have applied thro their friends for the place. Permit me to observe that it will be of importance to the United States that the person who holds that place be attached to the present administration. Mr. Byers is decidedly so, the others are not. Tis painful to see applications for offices under the administration who have uniformly spoken ill of the Exchange ever since the Adams system has been exploded.
. .

R. J. Meigs.

As seen in the letter below, William Tharpe was not only a friend of Doublehead, but he also acted as his attorney in some of Doublehead's business deals. Doublehead was heavily involved with business interests in operating "Stands and Houses of Entertainment" along public roads in the Cherokee Nation. Confirmation of these business deals is found in microcopy 208, roll 3, and number 1382. The following is a letter to Sampson Williams from Colonel Return J. Meigs in reference to his contract with William Tharp in the name of Doublehead and dated March 8, 1805, from South West Point.

In my letter to you 11 November 1803, I informed you of the conditions on which the stand at the forks of the road could at that time be taken from the establishment of a house of entertainment. Stating to you that although William Tharpe was interested in the stand, that the contract must be made with Doublehead, a Principal Chief on his name and that William Tharpe was authorized to act for Doublehead in making the contract.

In April then next following in April 1804, Mr. Tharpe brought forward to a Cherokee Council, proposition signed by himself, Thomas N. Clarke, and William Walton to take all the stands on the road for which they offered one thousand dollars per annum. The council took the proposition into consideration and came to the resolution that they would consent to the occupancy of all the necessary stands on the road. Six were pointed out exclusively by Thomas N. Clarke, Thompson Williams, William Walton, and Hugh Beatty at the rate of two hundred dollars per annum for each stand.

Of this I appoint you in my letter of the 14 April 1804. The gentlemen declined lately the stands on these terms of course this former contract remained unaltered. I have no copy of your agreement with Mr. Tharpe acting as attorney for Doublehead. He informs me it was similar in every respect – to that for Obeds River which has been transferred to William Walton. If there is anything due at this time for occupancy of the stand at the forks of the road, it is due to Doublehead. But William Tharp acting for

Doublehead may with propriety receive it. It is therefore accountable to Doublehead and to the Cherokee Nation for his agency in the [ ].

> *Sampson Williams Esq.*
> *Accept this the assurance of my [ ] respect.*
> *Return J. Meigs*

At this point it is important to note that Thomas N. Clark mentioned in the letter above was also an associate of Doublehead. Clark was in charge and responsible for the schooling and boarding of two of Doublehead's children including Bird Tail Doublehead and his half-brother, Tassel. Clark lived near South West Point and took a great deal of property from Doublehead's estate.

Some of the people operating the "Stands" were farming near the stores and were thought to be squatters or intruders on the Cherokee Nation; however, some of the operators were raising corn and other supplies to be sold in their stores. In order to prevent their farming operations from being moved by troops, they asked for permission to use the property near the stands for farming. The following letter is to Sampson Williams dated April 2, 1805, and is found in microcopy 208, roll 3, and number 1406. The letter is requesting a certificate to use the land. It appears that William Tharpe, attorney for Doublehead, is trying to prevent raising corn and other supplies by white folks for use at the stands.

> *The troops are out on the Indian frontiers and very properly removing intruders and I understand Tharpe is trying to persuade the officers to remove those persons that I have employed to raise corn and other supplies for the Fork Road Stand about four miles on this side of the stand near Barrens and c. I shall therefore thank you to send a certificate together with a permit for the land at the Fork Road.* On April 5, 1805, Colonel Return J. Meigs responds in a letter to Sampson Williams on the subject of removing intruders and stands on the roads in microcopy 208, roll 3, and number 1410.

In order to promote his business interests and get more involvement from government officials in providing equipment and provisions, Doublehead asks other Cherokee chiefs for greater cooperation. The following is a letter from Doublehead and lower Cherokee chiefs dated August 9, 1805, is to Principal Chief Black Fox and others asking for their cooperation in getting more provisions from the United States Government:

To: Black Fox, Dick Justice, Turtle at Home, Chinowe, Slave Body, Eusanalee,
Toochelar, Parched Corn Flour, Taugustuska

We have with much care and attention considered the results of the late Conference
[in July] with the Commissioners on the Highwassee, and we think that . . . we shall agree
to the request of our Father, at least in part. . . . the Agent had informed us that he could
not be Justified in continuing the presents of wheels, cards, and implements of husbandry
and in giving corn and provisions [in time of famine] as he had done before [unless there
was cooperation from us].
Doublehead, Tolluntuskee, Katigiskee,
the Seed, Sequeechee, Sikula, the Redbird

Doublehead operated a house of entertainment or a house of ill repute. A
Knoxville newspaper reported, shortly before he was assassinated, that Doublehead was
brave and generous with both white and red having experienced his liberality. Doublehead
wrote to an Indian agent asking aid for two poor middle-aged women living at his place
with large families composed entirely of girls. Some seem to think the two older women
were madams and the large numbers of girls were in the oldest business in the world.
Whatever the case, Doublehead was allowing a large number of females to live in his
house supposedly free of rent. The paper indicated Doublehead's house was a haven for
the needy.

In some of Doublehead's business deals, he is hesitant to come forth with payment
in a satisfactory manner. As seen in microcopy 208, roll 3, and number 1692, John
McAllister's sends a letter on September 26, 1806, and wants his pay from Doublehead.

Last spring Monte Bean passed Shoals and asked Doublehead to pay him.
Doublehead appeared unusually "lotcetory" to pay him but had only $10.00 in cash but if
Monte Bean would take beaver furs he would pay him up. Monte Bean is a celebrated
Rascal not worth one cent nor ever will be. Bean told Doublehead he had paid for cargo –
Doublehead says he will pay no one but Bean. Bean will go down the river next spring.

After Doublehead's death, Mr. John McAllister files a claim on Doublehead's
estate to obtain the money owed to him; however, John D. Chisholm claims the money was
paid to Bean. In microcopy 208, roll4, and number 2180, John D. Chisholm responds in a
letter relating to McAllister's claim on Doublehead's Estate from Highwassee, (Garrison)
dated November 2, 1808.

Doublehead paid Bean $20 for flour and steel in wrecked boat and promised
to pay a balance of $190.00 later. This he did in December 1806 or January 1807.

Chisholm advised Doublehead against paying Bean in horses. But Doublehead said he bargained with Bean and would pay him.

Mills and Ferries

Doublehead not only gets into the business of farming, raising cattle, owning stands and houses of entertainment, but he also gets into saw and grist mills. He requested more improvements for his people in the following: *"I, Doublehead, a principle Cherokee Chief, wishing to excellerate useful improvements in my Nations, and finding that Mills are much wanting in the Cherokee Country for the purpose aforesaid, determine to erect a sawmill and Gristmill on a stream on the South side of the River Tennessee."*

Samuel Adams with his family of sixteen persons has permission to pass into the Cherokee Nation at the Muscle Shoals. This permission is given me at the instance of Double Head in expectation that this family will by their industry & good conduct be of service in the plan of promoting Civilization amongst the Cherokees. 20th July 1802

Also, as seen in microcopy 208, roll 3, and number 1550, Doublehead and John Smith develop an agreement November 16, 1805, for a 10 year operation of a saw and grist mill.

Agreement to erect a Saw and Grist Mill "on a stream on the south side of the river Tennessee opposite Roy's Bent so called...John Smith Jr. of Roan County, State of Tennessee, lease for 10 years. Wit: John D. Chisholm, Hugh Beatty, Sam McAllister John Smith, Jr. and Doublehead

According to the Treaty of Tellico in 1805, Doublehead gained the right to operate a ferry at Southwest Point in Tennessee. It appears that Return J. Meigs was instrumental in getting ferry money for Doublehead and his associates. *Although the U.S. government hoped to keep ferry money for American interests, Commissioner to the Indians Return J. Meigs wrote to the Secretary of War in 1805 that the Cherokees kept their right to benefit by charging travelers.—I take this opportunity to inform you that the Road through the Cherokee Nation is now nearly opened for the traveling of Carriages. By the contract with the Indians for that road the income of the Ferries were reserved to them and to be put up to the highest Bidders.* (Ownby and Wharton, 2007)

Doublehead: Development, Roads, and Land

During the early interaction of the United States government with Doublehead and the Cherokee, commissioners encouraged the chiefs to allow them to improve and widen the old roads. In addition, they encouraged the construction of ferries and houses of entertainment; however, during 1801, Doublehead rejects the proposal of the commissioners for more land and roads.

Roads and Land

1801

"On this land there is a great deal of timber, pine and oak, that are much use to the white man. They send it to foreign countries, and it brings them a great deal of money.

On the land there is much grass for cattle and horses, and much food for the hogs.

On this land there is a great deal of tobacco raised, which likewise brings much money. Even the streams are valuable to the white man, to grind the wheat and corn that grows on this land. The pine trees that are dead are valuable for tar.

All these things are lasting benefits. But if the Indians are given just a few goods for their lands, in one or two seasons those goods are all rotten and gone for nothing.

We are told that our lands are of no service to us, but still, if we hold our lands, there will always be a turkey, or a deer, or a fish in the streams for those young who will come after us.

We are afraid if we part with any more of our lands the white people will not let us keep as much as will be sufficient to bury our dead."

Doublehead

According to "Georgia's Old Federal Road" by Ted Ownby and David Wharton, University of Mississippi, 2007, Doublehead opposed the construction of roads through Cherokee Country. *The leader of the Lower Town Chiefs, Chief Doublehead, made a long statement against new roads in 1801, arguing that Americans should not turn existing footpaths into wagon roads, that too much violence and theft had already occurred, and that conflict tended to breed hostility and more conflict. —When you first made these settlements there were paths which answered for them . . . . We do not wish to have them [wagon roads] made through our country. Our objections to these roads are these: a great many people of all descriptions would pass [along] them, and that would happen which has recently happened . . . ., and you would labor under the same difficulties you do now.*

In the late 1700s and early 1800s, Cherokees were divided about whether or not to allow the United States or the state of Georgia to build a road into their territory. In a general way, the Cherokees in the late 1700s and early 1800s divided between the Upper Town Chiefs, including Chief James Vann, and the Lower Town Chiefs, sometimes led by Chief Doublehead.

The following is Doublehead's speech against the Federal Road as reported in the <u>American States Papers</u>:

"Extract from the speech of the commissioners of the United States to the chiefs of the Cherokees, assembled at Southwest Point, September 4th, 1801.

Brothers: Your white brethren, who live at the Natchez, at Nashville, and in South Carolina, are very far removed from each other, and have complained to your father, the President, that the roads by which they travel are narrow and obstructed by fallen timber, with rivers and creeks, which prevent them from pursuing their lawful business with his red children and with each other.

Brothers: To remove these difficulties, and to accommodate his red children, your father is desirous to open wide these roads; but, as they pass over the lands of his red children, he first asks their consent to the measure, and is willing to pay them an equivalent for the indulgence to his white children.

Brothers: Your white brethren have also complained to your father, that, on these long roads, they have no place for rest or accommodation, which exposes them and their horses to much inconvenience and suffering. To remove this complaint, your father is desirous that his red children would consent to establish houses of entertainment and ferries, on these roads, to be kept by persons appointed by himself, who shall give security for their good behavior, and pay such annual rent to his red children, as may be agreed upon.

Brothers: This is a small request, made by your father; it is intended not to extinguish your rights, but to give value to your land, and make it immediately productive to you, in the manner of your ferry over Clinch river.

186

Brothers: You have been alarmed by songs of lying birds, and the talks of forked tongues. You have heard that your father would press you for further concessions of land, and, it has been said by some, even as far as the Big river. You will know, hereafter, how to listen to such thieves, liars, and mischief-makers, and will treat them as they deserve.

Brothers: Listen to us, and hear the truth. We stand up in this place between you and our white brethren and we are ready to speak from the one to the other. You white brethren want land, and are willing to pay for it. If you have any to sell, they will buy it from you, and if you can agree on the terms. But if you are not disposed to sell any land, not one word more shall be said on the subject.

Doublehead's reply*: The chiefs now have heard the talk of a father; and the sun is now lowering, and at the same hour to-morrow, we will deliver an answer; and the answer we shall give will be short, and we hope there will be no more of it: and we hope the commissioners will not insist on making a reply.*

Commissioners — When we have heard what you have to say, we shall know whether to reply or not.

The council adjourned, to meet again the next day, at one o'clock, P.M.

5th. —The commissioners met the chiefs, agreeably to adjournment, at one o'clock, P.M. when Doublehead rose, and spoke as follows:

Doublehead rose, and spoke as follows:

We shall commence to-day, notwithstanding the indisposition of one of the commissioners of the United States, and some of our own.

I am now going to speak. It is but yesterday that we heard the talk of our father, the President, and, to-day, you will hear ours. You are appointed by the United States to tell us the means devised for our interest; this was planned eight years past, for the welfare of our nation, big and small, done by our father, the President, who is now no more. It seems, it is by this plan, that means have been provided, to take care of the red people; and the present President, it seems, cherishes the same good wish towards us, which is pleasing to us, and we hold to it. I think that the new President ought to listen to our talks, and not throw them aside. We hope his good disposition towards us will continue, that our children may live in peace; and you, who are authorized by the President, have said, we ought not to listen to the crooked talks of those that are about us. In behalf of my nation, I am authorized to speak to you. There are a number of land speculators among you, who say we want to sell lands; we hope you will not pay regard to them; as they give them out for the sake of getting property. We hope you will not listen to these talks. The chiefs, the head-men of these frontiers, are, themselves, interested in these speculations, and they will give you fine talks, which are meant to deceive, as they are for their own interest. We think it is a shame that the land sellers should impose on the Government, and say, that we want to dispose of our lands, when we do not. When you first made these settlements, there were paths which answered for them; the roads you propose, we do not wish to have made through our country. Our objections to these roads are these: a great many people, of all descriptions, would pass them, and that would happen which has recently happened, and you would labor under the same difficulties you do now. We mean to hold fast the peace which is subsisting between you and us; to preserve this, we hope you will not make roads through our country, but sue those which you have made your land, and another, the Kentucky Trace. I expect you will think we have a right to say yes or no, as answers, and we hope you will say no more on this subject; if you do, it would seem as if we had no right to refuse. You, who are picked out by the Government, from among the first and best men of the United States, we hope you will take our talks, and assist us. Likewise, you, who are place on our borders, to see our rights maintained, that we may not be plagued by those people who want land. We consider General Wilkinson the general of the army of the United States, and we hope he will not insist on anything here, as we look to him as children do to their father; we remember the former talks: we were told the general was to preserve our lands, and not to let us be imposed upon. I am now done speaking for this day, and hope you will not say anything more about lands or about the roads.

Benjamin Hawkins
Indian Agent

The Commissioners' reply — What has passed between us shall be faithfully reported to the President, who knows best how to estimate it.

188

South West Point, 6ᵗʰ September, 1801
To the Honourable Henry Dearborn, Secretary of War.

Sir:
. . . The decided tone of "Doublehead" on the subject of their lands, his pathetic appeal to the justice and magnanimity of the government respecting the roads, and the pressing demands which followed them from himself and from Chuleoah for the fulfillment of existing treaties, and for the reparation of injuries recorded in blood, rendered it, in our judgment, unavailing and inconsistent with our instructions to press the conference further; while by dissolving it, we not only obliged the Indians, but gave them an impregnable testimony of the consideration and sincerity of the President. . . .
Jas. Wilkinson
Benjamin Hawkins
Andrew Pickens

1803

Even though Doublehead admonished the commissioners to say nothing more about building roads through Cherokee territory and ceding Cherokee lands the government was unrelenting. *The U.S. government made clear it was pressing the Cherokees for a road. In February 1803, Secretary of War Henry Dearborn wrote to agent Return Meigs, —The opening of the road through the Cherokee Country to Georgia has become highly necessary. He encouraged Meigs to offer —presents, to discuss putting up —public houses for travelers, and concluded that Meigs should tell the Cherokee chiefs, —We shall not consider the Cherokees as good neighbors unless they will allow their best friends, who are taking every means in their power to make them happy, to make a road*(Ownby and Warton, 2007).

In his letter of February 19, 1803, the United States Secretary of War Henry Dearborn is pressuring Colonel Return J. Meigs to get permission from the Cherokees to establish the Federal road through the Nation. The following is an excerpt of that letter:

"The opening of the road through Cherokee Country to Georgia has become highly necessary, and you will please to take the earliest opportunity of holding a conference with the principal Chiefs of the Cherokees to obtain it. You are authorized to make them some presents not exceeding 500 dollars for their consent. Additional presents may be made for the purpose, but in all events, we must have a road."

According to the Treaty Agreement of October 1803, Doublehead was given the rights to operate a ferry at Southwest Point in east Tennessee near the junction of the

Clinch River and Tennessee River. Doublehead's two daughters Gulustiyu and Nigodegiyu who married Samuel Riley lived at South West Point. Samuel Riley and his family operate the ferry for Doublehead. According to the treaty, *"the ferry at Southwest Point shall be put in the hand of our beloved chief Doublehead and the other two shall be rented by our agent to citizens of the United States to the highest bidders; the preference in Renting these Ferries shall be in favor of persons having connections to the Cherokee Nation...the Cherokee Nation and their connections will form a Turnpike Company for keeping the said Road in constant good repair"*. . .

Doublehead's Gifts

It would appear that Chief Doublehead would not change his mind initially on the construction of roads or relinquishing Indian land; however, when the proverbial carrot of money, property, and land for his personal use was waved in front of his eyes, he reversed his stand. According to a letter found in microcopy 208, roll 3, and dated February 1, 1805, Doublehead wants a road to come through Muscle Shoals.

"I have received a line from Doublehead, Kategishee and some others who live at the Shoals that they wish a road from Cumberland may pass-by the Shoals in such a deviation as to fall into the road to Georgia in a proper place."

Return J. Meigs

Doublehead built a road from Franklin County, Tennessee, to the Shoals and tried to get the government to connect it with the main road to the Tombigbee settlements. (McDonald, 2007) This road became known as Doublehead's Trace and was laid out on portions of the Old Buffalo Trail that ran from the French Lick (Nashville, Tennessee) on the Cumberland River. According to Walsh (1810), Meigs confirms that Doublehead had completed a road of 100 miles in length from Franklin County, Tennessee to his home at the mouth of Blue Water Creek in present-day Lauderdale County, Alabama.

LETTER FROM RETURN J. MEIGS, ESQ. TO THE SECRETARY OF WAR. *Hiwassee Garrison., 1st December, 1809.*

Sir,

I now transmit a general statistical table for the Cherokee Nation. This was attempted in 1806, having at that time the consent of the late secretary of war; but the Cherokees having some unfounded jealousy, that there was something in the measure intended to take advantage of them, and expressing some reluctance to the measure, it was

190

postponed until the last year. It has now been done with as much accuracy as possible, by the interpreters. If there is any error, it has probably arisen from a disposition in some to report a less number of persons, and of livestock than they actually have. The Cherokees on the Arkansas and White Rivers, are not included in the table now transmitted ; it is estimated that there is about 1000, including men, women and children, on the west side of the Mississippi; they have also many cattle and horses, some of them being very wealthy.

The table now forwarded, does not exhibit all their wealth; they have no inconsiderable quantity of cash in circulation, which they receive annually for the sale of cattle and swine. In 1803 they had not a single perch of wagon road in their whole country. In that year they consented at the request of the government to have a road opened for a communication between the states of Georgia and Tennessee. This road with its branches was opened by those states and is about 220 miles, on which they have a turnpike by agreement with the government, for which they are bound to keep the road in good condition for carriages. Since finding the advantages arising from roads, they have at their own expense opened upwards of three hundred miles of wagon road for communication between East and West

Secretary of War, Henry Dearborn

Tennessee. These roads intersect the first-mentioned great road at different points, except one road of 100 miles in length, opened by Doublehead, commencing at Franklin County, Tennessee, and runs to the Muscle Shoals, and it is contemplated to be continued to the navigable waters of Mobile. But to affect this interposition of the government will be necessary; because, from the Shoals to the navigable waters of Mobile, the road must cross lands claimed by the Cherokees and the Chickasaws.

Thus far, as exhibited by the statistical table have the Cherokees prospered by the pastoral life and by domestic manufactory ; but it must be understood that a spirit of industry does by no means pervade the general population ; the greatest number are extremely poor for want of industry. The hunting life is here at an end ; but a prediction for the hunters life pervades a great part of the Cherokees, and many are waiting to hear whether the government will give them the necessary aid and encouragement to migrate to the west side of the Mississippi. Notwithstanding this they have strong local attachment to the place of their birth, and to the sepulchers of their fathers. This being the case, to induce great numbers to migrate, they must be excited by advances of such kind as they need to establish themselves on the rivers mentioned; viz. arms, ammunition, beaver traps, blankets, and some provision of the bread kind, flour or corn, corn will suit them best. After the first year, they will want nothing of the government, except a factory for Indian trade, and a promise of protection by the government. These things once attained, and their attachment and friendship is secured forever—they will be proud of being closely connected with the United States, by whom they have been raised in improvement far above the western Indians.

I am, sir, very respectfully.
Your obedient servant,
Return J. Meigs

Later the Treaty of Tellico finally finalized the establishment of the Federal Road in 1805. The United States commissioners had been insistent enough about the Federal road through Cherokee territory to finally get it approved.

Of more than 100 Cherokee chiefs, only fourteen, including principal chief Black Fox, signed the treaty. Chief Doublehead, long an opponent of the Road, gained the right to a ferry and also the promise of a new boat for his own use. More secretly, James Vann received a series of privileges–ferry rights over the Chattahoochee, a contract to deal with U.S. postal workers, and also some promises to help some of his friends. Rumors of bribes and presents were so widespread that the language of the treaty made a point to rebut them, stating that the Cherokee chiefs were —not influenced by pecuniary motives.

Nicholas Byerst to Meigs – Doublehead may be bought, but it will be a hard matter to sell him.

Secretary of War Henry Dearborn writes to Meigs on October 8, 1805 about the price of land:

"The average price paid for Indian land in the last four years does not amount to one cent per acre and the highest price we paid for cession of Indian claims to land well suited and of good quality is two cents per acre."

The Treaty of October 25, 1805, in consideration of the foregoing cession the United States agree to pay $3,000.00 at once in merchandise, $11,000.00 in 90 days, and an annuity of $3,000.00 in consideration of 8,118 square miles of Cherokee land.

192

Secret Agreement

According to the *Territorial Papers of the United States* by Clarence Carter (1934), the United States makes a secret agreement with Doublehead that he does not refuse. *Following the transmission of the treaties to the Secretary of War by the commissioners, the latter addressed an explanatory communication to him, in which they set forth that by the terms of the treaty of October 25, 1805, there were reserved three square miles of land, "for the particular disposal of the United States, on the north bank of the Tennessee, opposite and below the mouth of Hiwassa." This reservation, they affirmed, was predicated ostensibly on the supposition that the garrison at Southwest Point and the United States factory at Tellico would be placed thereon during the pleasure of the United States, but that they had stipulated with "Doublehead," a Cherokee chief, that whenever the United States should find this land unnecessary for the purposes mentioned it was to revert to him (Doublehead), provided that he should retain one of the square miles to his own use, but should relinquish his right and claim to the other two sections in favor of John D. Chisholm and John Riley in equal shares.*

Doublehead's double son-in-law, Samuel Riley, resides on the property at Southwest Point. The John Riley mentioned in the secret agreement is actually the grandson of Doublehead and the son of Samuel Riley and Doublehead's daughter, Gulustiyu.

According to the *Territorial Papers of The United States*, the entire deal creates great controversy among fellow Cherokees concerning the "Doublehead Tract". *Colonel Martin, who was employed by Commissioner Meigs, also surveyed under the latter's direction during the same month the four small reserved tracts described in the treaty of October 25, 1805. One of these afterwards produced much controversy. The language of the treaty called for three square miles on the north bank of Tennessee River, opposite to and below the mouth of Hiwassee River. Colonel Meigs, who was one of the commissioners who negotiated the treaty and was there-fore entirely familiar with its intent, caused this tract to be surveyed adjoining the main line of cession, extending from Duck River to the mouth of Hiwassee and north of that line, which placed the tract opposite to and above the mouth of Hiwassee, instead of "opposite to and below" the mouth of that river.*

As above stated, while this reserve was ostensibly for the location of a military post and factory or trading establishment, it was really intended for the Cherokee chief Doublehead and other influential persons, as the price of their influence in securing from the Cherokees the extensive cession of land granted by the treaty.

South West Point and Hiwassee Garrison-1826 Tennessee Map

This was sought to be secured by means of a secret article attached to the treaty. This article was reported to the War Department by the treaty commissioners and made a matter of record, but it was never sent to the State Department nor to the Senate for the advice and con-sent of that body. After Agent Meigs had erected the Hiwassee garrison buildings on the tract, suit was brought in 1809 by Colonel Mc-Lung against the agent for the recovery of the land and mesne profits, basing his claim to title upon a grant from the State of North Carolina, of date long prior to the treaty of 1805. The suit was decided in the plaintiff's favor by the Tennessee courts. Subsequently, in 1835, John Riley made application to the Government for compensation for the loss of his one-third interest in this tract. The question was submitted to the Attorney-General of the United States for his opinion. He decided that the secret article, not having been submitted to the Senate for approval, was not to be considered as any part of the treaty; but that, if the commissioners had any authority for making such an agreement, the defective execution of their powers ought not to prejudice parties acting in good faith and relying on their authority; nevertheless, no relief could be had except through the action of Congress.

This secret article was also applicable to the small tract at and below the mouth of Clinch River, to the 1 mile square at the foot of Climberland Mountain, and to the 1 mile square on the north bank of the Tennessee River, where Cherokee Talootiske lived. The first mentioned tract was also intended for the benefit of Doublehead, who leased it February 19, 1806, to Thomas H. Clark for twenty years. Before the expiration of the lease Doublehead was killed by some of his own people. December 10, 1820, the State of Tennessee assumed to grant the tract to Clark.

The other two tracts alluded to of one square mile each were intended for Cherokee Talootiske. May 31, 1808, Talootiske perpetually leased his interest in the Cumberland Mountain tract to Thomas H. Clark. September 17, 1816, Clark purchased the interest of Robert Bell in the same tract, the latter deriving his alleged title under a grant from North Carolina to A. McCoy in July, 1793. This tract was also included in a grant from North Carolina to J. W. Lackey and Starkey Donaldson, dated January 4, 1795. The tract on Tennessee River, Talootiske sold to Robert King, whose assigns also claimed the title under the aforesaid grant from North Carolina to Lackey and Donaldson.

From the phraseology of the treaty in making these several reservations, it was concluded advisable in subsequent negotiations to secure a relinquishment of the tribal title thereto, which was done by the treaty of July 18, 1817. (Carter, 1934)

President Thomas Jefferson

President Thomas Jefferson also had his eyes on the prized territory along the Muscle Shoals that was controlled by the Lower Cherokees under the leadership of Doublehead. Jefferson was the first to propose removal of the Cherokees to the west of the Mississippi.

> *"Jefferson's Administration found itself constantly involved with the Cherokee....They controlled not only some of the most fertile lands of the great Tennessee Valley but also the most direct routes to the entire region....In late summer of 1804, Thomas Jefferson appointed two master Indian managers....to seek transfer of Indian lands in....northern Alabama. Daniel Smith and Return Jonathan Meigs were to pursue, nag, bribe, and cajole the Cherokee relentlessly in season and out....On October 24, 1804, at the Tellico Garrison the two commissioners signed a treaty with the Cherokee for the cession of a narrow strip of land in northeastern Georgia known as the Wafford Plantation....Meigs and Smith had driven an opening wedge, and now other cessions followed in quick order.*
>
> *Neighbors of the Cherokee in Tennessee and northern Alabama were the Chickasaw who in some areas claimed common land. At a site simply labeled 'in the Chickasaw country,' commissioners James Robertson and Silas Dinsmoor in late July of*

1805 struck a bargain with the Chickasaw for a tadpole-shaped parcel of land extending all the way from the Ohio River down into Alabama. The tail of the tadpole touched the Ohio River near Paducah, Kentucky, and its nose extended just below Huntsville, Alabama....The following October at Tellico, Meigs and Smith signed a pair of treaties with the Cherokee — one on the 25th and another on the 27th. In the first, the Cherokee relinquished title to a portion of the lands ceded three months earlier by the Chickasaw, lands to which they also had claimed ownership. They also ceded a large expanse of their lands in the upper Tennessee Valley, while reserving several small tracts for tribal use. In actuality, these reservations were intended for specific individuals, the most notable of them being a chief named **Doublehead***, who leased or sold land for speculative purposes. (Buried in War Department correspondence files are the details of these enterprising ventures, which reflect the complexity of Indian-white relationships.) This treaty also guaranteed American citizens "free and unmolested use' of proposed roads to Georgia and the Tombigbee settlements. The second of these tandem treaties relinquished title to minute parcels of land on the upper Tennessee River and provided free use of the road from Tellico to Tombigbee"* (Clark, and Guice,1989).

President Thomas Jefferson on January 8, 1806, gives a bribe to Doublehead:

The President of the United States presents to Doublehead the sum of one hundred dollars in consideration of his active influence in forwarding the views of the Government in the introduction of the arts of civilization among the Cherokee Nation of Indians and for his friendly disposition towards the United States and for the purpose of enabling him to extend his useful example among the Red people.

Land Deal after Doublehead's Death

In the letter below, Colonel Return Meigs explains how he acquired the land in the upper Elk River drainage that Doublehead had agreed to before his assassination. The deal between Meigs and Doublehead was completed nearly two months after his death. Meigs' letter was sent from Hiwassee Garrison on September 28, 1807, and is as follows:

Sir:
Sometime before Double-head's decease, I stated to him your request as expressed in your letter of the 1ˢᵗ of April last, that the convention line should be so extended as to comprehend all the waters of Elk river. He readily said, he would go with me, and selected three others on whom he could depend, and assured me, that the line should be so extended; but, on his being killed, I expected to meet with difficulty in effecting that business. A few days before I set out on that business, I communicated your request to a large council of chiefs, who were here, receiving their money on account of that

196

convention, and part of their annuity for the present year; from some, through ignorance, and others, from views of taking advantage to raise the compensation, I only received an evasive answer. I then invited the Black Fox, and some others, in whom I could confide, to go with me to the place of commencing the line; and on the 7th instant, met General Robertson and Mr. Freeman, at the Chickasaw Old Fields. When on the ground, we soon agreed that the line should be so run as to comprehend all the waters of Elk river, as will appear by the enclosed agreement; we then run such courses as the nature of the ground would admit of, until we intersected the first waters that fall into the Elk, then a direct line to the Cumberland mountain, and fixed a point on the side of the mountain, from which the rocky face of the mountain is the boundary to lands before ceded. With respect to compensation and presents, as you left it to our discretion, we did the best we could. There is upwards of two hundred families on the land, and all that part of it lying above the Tennessee line, surveyed into sections, and covered by land warrants. The Cherokees being in debt to the United States $1,823, I offered to cancel that debt as a compensation to the nation, for the alteration of the line; they requested to have it made up to $2,000, and $1,000 and two rifles, as presents to the chiefs transacting the business. General Robertson was fully in opinion with me, that we ought not to hesitate as to these terms, and they were agreed to.

I will state some of the reasons that induced us to these terms: 1st. Although they had not the right, they had the power to refuse to extend the line. 2dly. It would have required at least thirty days to have run the traverse, and the true line, at an expense of at least thirty dollars per day, so that near $1,000 is saved on that account. 3dly. To have marched a detachment to remove the inhabitants, would have caused considerable expense; it would have brought distress on the citizens, many of whom went on the land without any design to infract the laws.

These people now feel sentiments of gratitude towards the executive department, and the jurisdiction of the State will now be extended over them; it is really an acquisition to the State of Tennessee. With respect to the chiefs who have transacted the business with us, they will have their hands full to satisfy the ignorant, the obstinate, and the cunning of some of their own people, for which they well deserve this silent consideration. At the time the convention was made, everybody supposed that the waters of Duck river had their source more east than the waters of Elk river, and that the convention line would cover all the land which was in dispute between the Chickasaws and Cherokees. It is a handsome country, and is now settled cheap enough in all conscience. I am authorized by General Robertson to make this report in his absence.

I am, very respectfully, sir, your obedient servant,
Return J. Meigs

197

Lands leased by Doublehead

Lease Issues

After the Cotton Gin Treaty of 1806, Doublehead eagerly accepted settlers who wished to lease his reserved Cherokee lands.

Alford and Drew Lease

The following letter, found in microcopy 208, roll 3, and number 1775, is from Alford and Drew on January 12, 1807, to Doublehead, a principal chief of the Cherokees and other clans at the Muscle Shoals and John D. Chisholm.

Sirs:

We wish to live at the Shoals. We will conform to laws of the Cherokee. We are willing to settle at the Shoals and help Doublehead's people with farming, raising cotton, and other produce, together with house building.
Sincerely,
Hutson Alford and Newit Drew

The following letter to the Indian Agent Return Jonathan Meigs from Doublehead shows he approves of Alford and Drew getting permits to lease land from the Cherokee. His letter was written from Shoal Town and penned by John D. Chisholm, agent to the Cherokees. It appears that Doublehead had to get permission from the agent before he could lease Cherokee lands to settlers. The letter is found microcopy 208, roll 3, and number 1776. The following is Doublehead's letter to Return J. Meigs on January 14, 1807, by John D. Chisholm, agent to the Cherokees from Shoal Town at Muscle Shoals.

Friend and Brother:

I send my friend Chisholm to you to lay before you several matters together with the concerns of Jonathan Arnold, which died in this place and I believe has been robbed of considerable sum of money. I have laid it before Governor Williams. He had desired me to send Chisholm to you with the information about the business. I hope you will assist Chisholm in all my business. I wish to hear about the saw mill and the land at Highwassee. I have desired my friend to consult with you and get you to write the President.

I (Doublehead) am not able to ride or I should have come – I send you letters from two good men (Hutson Alford and Newit Drew) whom Kattygesky and I want to live here. I have consulted with Katty Gisky. Please give them permits.

Your Friend and Brother,
Doublehead

Drew Court Case

In the following court case Newit Drew tries to claim the land leased to him by Doublehead and John D. Chisholm after Doublehead's death. According to the case as given by John Proffatt in *The American Decisions* printed in 1886, Doublehead as an Indian had only a life estate in the property given him by treaty. Also as an Indian, Doublehead could not convey ownership in the land he received by treaty.

Drew Vs. Clarke.
"Relief After Judgment At Law. A court of equity will give relief, after a judgment at law, where the legal remedy is not plain, and where the defendant answers and the cause is heard upon its merits, and when it clearly appears that the complainant is entitled to relief in some jurisdiction.

Mistake of Law. If a man is clearly under a mistake of law which is occasioned by the representations of the other party, he can be relieved as in case of a mistake in matter of fact.

Bill in equity to be relieved against a judgment on a bond assigned to the defendant, and given by the complainant in consideration for a lease of land to Doublehead and Chisholm, in which land, as complainant subsequently ascertained, Doublehead merely had a life interest. The facts further appear from the opinion.

Haywood, for the complainant, urged that there had been a mistake as to Doublehead's interest, against which equity would relieve…and that there were cases where equity would grant relief, although ample redress might be had at law…

Hayes and Whiteside, contra, contended that the complainant ought to have defended himself for the non-performance in the action at law…and that a mistake as to the law would not excuse the performance of a contract.

By Court, White, J. The bill charges that Doublehead, a Cherokee Indian, represented that by virtue of a treaty between the United States and the Cherokees, he owned in fee-simple a certain tract of land; that the complainant, believing the representation, agreed to take a lease on a part of it for the term of ninety-nine years; and that to secure the payment he executed his bond to Doublehead and John D. Chisholm, for six hundred and sixty-six dollars, payable two thirds in property and one third in cash at a future day. That shortly afterward Doublehead died, when the complainant discovered that he had only a life estate in the land, and also that the same tract had been, before the grant to Doublehead, granted by the state of Georgia to Zachariah Cox & Co.; that the defendant received an assignment on the bond after it became due, and with a full knowledge of the failure of the consideration, and that he had brought a suit and recovered a judgment. The answer of the defendant states that the bond was assigned to him after it became due; that he knew at the time of the assignment that the bond had been given about land which Doublehead claimed by virtue of a treaty, but that the treaty is a public law of which the complainant was bound to take notice. The defendant also alleges that he does not know what interest Doublehead pretended to have, and that the complainant agreed to take it as a risking bargain.

Now proof has been made by either the complainant or the defendant; but it has been insisted that enough is admitted by the answer to entitle the complainant to relief. It seems undeniably true that the defendant can stand in no better situation than Doublehead. The bond, if negotiable, was assigned after it became due, and therefore the assignee is affected by any equity which would have affected the obligee. Again, the bond was in part payable in property, and the assignment, even if made before it came due, would not draw after it those consequences attached to negotiable papers.

The question must therefore be now examined as if the suit were between the complainant and Doublehead's representatives. The treaty was entered into on the seventh day of January, 1806. By the first article of it the Cherokees relinquish to the United States all right, title, interest and claim to all that tract of country which lies north of the Tennessee River and westward of a line directed, etc., excepting two described tracts, etc., "which first reserved tract is to be considered the common property of the Cherokees who now live on the same, including John D. Chisholm," etc. Doublehead's name is not mentioned in the reservation, but it is presumed he was one of the Indians who lived upon it. From the words of the treaty, as well as the spirit of it, it would seem that as to the excepted tract the Indian title is not extinguished, because it is appropriated by the Indians themselves to a particular part of their nation. It is certainly true that in the reservation there are no words of inheritance by which to transmit the interest to the heirs of those for whom it was reserved. But to whom it is to belong after their death, whether to the whole nation or to any particular part of it, in the view which the court has taken of the subject, is perfectly unimportant. The bond was given by a citizen of the United States to an Indian and an Indian countryman, to secure the consideration money for an interest in a tract of land, to which the Indian title was not extinguished.

200

By the act of congress, entitled "An act to regulate trade and intercourse with the Indians and preserve peace on the frontiers," passed in the year 1806, it is enacted "that no purchase, grant, lease, or other conveyance of lands, or of any title or claim thereto, from any Indian, or native, or tribe of Indians, within the bounds of the United States, shall be of any validity in law or equity, unless the same be made by treaty or convention entered into pursuant to the constitution," etc. It is conceived this section of the act of congress operates directly on this contract, and renders null whatever agreement the complainant and Doublehead may have made with respect to the land. The complainant could not legally acquire any interest in the land by virtue of the agreement. In point of fact he does not appear to have derived any benefit therefrom, and the bond must be considered as one for which no consideration whatever was given.

In ordinary cases, if one gave his bond without consideration, and at the time of giving it expected he was receiving a consideration, he can only be relieved in equity because a want of consideration, or the failure of the consideration, cannot be inquired into at law. But in this case it has been urged that a court of equity ought not to interfere, because by proper pleading the complainant could have made an effectual defense at law. It appears certainly true that if a party has a plain legal remedy, and from his own negligence or default does not avail himself of it, a court of equity ought not to hear his complaint.

It had been already stated that if this were an ordinary case the want of consideration could be inquired into alone in this court. What then is there to confine it exclusively to an investigation at law? The counsel for the defendant answer that the jurisdiction of this court is ousted in consequence of the act of congress which makes void purchases of the kind now before the court. The answer is by no means satisfactory. The act of congress is entirely silent as to the effect of an instrument given to secure the consideration money for a lease or conveyance of this kind. The "purchase, lease or conveyance" is made void; but whether the purchaser is to be relieved as to the consideration, and if he is, in what court, the statute gives no directions. At all events it cannot be said to be a case in which a plain defense at law could have been made; and yet it is most obvious that the complainant is entitled to relief somewhere.

It has been further urged that the treaty and act of congress are public laws, of which the complainant must be presumed to have had knowledge, and, therefore, he cannot be relieved. It is evident that Drew expected to derive a benefit from the contract when he entered into it; this expectation must have been raised by Doublehead, or some person in his behalf, as his name is not mentioned in the treaty; and if a man is clearly under a mistake in point of law, which mistake is produced by the representation of the other party, he can be relieved as well as if the mistake were as to a matter of fact.

The injunction must be made perpetual." (Proffatt, 1886)

Doublehead probably thought he actually owned the land he had received in treaties and secret agreements. By the same token, Drew actually thought he owned the property he had acquired from Doublehead; however, it appears the court did not agree with Drew.

Thomas Norris Clark Lease

Thomas Norris Clark appears to have benefitted greatly from his relationship with Doublehead by receiving land and property after Doublehead's death. For boarding and schooling two of Doublehead's boys Bird Tail Doublehead and Tassel Doublehead, Clark took some 20 slaves, many horses, and was given land that had originally been given to Doublehead and his family by treaty; however, the treaty concluded on July 18, 1817, relinquished all of Doublehead's claims to his land given by the Cotton Gin Treaty of January 7, 1806.

The treaty of July 18, 1817, and proclaimed December 26, 1817, was held at the Cherokee Agency, in the Cherokee Nation, between Major General Andrew Jackson, Joseph McMinn, governor of Tennessee, and General David Merriweather, commissioners of the United States, and the chiefs, headmen, and warriors of the Cherokee Nation east of the Mississippi River, and those on the Arkansas River, by their deputies, John D. Chisholm and James Rogers, duly authorized by written power of attorney. The material provision number 10: The Cherokee Nation cedes to the United States all claim to reservations made to Doublehead and others by treaty of January 7, 1806 (American Ethnology Bureau, page 213, 1887).

In 1835, John Riley, the son of Samuel Riley and grandson of Doublehead, made application to the United States Government for compensation for the loss of his one-third interest in his tract of land near the junction of the Clinch River and Tennessee River that was given in the secret agreement. The application was submitted to the Attorney General of the United States for his opinion. He decided that the secret article, not having been submitted to the Senate for approval, was not to be considered as any part of the treaty; but that, if the commissioners had any authority for making such an agreement, the defective execution of their powers ought not to prejudice parties acting in good faith and relying on their authority; nevertheless, no relief for John Riley could be had except through the action of Congress.

This secret article was also applicable to the small tract at and below the mouth of Clinch River, to the one mile square at the foot of Cumberland Mountain, and to the one mile square on the north bank of the Tennessee River, where Cherokee Tahloutuskee lived. The first mentioned tract was also intended for the benefit of Doublehead, who leased it

202

February 19, 1806, to Thomas Norris Clark for twenty years. Before the expiration of the lease Doublehead was killed by some of his own people. On December 10, 1820, the State of Tennessee assumed to grant the tract to Clark.

The other two tracts alluded to of one square mile each was intended for Cherokee Tahloutuskee. On May 31, 1808, Tahloutuskee perpetually leased his interest in the Cumberland Mountain tract to Thomas Norris Clark. On September 17, 1816, Clark purchased the interest of Robert Bell in the same tract, the latter deriving his alleged title under a grant from North Carolina to A. McCoy in July, 1793. This tract was also included in a grant from North Carolina to J. W. Lackey and Starkey Donaldson, dated January 4, 1793. The tract on Tennessee River, Tahloutuskee sold to Robert King, whose assigns also claimed the title under the aforesaid grant from North Carolina to Lackey and Donaldson. (American Ethnology Bureau, pages 191-195, 1887)

It is uncertain if Thomas Norris Clark was given all the tracts of land that he had leased by the State of Tennessee, but for sure Clark received the tract of land below the mouth of the Clinch River. It appears that no other individual benefitted as much as Thomas Norris Clark from the death of Doublehead.

Other Legal Problems with Leases

In microcopy 208, roll 3, and number1781, John D. Chisholm's letter respecting the reserve of Doublehead on January 25, 1807.

Muscle Shoals –
Some disposed persons in Cumberland Country have tried at the last Federal Court held at Nashville to have presented to grand jury certain citizens supposed to have purchased land from Doublehead. Doublehead has not sold an acre of land. He has leased some of the ground reserved for him and those that live on it, these to teach Indians farming and quit hunting. Since I have heard of the affair of Mr. Burr, it reminds me of a drifter who come through here. Claims to be a millwright – Has gotten in jail in Nashville for debt. Burr had gotten him out, gave him a horse and advised him to the Creek Nation. He had no passport. Man had gotten lost. While I talked to him, he kept saddle bags close to him. Chisholm thought he was peddling counterfeit money. But I think he was on other business. You might inquire of the jailer at Nashville.

I have been out with Commissioners from Tennessee about a road recognized by Treaty of Tellico from Franklin to the Tombigbee River, not to exceed 180 miles from Nashville to where vessels can come near Mobile.

John D. Chisholm

Letter to Secretary of War enclosing Chisholm letter above was sent on February 12, 1807.

Some persons under improper impressions endeavored to have persons who dealt with Doublehead indicted but prosecution could not be sustained. Government officials want to provide Indians with 30 plows, 100 oxen, and 150 cows.

In microcopy 208, roll 3, and number 1792, the letter is addressed to General Daniel Smith on February 12, 1807.

Burr Plot mentions that Doublehead has not sold an inch of land at the Shoals as has been reported-so he assures me. He has leased land to five persons – Good Citizens – our advice to him from Nashville in June last was not to dispose of any of that land. He had previously bargained as I presume. He then reduced the transaction to the nature of a lease. There had been some prosecutions against the persons said to have purchased from Doublehead but they have come to nothing.

In microcopy 208, roll 3, and number 1801 contains a letter from the Secretary of War dated March 2, 1807. "Doublehead and his neighbors ought not to sell any of their lands to individuals or lease them for more than 21 years."

Leased Lands

Cherokee Receipt Books, Journal of Colonel Return J. Meigs, War Department 1801-1809, Number 67, pages 91-96, Doublehead's Reserve. Indenture make 3rd day of August 1807 between John D. Chisholm on behalf of himself and attorney in fact for Doublehead, an Indian Chief in the Cherokee Nation of the one part and Ezekiel E. Park V, John Towers, Daniel Flournay, Joseph Phillips, Zach Phillips, Tyre Dobny, Jacobs Mitchell, Henry Lucas, John T. Colquet, Abraham Heord, William Randal, Willis Randal, Sam E. Hemphill, Peter Robinson, Bartlet Towns, Zac Sims, Isham S. Fannin, George Heard, Thomas Heard, Cuthburt Collier, Robert Lucas, William Harris, Stephen Gatlin, Robert Sims, Andrew Baxter, John Coffee, John Lucas Jr., Adam Hunter, Thomas Ligon, Thomas Cooper, William Watson, and Oliver Porter of the State of Georgia of the other part: lease formed to the aforesaid lessees: tract or parcel of land on the north side of the Tennessee River at a place known as the Muscle Shoal bonded southward by the Tennessee River, westward by a creek called Tee-kee-ta-no-eh (Cypress), eastward by Chee-wa-lee (Elk River), and from a point ten miles north on Elk river to same on Cypress Creek except the following investors in said tract.

204

Widow Smith & Brother	2,560 acres	John Crudep	480 acres
William Burney	12,000 acres	Captain John Johnson	1000 acres
Dr. McPherson	12,000 acres	Town & Ferry	640 acres
Captain John Hays	6,000 acres	P. Moore	640 acres
Lodwich Moore	600 acres	Frederick Peeler	12,000 acres
Doublehead	1,500 acres	Thomas Butler	1,200 acres
John D. Chisholm	1,000 acres	Calwell Estridge	200 acres
John Cragmiles	640 acres	William Stevens	100 acres
Hudson Alford	800 acres	William Hester	100 acres
			53,460 acres

To the above company a 99 year lease – renewable for 900 years – consider it to be paid in 4 installments.

National Archives Microfilm Publications, Records of the Cherokee Indian Agency in Tennessee 1808-1809, Microcopy 208, roll 4, number 2231,Correspondence and Miscellaneous Records 1808-1809, Names of Tenants on Doublehead's Reserve, May 25, 1809. Original Leases 20….Under them 18.

A Man Name Unknown	Josiah Glover	Adam Lackey
Hudson Alford	Mr. Hatch	Mr. Longane
Julius Alford	Harmon Hays	James Milstead
Samuel Anderson	John Hays	Zellous Milstead
Mr. Birdwell	Thomas Hays	Benjamin Moore
William Burney	Mr. Hemphill	Dr. McPherson
Gabriel Butler	Thomas Hull	Fredrick Peeler
John Butler	Moses Jones	Dr. Potter
Richard Butler	David Keeler	Benjamin Rays
Thomas Butler	John Keeler	James Taylor
Clark & Hall	Mr. Keeler	Finey Thomas
James Cummings	Mr. Keeler	William Weir
Cullin Earp	Mr. Kooley	

National Archives of Microfilm Publications, Records of the Cherokee Indian Agency in Tennessee 1801-1835, Microcopy 208, roll 4, number 2311, Correspondence and Miscellaneous Records, 1808-1809, Intruders on Shoals Creek, May 23-24, 1809.

Daniel Beeler	East Branch	George Circle	East Branch
Jonathan Chambers	East Branch	Sterline Clack	SW Branch

James Coe	SW Branch	Wm McConnel	W Fork
John Crawley	SW Branch	Wm McFenal	E Branch
Moses Crout	W Fork	Alex Mackey	E Branch
Mr. Ben Cutbeard	W Fork	Mays	SW Br. 2 in family
John Haley	SW Branch	Joel Phillips	W Shoals Creek
Richard Haley	SW Branch	Mr. Hugh Randolph	E Branch
Ezek'l Heraldson	E Fork	Spires Roach	SW Branch
Jno. Higgs	E Branch	Thos Robinson	W Fork
Simon Higgs	E Branch	Fred Shalley	W Shoals Creek
William Hinson	W Shoal Creek	Jno. Shoate	W Fork
George Hoge	W Shoal Creek	Wm Shoate	W Fork
Sam Inmand	W Fork	Jas Tade	W Shoals Creek
Wm McCann	W Fork	Jno. Welch	E Fork

Intruders on West Bank of Elk River 27 May 1809.

Andrew Coffen	W Bank	Mr. Peaton	W Bank
Mr. Freeman	W Bank	James Radish	W Bank
Geo Harper	W Bank	Jno Reynolds	W Bank
Jno Manasce	W Bank	Reuben Riggs	W Bank
Jno Payne	W Bank		

Chickasaws want White Intruders Removed

In microcopy 208, roll 4, and number 2303 is General James Robertson's letter from Nashville, Tennessee, on May 6, 1809. *"The Chickasaws have been meeting in council. I am now assured that if the white people are not removed off of Doublehead's reserve by government that the Chickasaw will take measures to do it."*

According to the Territorial Papers of the United States by Clarence Carter (1934), the Chickasaws pushed for removal of the intruders and the United States recognized Chickasaw claims. The Chickasaws succeeded in having the intruders removed from their lands and inadvertently the building of Fort Hampton in Limestone County, Alabama, for that purpose.

In the meantime the Chickasaws, having learned that the United States had purchased of the Cherokees their supposed claim to the territory as far west as the Tennessee River, including a large region of country to the westward of the limits of the cession of 1805 by the former, construed that fact as a recognition of the sole and absolute title of the Cherokees thereto, and be in consequence very much excited and angered. They were only pacified by an official letter of assurance from the Secretary of War, addressed to Maj. George Colbert, their principal chief, wherein he stated that in purchasing the Cherokee right to the tract in question the United States did not intend to destroy or impair the right of the Chickasaw Nation to the same; but that, being persuaded no actual boundary had ever been agreed on between the Chickasaws and Cherokees and that the Cherokees had some claim to a portion of the lands, it was thought advisable to purchase that claim, so that whenever the Chickasaws should be disposed to convey their title there should be no dispute with the Cherokees about it.

Petition to Stay on Chickasaw Land

According the Territorial Papers of the United States, Mississippi Territory, Elk River, Sims' Settlement, September 5, 1810, the intruders on Chickasaw lands petitioned the President and Congress to allow them to stay.

To his Excellency James Maddison President of the United States of America and the honourable Congress assembled:

We your petitioners humbly sheweth that a great many of your fellow citizens have unfortunately settled on what is now called chickasaw land- which has led us into difficultys that tongue cannot express if the orders from the ware department are executed in removeing us off of said land. However in a government like ours founded on the will of the people we have reason to hope and expect that we shall be treated with as much lennity as the duty you owe to Justice will permit. We therefore wish, Without the shade or colour of falshood, to leve to your consideration the main object of our setling of this country In the first Place, we understood that all the land on the north side of tennessee river was purchased of the Indians which was certainly the Case, and further we understood that this was congress land as we call it and by paying of two Dollars per acre we should obtain An undoubted title to our lands and avoide the endless law suits that arise in our neighboring states in the landed property under these and many other impressions of minde that appeared inviteing to us to setle here a great many of us solde our possessions and Came and settled here in the winter and spring of 1807 without any knoledg or intention of violating the laws of government or Infringing on the right of another nation and we remained in this peacefull situation untill the fall of 1807 when General Robertson Came on runing the chickasaw boundary line and he informed us that, though the cherokees had sold this land, yet the chickasaws held a clame to it as their right. And now as booth nations had set up a clame to this land and Government haveing extingushed the cherokee clame; and we who are well acquainted with the boundarys of this country do think in Justice that the cherokees had undoubtedly the best right to this land we could state our reasons for thinking so, in many cases, but we shall only refurr you to one particular, that is when Zacheriah Cocks made a purchase of parte of this country and came in order to settle it he landed on an island in the Mussell Shoals, and was making preparations to in garrison himself but when the Cherokees Understood his intentions they got themselves together and sent in messingers to him telling him if he did not desist and remove his men out of their country they would certainly imbody themselves and cut him off. And Cocks took the alarme. And left the Island in the night. And if the Cherokees had not defended this country at that time it may be persumed that it would have been taken from the Chickasaws without asking of them anything about their right to it. For the Cherokees do say that they have held an antiant clame to it which they never lost by sword or treaty untill extinguished by government. And should this be the camse and appeare to your satisfaction that the Cherokees had at least as good a right as the Chickasaw and you haveing that right invested in you-and you are allso willing to pay the Chickasaw for their clame and they refuse to sell it where then can there remain a single doubt In the publick Minde of doing the Chickasaws any kind of unjuistice in makeing use of the Cherokee clame and saying: if they will not take a reasonable price for their clame we will not remove our fellow citizens off which will bring many women and children to a state of starvation mearly to gratify a heathan nation Who have no better right to this land than we have ourselves And they have by estemation nearly 100000 acres of land to each man Of their nation and of no more use to government or society than to saunter about upon like so many wolves or bares whilst they who would be a supporte to government and Improve the country must be forsed even to rent poore stony ridges to make a support to rase their famelies on whist there is fine fertile countrys lying uncultivated and we must be debared even from inJoying a small Corner of this land but we look to you the boddy of government as a friendly father to us and believe it Compleatley within your power Whilst you are administering Justice between us and the Chickasaws to say with the greatest propriety that we have once purchased this land and we will not remove our fellow citizens off but let them remain as tennants at will untill the Chickasaws may feell a disposition to sell us their clame therefore we your humble petitioners wish you to take our standing duely into consideration and not say they are a set of dishoneste people who have fled from the lawes of their country and it is no matter what is done With them.for we can support our carractors to be other ways and it is our wish and desire to protect and supporte our own native Government we must informe you that in the settling of this country men was obliged to expose themselves very much and the Climate not helthy a number of respectable men have deceased and left their widows with families Of alphan [orphan] children to rase in the best way they can And you might allmost as well send the sword amongst us as the fammin the time being short that our orders permits us to stay on we wish you to send us an answer to our petition as soon as posable and, for heavens Sake Pause to think what is to become of these poore alphan families who have more need of the help of some friendly parish than to have the strictest orders executed on them who has not a friend in this unfeeling world that is able to asist them Either in geting off of said land or supporting when they are off we are certain in our own minds that if you could have A true

208

representation of our carractor the industry we have made and the purity of our intentions in settling here together with the justice of our cause you would say in the name of God let them stay on and eat their well earned bread. Perhaps our number may be fare more than you are apprised of from the best calculation that we can make there is Exclusive of Doubleheads reserv 2250 souls on what is called Chickasaw land and all of us could live tollerabie comfortable if we Could remain on our improvements but the distance is so great if we are removed off that we cannot take our produce with Us and a great many not in a circumstance to purchase more will in consequence of this be brought to a deplorable situation We shall therefore conclude in hopes that on a due consideration we shall find favour in the sight of your most honourable Body which will in duty binde your petitioners to ever Pray &c.

Sims	Wm Cooper	Wm. Kile
James Sims	Wm Conway	Samuel Bradley
Michael Odaniell	Charles Easely	William Adams
Thomas Skagg	John Scaggs	Roland McKenny
Wiliam Payne	John Eppler	James McKenny
Berry Matlock	Jonathan Eppler	John McKenny
George Brown	James Neill	Ruben McKenny
James Reynolds	Isham Brown	Robert McKenny
Larkin Webb	James Brown	William McKenny
Isaac Crowson	Abraham Brown	John Lynn
Benjimen Osbourn	Edward Davis	Elijah Price
Robert Cravens	Rawleigh Dodson	John Hogges
Andrew Arnett	Aaron Luisley	Calvin Wittey
Jonathan Cochron	Simon Foy	Caleb Juett
Hoseph Bradley	Benj. Murrell	Isaac Murrell
James Wooley	James Ball	George Arbuthnot
Henry Lysby	[MS illegible]	Francis Daugherty
Isaac Gibson	John McCutchen	Bejman Carrel
Samuel Easely	David McCutchen	Asa Magge
David Simon	John Calwell	Sammell Preed Jun
John Hoddge	John Bidell	Sammul Preed
John Coward	John Rosson	James Preed
Charles Skaggs Sen	Simon Rosson	Christopher Baylor
Charles Skaggs Jur	Richard Linville	Marckel Stockdon
Charles Williams	Wm. Nelson	Thomas Redus
William Adams	John Nelson	Abraham Sims
Wm Bowling Sen	James Ford	Richard Murrell
Wm Bowling Jr	James Caldwell	John Daugherty

James Hodge
James Hood
William Mayer
William Hodge
William Hoodser
Edmond Fears
William Hood Jr
Ely Robertson
Samuel Robertson
Michel Robertson
John Allon
John Sessoms
Amos Moor
William Ellis
John Thomas
Joshua Perkins
Issac Fraey
Lovill Coffman
Cornelius Gatliff
James Redey
John Panton
Jesse Panton
William Hooker
Thomas Pool
Philmer Green Senr
Jere. McKellins
Reuben Riggs
William Candon
James Riggs
Robert Tayler
Enoch Tayler
John Tayler
Jas Wilder
Fracis Ascaugh
Joab Arbagh
Jas. Wherrey
John Bell
Benjamin Russell
Edward Frost
Jas. Anderson

Joseph Evans
Henry Evans
John Scallern
Jacob Scallern
John Wainwright
John Myers
James Green
John Mowery
Alexander Dutton
George Fergel
John Sauls
Reel Matcok
John Bartell
John Kim
Andr Jackson
Henry Miller
Henry Cross
Jonathan Adams
Thos. Adams
Robt. Wallis
James Isaac
Hardin Hulsey
William Hill
Jas Miller
John Hamlin
Samuel Smith
Ellexander Smith
Felps Smith
Wm. Smith
Bryan Smith
Jonathon Greenhow
Wm. Greenhow
Greenbery Greenhow
John Croslin
Abraham Miller
Robert Foury
Joseph Calvert
James Mossy
James McMahhan
Jessy Cooper

David Miller
Levi Cummins
Mark Mitchell
Allen Cotton
John Cotton
William Cox
Thomas Hardy
George Loften
John Tayler
John Reed
Elkin Tayler
Lennard Lofton
Joseph Foster
Abraham Kirkelot
John Kirkendall
Jos. Jones
Levi Cooper
John Cooper
John Paine
Fuller Cox
Sami Cox
Joseph Looker
William Riggs
Bridges Freeman
Charles Hulsey
Beverly Philips
Shaderick Cross
Benjamin Ishmal
Benjn. Cross
Benjamin French
Henry Croslin
Jessey Richardson
Joseph England
David Dudden
John Crage
Michal Trimble
Elisha Rainbolt
Jas Craig
John Mitchell Snr
Elisha Garritt

210

John Mitchell Jnr
George Mitchell
Wm. Smith
Jno. Sanders
Reuben Sanders
Joseph Carnes
Wm Carnes
Redden Crisp
Wm. Black
Levi Black
Jos. Keen
John Allman
Walter Tremble
Elye Hornback
Wm. McGowen
Robt. Hodges Jnr.
Robert Stenson
John Smith
John Runnels
Francis Bird
Thos. Henderson
Shadrach Morres
Lewis Tacket
William Kellett
Joseph Kellett
James Kellett
James Humphrs
[Humphreys?]
William Humphrs
Charles Smith
William Stephens
Samuel Nelson
George Honbre
Joel James
Henry McGuin
Wm Mullin
Thomas Mullin
John Toliver
Matt Smith
James Mullens

Jaret Brandon
James Smith
John Miller
Elijah Major
James Major
John Trimble
Joshua Brunson
David Parker
John Ray
John Carnham
Jacob Pyeatt
James Pyeatt
Aron Gibson
Cabot Turner
Isack Shipman
John Hakins
George S. Wilson
Josha Bruntson
James Slaughter
Jesop Luster
John Luster
James Luster
Robert McGowen
DanI McIntyre
Alexr Masky (or Marky)
John Chambers
Thos Price
Joel Philips
Wm. Stinson
George Hauge
Ezek. Smith
Wm Smith
Andrew Smith
Jame McConel (or
McCarrel)
Sami McConell
Jams M. McConell
William Chambers
Jno. Webb
George Bankhead

Jno Bankhead
Michael Shaly
George Shaly
Fredrich Shaly
Moses Crosen
[Crowson?]
Moses Chot
John Vans
Duncan McAntire
William Voss
Alex Miller
William Cochran
John Welch
William Welch Senr
Beverly Luster
David Luster
Jas Bevers
Jonathan Burleson
John Burleson
Mathew Brunston
William Slaughter
Jonathan Blair
John Billinsly
Johnathan Greenhow
Clouds Greenhow
Alexander Moor
Robert Moor
John Umphres
[Humphreys?]
Archable Tremble
James Garner
John Bell
James Burlston
Robert Thresher
David Thompson
John Roguey(?)
David Capshaw
Malachi Reeves
Robert Gresham
Amos French

William W. Capshaw
George Ogel
George McCown
David Allerd
William Magers(?)
Harda Allerd
Georg Cooper
David Water
John Wager
Harmon Horn
Banra Devon
John Gebbens
Robt Gebbins
Saml Gibbons
James Gibbons
Jos. Gibbons
Clemen Arman(?)
Mathew Brewer
James Norman
Aaron Shote
John Shote
John Wynn
M. Armstrong
Thos. Dodd
Isaac Perrett
Jeremiah Rowlen
Mitchell O'Neel
Jessy Dillion
Tiery O'Neel
Hirram O'Neel
Joseph Brunson
John Parmerly
Richard Robertson
George Taylour
Ellken Taylor
John Taylour Junr.
Robert Taylour
Hanum Taylour
John Taylour Sen.
Thomas Read

John Read
Wm. Taylour
Nathanniel Hannet
[Hamet?]
James Dunahoo
James Long
John Cooper
Leire Cooper
James Dunham
Alexr Dunham
Thomas Brighton
Names of the Widows
Damarias Bowling
Amerida Hatton
Betsey Williams
Mahaley Robertson
Gilly Crowson
Milly Hogwood
Drankey(?) Medders
Patsey Carter
Caty Lawrence
Joan Black
Ann Johnstons
Susan Wigges
Betsey Cooper
Ann Grin(?)
Elizebeth Sims
Grizell Sims
Polly Prigman
Sally Williams
Any Taylour
Christiana McRavey
Men's Names
Abner Camnon (or
Camron)
Jessey Beavers
John Hoaton
Robert Hoaton
Nicholess Boren
James Boren

Abner Boren
Henry Davis
Benjamin Land
Andrew Blithe
Jacob Blithe
Wm. Lilly
Obediah Martin
Wm. Martin
Henson Day
Andrew Pickins
Joseph L. Jones
Hugh Bradon
Adam Burney
James Burney
Wm. Ferrell
Owen Shannon
William Cooper
Jas. Braden
James Steward
John Cooper
Levi Cooper
Chale Dever
John Black Junr
Prier Kile
Reuben Smith
Isac Lann (or Lanse)
Eli Tidwell
Millin Tidwell
Eli Tidwell
Daniel Kinny
Owin Shannon Se.
James Renn
H. T. Hendry
Jos L. Hendry
William Cramer
William Murrell
William Smith
John Smith
John Black Senr

212

Gabriel Tayour [Taylour?]

Natheniell Harbin(?)

Jessee Harbin

James Harbin

Robert Wood

Millenton Tidwell

James Leath

Edward Shoat

Vantenten [Valentin?] Shoat

John Taylour

Benjamin Tutt

Thomas Kile

James Pickins

[Endorsed] Petition (addressed to James Madison, President of United States by 450 of the Intruders upon the Chickasaw Territory: Rece^d Oct. 1st 1810.

Simon Foy and Thomas Dodd *are not on the 1812 Giles tax list, but are mentioned by McCallum as early Elk River settlers. Both are also on the 1809 intruders list.*

Fort Hampton at the Doublehead Reserve became home to the soldiers' whose duty it was to rid the reservation lands of "intruders."

Doublehead Conspiracy

A long term conspiracy to assassinate Doublehead developed over several years. Many of the Upper Cherokees disliked the control Doublehead exerted along the Tennessee River Valley trade routes. They envied the favor he found with the United States government officials, who tried to influence him with land deals. Many disliked his brutality in his dealings with the killing and eating of Overall and Burnett, Cavett's Station murders and the small boy who was captive, and also the murder of his fifth wife who was the sister-in-law of James Vann. Many hated the land leases along the Muscle Shoals of the Great Bend of the Tennessee River he was making for personal gain and money.

Letters Seeking Meigs' Support

The Glass, Doublehead, and other chiefs write to Colonel Meigs on March 23, 1805, asking him to tell the young chiefs they did not sell Cherokee lands.

"We should be glad for you to write us that we sold no land to you. Such a letter is needed to satisfy the young men that we sold no land . . . the young warriors is trying all they can to put us out of place, but we hope to do everything for the good of our Country."

On October 3, 1806, Doublehead writes to Colonel Meigs letting him know of his concerns about ill will toward himself from younger chiefs. It appears that Doublehead sees the handwriting on the wall and it is telling him that he is in trouble with his people as follows:

"You know very well that this annuity could not support the nation in clothing or houseall furniture; it is the Traders that Brings these things to us and it is the same with the white people; we cannot live without Trade, for the Trader brings his hoes, axes, hatchets, and Brass and Tin Kettles, powder, ect. amongst us and our people has got indebted to them.

. . . you know and so do the marchants that I can pay my debts myself, but some who are in debt are poor people and the best hunting ground now belongs to the United States and I can't see how the poor Indians is to pay their debts if the nation would not use its tribal resources to do it. It seems hard to Take away from a family that has but two or three cowes to pay the Trader with it.

It seems that my people think hard of me, and if you know of anything I have done that is not Right, Tell it to the people. Such great and Good men as the young chiefs pretend to be ought to be ashamed. Their behavior has hardly been unselfish in the past: when the annuity was given out did they not keep some of the Best goods and say that they would give in money to the nation, and where is that money?

. . . [I can] quit my nations Concearns and goe hom and mind my own Buisness."

Again Doublehead appeals to Colonel Meigs on January 14, 1807, speaking of the enemies of improvement. He probably knows a conspiracy against him is building and probably perceives that Meigs is not helping his situation:

"Desing and foolish persons that are Enemies to the improvement and Civeliation of their People, Enemies to all Improvement, Enemies to all that wish to improve the Blessing that the great and good all-being has Blessed them with; their Eyes and Ears are shut to such things as they ought to know."

Charles Hicks voices his dislike for Doublehead found in microcopy 208, roll 3, and number 1681. Charles Hicks sends a letter on August 19, 1806, a little less than a year before Doublehead's assassination, expressing the dislike for Doublehead by the Upper Cherokees as follows:

"I can assure you that the upper (Cherokee) is very much exasperated at the language of Doublehead that you in the United States is to furnish him two or three thousand men to uphold his authority and he further said that you are not to listen to any solution that the upper towns may make you – but you would listen to his, Doublehead's talks, and his part of the nation and that you had promised to visit him and George Colbert (Doublehead's double son-in-law) – and about other land jabbering which appears to be probability from the amount given on that subject."

Letters Complaining of John Rogers

Doublehead's Letter

In microcopy 208, roll 3, and number 1562, Doublehead's letter of October 3, 1806, is complaining of the talk at Sawta in July last and complaining of John Rogers. The letter from Doublehead is addressed to Colonel Return J. Meigs.

the 3 Oct 1806

Friends & Brothers:

  It is thirteen nights, ago since the talks was at Wills Town, thoe I expect you have been informed before this, I was sick at the time and lay within a quarter of a miles of the place, I expect that you have been informed you what John Rogers head man had to say at the talk, that is some of the half breeds, and expects that you will send their talk to the Secretary of War, perhaps that John Rogers talk will go further than the Secretary of War tells on the President, he thinks that he and his party can out do the United States. The treaty was made and concluded on by both parties last December in the presence of all the great men of the United States. Since that, there was a meeting called at Estaneley and there some people objected the treaty such as Rogers Party, since that there was a meeting called at Sautey on the Tennessee where you and the old chiefs had a talk and had all your talk and papers on it, and there you and the chiefs all agreed and confirmed the treaty that we made with the President and the Secretary of War, if the United States has appointed a fifth white man to consult with the Indians, I do not know of it, I knowed there was one appointed for this nation that is yourself and Colonel Hawkins from the Creeks, and one for the Chickasaws and one for the Choctaws, but we did not know that John Rogers was appointed by the United States to meddle on concerns with public business and throw the President's talks aside, if so the chiefs would be glad the Secretary of War would inform them and keep Rodgers and confuse the people in this nation and keep them distracted, Rodgers informed the counsel at Willstown and the people at large, that you told him that he must press on the minds of the people to agree of dividing the land in their country, and that it was the secretary's talk likewise and that he might by so doing become very rich, that he might buy the poor Indians lands with whiskey. These words he spoke in public and there is another thing I expect that the great men that meets in Congress do not sign the President's name to paper when he is a sleep, these people sent you their talk has done that signed the Black Foxes name to that letter when he was asleeping, I think it is a great shame to try to deceive the Secretary of War by signing our old head man's name to that paper and when he was not at the head of that talk – as to the objecting against paying the traders their debts against us, is because they think I owe a great deal to my Friends the merchants but you know and so do the merchants, that I can pay my debts myself and it is but five or six years ago since I began to talk a little, but for all that I can pay my debts - now my friends ever since the treaty of Holston there has been a compensation allowed to this nation, and the great men of the United States abed the payment ever since that treaty, you no very well that this annuity could not support the nation in clothing, or house all furniture, it is the Traders that brings those things to us and it is the same with the white people. We cannot live without trade, for the traders bring hoes hatchets and brass and tin kittles powder and such amongst us, and our people has got indebted to them and some are poor people, and the best hunting grounds now belongs to the United States and I can't see

216

how the poor Indians is to pay their debts – it seems hard to take away from a family that has but two or three cows and pay the trader with it, now I give you my talk it seems that my people think hard of me, and if you know of anything that I have done that is not Right, tell it to the People, I always think that I follow the Talk of the Council. You remember the time when the chief give consent that there should be a public road through the nation, at the same time the chiefs agreed that I should keep a ferry at South West Point and that Thorp should join with me – Sometime after Riley joined with me and that I might have the land that lied over against the point and use that up or down the river where it pleased, but you can look over your papers and see the agreement made, show it to the people that makes themselves busy in my affairs – they ought to look back and see themselves. You remember very well some time ago at Tellico Block house that you give out publick money to these men that is always a talking, and what have they done with it, and when the annuity was give out did they not keep some of the best goods and say they would give in money to the nation, and where is that money, no these men never look back and see what they have done. I might be mistaken in these such men they may be fitten to rule the country, the people at large may see that they mean to do justice, because they have turned the little Tarripine out of his house that lived at the mouth of Highwassee, that shows how good these men is that man has lived there a long time and he has the best right to that place and keep a ferry at the place and not for them half breeds, such great and good men as they pretend to be ought to be ashamed and not do so and as to myself, I have been this frontier on fifteen years in public business, and the old chiefs that first authorize me to do public business is dead, and I now lived on the land that the Chickasaws sold to the United States as the United States was good enough to give me some of it. I will now go home and mind my own Business – and from the day forward I quit my nation concerns-I do not say I quit the United States Talks. I hold that fast and I beg you as a friend to correct my letter, as I would you to make this public in print that everybody may see it.

Your Sincere Friend,
Doublehead.
Col Meigs

John Lowery's Letter

John Lowery sends a letter to Colonel Return J. Meigs complaining of John Rodgers and company's talk at Sowta in July 1806.

October 23, 1806

I will try to explain what has taken place since I saw you at Sauty. You recollect the laws made and all the chiefs signed their names to it.

Now there has been a talk by some of the gossiping chiefs and indeed some of them, not chiefs, atole trying to break that law. What the country coming to if the young simple drunken chiefs can break the law the old chiefs made. You remember that when the talk was held at Sauty that there was one or two that tried to break it then and I don't doubt but they would have broken it then if they had sat still and saw nothing. What was done was right and I signed my name to it.

Now I must inform you what I saw to the old chiefs when they were holding this last talk. I told "Chiller" to tell Black Fox and all the old headmen not to sign their names to it.

I was so uneasy I took the trouble to hunt the Path Killer and told him not to sign his name for their talk was for nothing. Hunted the Black Fox and found him asleep and I was much pleased to think that he was not where the talk was. Black Fox's name and Jacks were forged to the talk they sent you. Those at that talk were John Walker, Will Saeey, John Watts, Young Wolf, George Fields, Dick Fields, James Brown, John & Colaquashie Spears, Charles Hicks. Now the whites, Rogers, Mr. Rose. Mr. Vance, Mrs. Macdonnel,

John Lowry

Black Fox's Letter

Principal Chief of the Cherokee Nation Black Fox wrote a letter on October 23, 1806, to Colonel Return J. Meigs. Black Fox was confirming the talks at Sauta last July and requesting the money to be kept until he comes up to receive it.

Cherokee, Turkey Town, 23 October 1806.

Sir & Brother:
You are appointed by the United States to act in this nation agent for us and that you should do justice to us if you see anything that was against the interest of our nation. My young chiefs will inform you what they know.

Brother we had a meeting at Sautey on Tennessee and there I and the rest of the chiefs agreed to the talks was made at Washington. The meeting we had there was a handsome one and both parties agreed to the talks and we are determined from this council to hold that fast and those men first appointed should act as before mentioned and you know their names.

When you return home from the line, I shall expect to hear from you. We shall be ready to go up to receive our annuity. Give us notice some few days before hand that we may get ready. The money you keep till I come to pay the traders. We have stopped the head Bird and his party from going to war against the Osages – I am your friend and his Brother

Black X Fox mark
Wrote and compiled by John Thompson

Samuel Riley's Letter

Doublehead's son-in-law Samuel Riley sends a letter about John Rogers as found in microcopy 208, roll 3, and number 1729. Samuel Riley's letter is dated November 29, 1806, and concerns the annuities and John Rogers. Riley also discusses John W. Hooker who was the United States Factor at the public store at Tellico in Tennessee.

I inquired respecting of Rogers conversation against government and was told by two respectable men as follows that Mr. Hooker told him that when he was the North that in conversation with Mr. (Thomas) Jefferson. He ask him if he could get the Cherokees to run in-debt to the amount or ten or twelve thousand dollars in the public store. Mr. Hooker told him for answer fifty thousand, well says he, that is the way I intended to get their country for to get them to run in-debt to the public store and they will have to give their land for payment. Mr. Hooker's answer was if that is your determination you must get some other person to keep the store.

I am yours to serve,
Samuel Riley

According to microcopy 208, rolls 6 and 7, and number 3380, John Rogers gives testimony on the Cherokee-Creek Boundary. *"On December 22, 1815, John Rogers gave a deposition on Cherokee-Creek Boundary. John Rogers, age 69 years, lived in Creek Nation from 1768-1780."* John Rogers, a white man, married a Creek Indian lady and they had a son, James Rogers.

Death of Doublehead

Eventually, Doublehead paid with his life for taking government handouts to benefit him personally and for his ironclad control of cotton trade down the Tennessee River. Doublehead's family and friends controlled a large section of the Tennessee River from the Mississippi State line through the middle of east Tennessee. Doublehead's executioners used his practice of securing personal gain at the expense of the Cherokee Nation as the prime reason for his planned assassination.

Other reasons which led to the decision to kill Doublehead included his brutality especially in the murder of his wife who was the sister-in-law to James Vann. Doublehead's actions at Cavett's station in the killing of the family who had just surrendered along with the tomahawk killing of a small boy that was taken captive created strong resentment with James Vann and Major Ridge who witnessed the gory scene.

Another factor included the government annuities which were distributed among Doublehead's friends of the Lower Cherokees. Alex Saunders had complained to President Thomas Jefferson the year before the assassination that the Upper Cherokees were not getting their fair share. President Jefferson told Saunders that the government gave the annuities to the chiefs and headmen and it was their responsibility to distribute the money fairly.

A big reason Doublehead got into trouble with the Upper Cherokees was the leasing of Cherokee lands for his monetary gain to white farmers. However, the final straw was giving some of the favorite hunting grounds of the Cherokee to the government for personal gain in large tracts of land set aside specifically for Doublehead.

Assassination Accounts

In August 1807, the Cherokees were to receive annuities from the government at Hiwassee Garrison. On the same date, the Cherokees had prepared for a stickball game and played the game near the garrison which was close to the Hiwassee River in east Tennessee near present-day Calhoun, Tennessee. Stickball was the recreational sport of the Cherokee Nation, and attracted large crowds which gambled on the outcome. At this stickball game in August 1807, more than a thousand Cherokee Indians were present and others from Hiwassee Garrison including many white traders attracted by the prospect of selling their goods to the Cherokee.

One account of Doublehead's death is an eyewitness Caleb Starr, after the stickball game was over late that afternoon Doublehead mounted his horse and was preparing to leave when he was approached by a drunken Indian by the name of Bone Polisher and his friend. The two became belligerent and accused Doublehead of being a traitor to the Cherokee Nation for selling the lands of the Cherokee people. For a while Doublehead sat silent on his horse and remained calm; however, the two continued to become more angry and abusive grabbing the reins of Doublehead's horse.

Bone Polisher's friend swung at him with his tomahawk, which Doublehead received on his left arm and nearly severed his thumb. Doublehead drew his pistol snapped it at his assailant. As Bone Polisher then rushed him, Doublehead drove the cock of his gun into Bone Polisher's skull killing him instantly.

Sometime after dark, Doublehead, who had been drinking, went to Walker's Ferry on the Hiwassee River near present-day Calhoun, Tennessee. The ferry was owned by John Walker, Jr. who was one of James Vann's close associates. In July 1834, John Walker Jr. would be killed by James Foreman, the grandson of Doublehead, and Anderson Springston, the son of Doublehead's wife Nannie Drumgoole and half-brother to Bird Tail Doublehead. Bird Tail Doublehead, son of Doublehead and Nannie Drumgoole, was only twelve when his father was murdered. At the time of his father's death, Bird Tail was boarding and receiving schooling while living in the home of Thomas Norris Clark.

Doublehead entered John McIntosh's Tavern and continued his drinking. Among those whom he encountered there was The Ridge, who had turned against Doublehead after his actions at Cavett's Station. Ridge and James Vann had planned for a long time to assassinate Doublehead; however, this night Vann was too drunk to carry out the deed (Ridge would later become known as Major Ridge). Accompanying Ridge was a half-breed known as Alexander (Alex) Saunders, who had complained to President Thomas Jefferson a year earlier that Doublehead was preventing the Upper Cherokees from getting their fair share of the government annuities. Another person at the tavern was John Rogers, an old white man who had long resided in the nation and whom Doublehead a year prior had warned his friend Colonel Return J. Meigs that Rogers was a trouble maker. Rogers began to revile Doublehead, much after the manner of Bone Polisher. The event escalated to the shooting and wounding of Doublehead.

Doublehead's friends set out with him for Hiwassee Garrison, but fearing they would be overtaken, turned aside, and concealed him in the loft of Schoolmaster James Black's house. The next morning, two warriors of the Bone Polisher's clan traced Doublehead by his blood to his hiding place. At the same time Ridge and Saunders came galloping up, shouting the war whoop. Sam Dale and Colonel James Brown, of Georgia, followed them. The wounded chief was lying on the floor, his jaw and arm terribly lacerated. Ridge and Saunders each leveled their pistols, but both missed fire. Doublehead sprang upon Ridge and would have overpowered him had not Saunders discharged his pistol and shot him through the hips. Saunders then made a rush on Doublehead with his tomahawk, but the dying chief wrenched it from him, and again leaped upon Ridge. Saunders seized another tomahawk and drove it into his brain. When he fell another Indian crushed his head with a spade. The last Chickamauga Cherokee Chieftain now lay dying on the floor. Caleb Starr said he rushed upstairs and took Doublehead by the hand as he drew his last breath.

Caleb Starr Version 1838

The following is the actual testimony on Doublehead's death and is found in the Records of the Bureau of Indian Affairs, RG 75, Entry 236 (Estate of Doublehead). The following is the statement of an eyewitness account of Caleb Starr made on August 11, 1838, about the killing of Chief Doublehead:

Caleb Starr makes oath that he was very well acquainted with the Chief Doublehead and has often heard the Cherokees speaking freely of Doublehead's wealth and understood that he was well off at the time he was killed, and that he amassed a large quantity of personal property at that time. Affiant was at the ball ground the day before he was killed and on the same evening Doublehead got wounded, and it occurred as follows: Late in the evening a Cherokee came up to Doublehead while setting on his horse and seized the bridle's reins and said to him, "You are friendly to the whites and trying to sell our country, and you ought to be killed." Doublehead told him to let go the bridle for he was drunk and did not wish to be bothered with him. The Cherokee refused to let go, and the Doublehead drew one of his pistols and threw out the priming in order to snap it at his assailant and exterminate him, but there was not enough left to cause it to discharge and he shot the other Cherokee, who drew his tomahawk and cut off Doublehead's thumb all but the skin which it hung. Then Doublehead struck the other with the cock of his pistol and sunk the cock deep in his skull and _____ he died. After which we had _____ the thumb of Doublehead, he was shot in the jaw and he fell and one John McIntosh took him and concealed him where a school master lived near the place where the fort now stands. The next morning, the Indians Ridge and Saunders found him and attacked him and Ridge shot him and Saunders used the tomahawk and both of them finally after a long struggle killed him. Saunders struck the tomahawk in his forehead _____ across just above his nose and struck it so deep that Saunders said it took both of his hands to pull it. Affiant ran up the stairs and took him by the hand just as he was drawing his last breath...

Sworn to and subscribed before me,
11th of August 1838
James / Liddel

Caleb Starr
(Signature)

General Sam Dale Version 1860

One prominent Georgian Indian trader attending the festivities was General Sam Dale, famed for the famous Indian canoe fight. In addition, the leading Chickamauga Cherokee Chieftain Doublehead, who was the most powerful figure of the Lower Towns, was also among the crowd. Doublehead had two daughters who married Samuel Riley that lived nearby at Southwest Point; therefore, Doublehead exhibited his confidence as he approached Sam Dale, of Mississippi. Doublehead called out Sam Dale in the vast crowd, *"Sam, you are a mighty liar".*

The following version of Doublehead's death is found in the *Life and Times of General Sam Dale* by J. F. H. Claiborne, produced by Harpers and Brothers Publishing, and printed in 1860:

"In 1803, Colonel William Barnet, Buckner Harris, and Boderic Easely were commissioned by the President to mark out a highway through the Cherokee nation. Ellick Saunders, a half-blood, and I were selected as guides. The road having been established, I united with Jo Buffington, a half-blood, and set up a trading-post on Hightower River, among the Cherokees. We chiefly exchanged our goods for peltries, which we wagoned to Charleston.

While thus enrolled I witnessed the death of Double-head, the great chief of the Cherokees. I had gone with several pack-horses, loaded with merchandise, to a great ball-play Old Hiwassee River, where more than a thousand Cherokees, the officers from Hiwassee Fort, and numerous traders had assembled. The chief affected to receive me with severity, and said, "Sam, you are a mighty liar." I demanded why he insulted me in public. He smiled and said, "You have never kept your promise to come and see me. You know you have lied." He then produced a bottle of whisky, and invited the officers and myself to drink. When we had emptied it I offered to replenish it, but he refused, saying,

"When I am in the white man's country I will drink your liquor, but here you must drink with Doublehead."

When the ball-play ceased I was standing by the chief, when the Bone-polisher, a captain, approached, and denounced him as a traitor for selling a piece of the country, a large and valuable tract near the shoals of Tennessee River, to a company of speculators. The great chief remained tranquil and silent, which only aggravated the Bone-polisher, who continued his abuse with menacing gestures. Double-head quietly remarked, " Go away. You have said enough. Leave me, or I shall kill you." Bone-polisher rushed at him with his tomahawk, which the chief received on his left arm, and drawing a pistol, shot him through the heart. Foreseeing trouble, I left immediately for Hiwassee Ferry.

Sometime after night Doublehead came in, evidently under the influence of liquor. One John Rogers, an old white man, who had long resided in the nation, was present, and began to revile the chief in the manner of Bone-polisher. Doublehead proudly replied, "You live by sufferance among us. I have never seen you in council nor on the war-path. You have no place among the chiefs. Be silent, and interfere no more with me." The old man still persisted, and Doublehead attempted to shoot him, but his pistol miss fired; in fact, it was not charged. Alex Saunders, and Ridge, a chief, were present. Ridge extinguished the light, and one of them fired at Double-head. When the light was rekindled, Ridge, Saunders, and Rogers had disappeared, and the chief lay motionless on his face. The ball had shattered his lower jaw and lodged in the nape of his neck. His friends set out with him for the garrison, but, apprehensive of being overtaken, they turned aside, and concealed him in the loft of one Mr. Black, a schoolmaster.

In the meantime, two warriors, of the clan of the Bone-polisher, who had been designated to avenge his death, traced Doublehead, by his blood, to the house where he had been concealed. At the same moment Ridge and Saunders came galloping up, shouting the war-whoop. Colonel James Blair, of Georgia, and I followed them.. The wounded chief was lying on the floor, his jaw and arm terribly lacerated. .Ridge and Saunders each leveled their pistols, and each missed fire. Double-head sprang upon Ridge and would have overpowered him, but Saunders discharged his pistol and shot him through the hips. Saunders then rushed on him with his tomahawk ; but the dying chief wrenched it from him and leaped upon Ridge, when Saunders seized another tomahawk and drove it into his brains. When he fell, another Indian crushed his head with a spade.

It was a dreadful spectacle and most cowardly murder. Doublehead was a renowned chief. In single combat he never had a superior. He wielded much influence by his oratorical abilities, and was often compared with his predecessor, the "Little Turkey," the most famous and popular of all the Cherokee chiefs. The cupidity of speculators, who

224

have so often robbed and ruined the Red Men, tempted him to sell a portion of his country. From that moment his death was resolved upon. The rencounter with the Bone-polisher, where he acted strictly in self-defense, merely precipitated his fate. He perished apparently upon the Indian maxim of blood for blood, but was really the victim of conspiracy" (Claiborne, 1860).

Cherokee Tragedy Version 1970

Another version of Doublehead's Death is from Cherokee Tragedy by Thurman Wilkins and published by The MacMillan Company in 1970 as follows:

"The resentment grew more bitter still when news leaked out that a secret agreement, unsanctioned by the Cherokee council, had reserved two tracts for Doublehead's use at the mouths of the Clinch and Hiawasee rivers. To make matters worse, a similar reserve at the mouth of Duck River was held for Tahlonteskee, Doublehead's kinsman. As a result, many Cherokees considered Doublehead a traitor. His leasing of farmlands to white men on the tracts he had secured at Muscle Shoals through the treaty he had signed at Washington in December 1806 added fuel to the fire. Moreover, another land deal with Colonel Meigs was brewing in the summer of 1807. But Doublehead's land manipulations were only one reason for his having become the most abhorred chief in the Nation. "As he sought office with selfish views," McKenney wrote, "he very naturally abused it, and made himself odious by his arbitrary conduct. He not only executed the laws according to his own pleasure, but caused innocent men to be put to death who thwarted his views. The chiefs and the people began alike to fear him."

Certain principal men- the Vann faction led the movement- determined that he should die for his crimes. The Ridge, Alexander Saunders, and James Vann were "selected" as his executioners. The Ridge had detested Doublehead since the outrage at Cavett's Station, but Vann had a family score to settle. Doublehead had married the sister of his favorite wife and had treated her brutally, having Beaten her when she was pregnant until she died. The Vanns regarded the death as murder; revenge became a paramount issue in their household. Vann's wife had even vowed to seek vengeance with her own hands and she pushed her husband to act. He was still incensed over a row he had had with Doublehead in Washington when he had called the Speaker a traitor. "High words [had] ensued," according to Payne, "and dirks were drawn; but the parties were separated and no blood was shed." Now, however, Vann volunteered to execute the "traitorous murderer," with the help of Saunders and The Ridge. The three decided to stage the execution before a large assembly, the August meeting of the Cherokees to collect the tribal annuity from the American agent.

On the way to the agency at Hiawasee, Vann fell ill and could not proceed. He yielded "the honor of destroying Doublehead" to Saunders and The Ridge, and they decided to eliminate the chief not as a wife-killer but as a traitor and a lawless speculator in Cherokee lands. On reaching Hiawasee, The Ridge went with Saunders to Mcintosh's tavern to wait for Doublehead's arrival. While they waited, the chief paddled up to Hiawasee in his canoe and, without their knowledge, rode off on horseback to a ball-play three miles away. He did not return to town till long after dark, and when he entered the tavern, he seemed excited, half drunk. There was a bandage on his hand. An old white man named John Rogers began to revile him.

Doublehead replied: "You live by sufferance among us. I've never seen you in council or on the warpath. You have no place among the chiefs. Hush and interfere no more with me."

Someone suddenly seized a candle that flickered on the table and held it close to Doublehead's face. A moment later The Ridge darted and blowing the candle out, he shot Doublehead through the jaw near the lower part of the ear. In the darkness he and Saunders slipped from the tavern, thinking their purpose had been achieved, that the traitor was dead.

Soon they heard that Doublehead had killed another man that afternoon. The ball-play had drawn a large crowd, and at dusk while the spectators milled from the field, excited over the bloodiness of the game, "the whiskey kegs of the whites met them in every direction." Many were soon tipsy, including Doublehead and a warrior named Bone-Polisher, who approached the chief as he sat astride his horse, and grasping the bridle, called him a traitor. Doublehead ordered him to release the bridle and go away or he would kill him, but Bone-Polisher became more abusive. Doublehead drew his pistol; he threw the priming out, intending merely to snap it at his assailant to intimidate him. But enough priming remained to discharge the pistol. Bone-Polisher retaliated with a blow from his tomahawk, chopping off one of Doublehead's thumbs, "all but some skin by which it hung." After that Doublehead lashed out with his pistol and drove the cock so deep into Bone-Polisher's skull that the warrior died. And so more blood had flowed to justify The Ridge's act, if it needed vindication.

But The Ridge and Saunders also learned that Doublehead was still alive, though his jaw was shattered, with the ball lodged in his neck. They heard that during the night the tavern keeper had moved the chief to his house, thrusting him in secret through a back window; that, later still, Doublehead was spirited off to a safer place. It took Saunders and The Ridge till after dawn to find the new hiding spot- the loft of a Mr. Black, who taught in Gideon Blackburn's school. With war whoops they rushed into the room where

226

Doublehead lay, two men of Bone-Polisher's clan joining their company. As they approached, the wounded chief sprang up, drew a dirk, caught at a pistol, but "the sheet clung to his limbs & clogged his heels." The Ridge and Saunders leveled their guns at him, but both missed fire. Doublehead sprang on The Ridge and grappled at him with a terrible, desperate strength, till Saunders reprimed his pistol and shot him through the hips. Then Saunders drove his tomahawk into the chief's forehead with such force that it took two hands and a foot against the cloven skull to pry it loose. A third Indian pounded the head with a spade and crushed it to a pulp.

After the killing, The Ridge "addressed the crowd who were drawn together by this act of violence, and explained his authority and his reasons." No one mourned the slaughtered chief, unless it was Meigs, who had a treaty to conclude; nor was there any retaliation. The consensus was that, however crudely, justice had been done.

Doublehead's death on August 9, 1807, benefited the Cherokees in a number of ways, including increased tribal unity. It led to the entire abolition of the Blood Law at the Council of Broomstown on September 11, 1808, which abrogation was reaffirmed in 1810 at Oostanaula. As most Cherokees felt that the destruction of Doublehead was justified and that his relatives should not be forced by clan responsibility to take revenge, there was an incentive to remove the question from the jurisdiction of the clans and base punishment on a sounder principle than mere retaliation. Gideon Blackburn, spurred by the fact that "the execution" had taken place in the house of one of his teachers, encouraged sentiments for reform among a number of principal men. And when the Cherokees came together at Broomstown, they took pains to negate the Blood Law when framing their first written constitution. In reporting the reforms to Jedidiah Morse, Blackburn declared that "All criminal accusations must be established by testimony; the infliction of punishment is made a governmental transaction." This provision in itself proscribed the Blood Law as an instrument of clan revenge. But the question was resolved even more specifically. "One law," Blackburn wrote, "is that no murderer shall be punished until he has been proved guilty before the council." Thus, The Ridge was legally immune from retaliation from Doublehead's clan, though enforcement of the new provisions was another matter" (Wilkins, 1970).

The Cherokee Tragedy above states two benefits from Doublehead's assassination, tribal unity and abolition of Blood Law. First, 1,131 of Doublehead's relatives and friends left for the west shortly after his death and became the Old Settlers or Cherokees West. Not a whole lot of unity when a large number of the Lower Cherokees left their homes for a distant land because of Doublehead's assassination. Doublehead's family may not have mourned, but many were upset enough that they left the country. Second, evidently someone forgot to tell the family and friends of Doublehead that the Blood Law had been abolished.

Major Ridge Assassination

Major Ridge, members of his family, and some 70 other Cherokees who were killed by their own Cherokee people found out Blood Law was still in practice with the Old Settlers in the west; therefore, Ridge eventually paid the supreme sacrifice for the assassination of Doublehead. Some claim Ridge's death was due to him signing the Treaty of New Echota, which gave Cherokee lands east of the Mississippi River to the United States Government; however, his assassins were already in the west waiting for him to arrive. Many claim that the Ross faction, who opposed the Treaty of New Echota, was responsible for the assassination of Major Ridge; but remember, John Ross and Colonel Return Jonathan Meigs were good friends with Doublehead's family. Regardless, Doublehead's son Bird Tail Doublehead, Bird Tail's half-brother, and other relatives were the ones who actually assassinated Major Ridge and most had been in the west since 1809 some 30 years before the signing of the Treaty of New Echota.

Mayor Ridge

Bird Tail Doublehead, James Foreman, Anderson Springston, Isaac Springston, James Hair, Jefferson Hair, and some 40 other Cherokees were members of the assassination teams that killed Major Ridge, his family members, and friends a little over 30 years after Doublehead was assassinated. These Cherokees were mostly relatives or friends of Doublehead seeking revenge. Bird Tail was the son of Doublehead by Nannie Drumgoole Springston. James Foreman was the half-brother of Bird Tail Doublehead by Nannie and John Foreman. Anderson and Isaac Springston were also the half-brothers of Bird Tail Doublehead by Nannie Drumgoole Springston, Doublehead's third wife. Anderson and Isaac Springston were also brother-in-laws to Doublehead's granddaughter Elizabeth "Betsy" Foreman who married their brother, Edley Springston.

It was not a good idea for Major Ridge, his family, and others in Doublehead's assassination party to move west to the home of Doublehead's family and friends, who were the Old Settlers. You can bet they had a long time to plan on Ridge's assassination and waited on his arrival west of the Mississippi. Not only was Major Ridge shot five times and died on June 22, 1839, but also his son John Ridge and his nephew Elias Boudinot were assassinated the same day within a few hours. John Ridge was stabbed by some 30 assailants and Elias Boudinot was stabbed and an ax drove into his skull like Doublehead.

John Ridge

Elias Boudinot

Elias Boudinot's brother, Stand Watie was warned and escaped assassination. Watie later shot and killed James Foreman in May 1842, and Anderson Springston on March 22, 1866, supposedly in self-defense. He was arrested, tried in an Arkansas Court, and later released. After becoming the last Confederate General to surrender during the Civil War, Stand Watie died September 9, 1871.

Ridge's family moved west shortly after the Treaty of New Echota was ratified by the United States Congress on May 23, 1836. The main portion of eastern Cherokees started their move west in October 1838 and ended in March 1839; therefore, it did not take Blood Law long to avenge Doublehead's death after his killers reached the west.

Letters of Doublehead's Death

Letter from Captain Addison B. Armstead, August 9, 1807

Microcopy 208, roll 3, and number 1889, Captain Addison B. Armstead's letter stating his problems and opposition in the arrest of James Chisholm dated August 9, 1807, from Hiwassee Garrison, Tennessee.

Sir:

Agreeable to your instructions I set out on the 9th Inst. In pursuit of James Chisholm, an intruder on the Cherokee Tribe of Indians on my arrival at the place where I calculated on finding Chisholm, I was grossly insulted by a Cherokee Indian who charged his horse on me with drawn pistol. I was entirely unarmed having lost my rifle in the crowd. A considerable number of the principal men of the nation were present who would not take the least trouble to reduce the Indian to order/save one Sequechee. The only satisfaction was to beat the fellows with my fist. Soon after this I found Chisholm who I immediately took prisoner and confined. After riding with him about an half a mile, I was overtaken by a large party of Indians, one of them a Chief by the name of Wiliowee who was armed with a rifle, ordered me in the most peremptory manner to release the prisoner which I contemptuously refused.

I then passed onto Walker's ferry where I was overtaken by James Rodgers a half breed with a drawn knife and pistol and John Rodgers his father, a white man. This fellow James Rodgers said he had come to release James Chisholm or die in the attempt. I argued with him for some time to no effect. He persisted in his intention. I then called on Mr. Samuel C. Hall to assist me in the defense necessary to keep the prisoner. He drew a pistol and I got another and in that way we kept him from releasing Chisholm. Old Rodgers wished me to believe that he wished his son to desist but it was evident to me and every gentlemen, by that so far from chiding his son, he encourages him, he requested James Rodgers to ask the prisoner if wished to be untied and observed if he answers in the affirmative you may act as you like at the same time observed that he never raised a son that was afraid of a pistol – This John Rodgers is in my opinion one of the most disaffected people in the Cherokee nation and if he is not removed from the Indians he will become there ruin for I am confident he would do everything in his power to thwart any orders that you may give for the good of the Cherokees and after being convinced there threats could not have the desired effect – they left me and I not being able to cross the river returned to Mr. Blacks where I had not been long before John Rodgers come in and said Chefulalalaga/alias Doublehead/was shot. He had all the appearance of being the assassin as he was bloody from the collar of his shirt to his shoes and was very much

230

agitated. During his stay some person come in and said Doublehead was not dead. John Rodgers observed if he was not dead he should die saying he/Chequlaluga/had snapped a pistol at him.

I sincerely console with you on the loss of our greatest friend among the treacherous and savage nation. This friendship is not to be calculated or individually. If it is nationally as was truly proved in my case, I have done everything to render myself popular among them which I thought I have effected in an eminent degree but when they saw me in difficulty not one interfered except one already mention Sequechee/Doublehead's brother.

I am sincerely respectful,
Captain Addison B. Armstead

Letter from Samuel C. Hall, August 9, 1807

Microcopy 208, roll 3, number 1891, Samuel C. Hall's letter relating to Doublehead's death on August 9, 1807, to Captain Addison B. Armstead, Commander of Highwassee Garrison.

Dear Captain Armstead:
As to the conduct of John Rodgers, I have but one opinion, which is that he merits (two unknown words) and show that he is at the moment in a situation which the agency can probably take hold of him, upon a change of the murder of Doublehead – his being a white man exempts him from the plea which a Cherokee might consider their law and make use of, which is life for life, admitting that Doublehead did kill the other, which has not yet been proven. My reasons for supposing that Rodgers was in fact Doublehead's murderer are simply those, all of which I believe you have also a thorough knowledge of.

In the first place it can be proven that Rodgers was present immediately preceding this massacre, in the company of Doublehead, and that they were upon terms of hostility at that time.

The second fact is that the murderer of Doublehead did, instantly, after the murder, mount Doublehead's horse and make his escape there on.

The third fact is that in a few seconds, Rodgers made his appearance the Bloods with all the makes of one assassin, being literally speaking covered with gore from his neck downwards, mounted upon Doublehead's horse. Informed us that Doublehead was killed and exulting at the same time at the act.

I have already taken the only legal opinion which can be had here, which is decidedly that these facts will warrant his arrest upon a charge of murder, the circumstances being as strong as circumstances can go to establish a fact.

If you coincide with me in opinion, will it not be admissible, without loss of time to consult Colonel Meigs upon the business – so atrocious an act ought not to go unpunished – and the character of this man so infamous – his residence among the Indians productive of such dangerous threats that I think this is the time to strike a decisive stroke, and I assure you this is the general sentiment presiding here.   If Colonel Meigs begins to act in the business, and wishes any further be legal advice, I will with pleasure take a trip to Knoxville, and obtain the best the place affords.

Mr. Bell left us this morning for Nashville, nothing new here, all the papers which could be procured are forwarded to you. I expect to be down in about five days. Tell them May God bless you and take you unto his holy dwelling.

Samuel C. Hall

Letter of Colonel Joseph Phillips, August 15, 1807

Microscopy 208, roll 3, and number 1884, Colonel Joseph Phillips testimony relating to the Death of Doublehead who was killed on the 9th instant August 1807, Highwassee Garrison, August 15, 1807.

The following conversation took place between several unnamed persons living in the Cherokee Nation and myself.   George Saunders observed that the Indians were much displeased with Doublehead and Chisholm, and he expected they would be called to account at the ball play. I told him it would be too rash to take matters into their own hands and they ought to complain to Colonel Meigs for justice. They said Meigs was as bad as Doublehead and Chisholm.

David Maeenncley informed me that Doublehead was killed and that prior to his death he had killed another man. He said this was not the cause of Doublehead being killed for the man that killed Doublehead did not know another man had been killed by Doublehead. It had been previously determined that the Ridge was appointed to execute the business and was so prepared.

John Rodgers informed me that the man who killed Doublehead did not know that Doublehead had killed another and that Doublehead throwed out the primer out of his

232

pistol before he shot the man and he was convinced he did not mean to kill but rather scare him.

Joseph Phillips

Other Letters

In a letter found in microcopy 208, roll 4, number 1906, Captain Addison B. Armstead makes the following statement to Colonel Return J. Meigs, on August 27, 1807.

"We think if old Rodgers will come forward and ask pardon for his offense and give his on up for punishment that it will be well to forgive once now."

Three days after Captain Armstead letter to Meigs, Dr. Allen Burd Grubbs according to microcopy 208, roll 4, number 1907, in a letter to Colonel Return J. Meigs on August 30, 1807, requests forgiveness for Rogers. Dr. Grubb, who was from Pennsylvania, had married a Cherokee woman and knew John Rogers. He was a respected citizen and requested that the incident concerning the arrest of James Chisholm be dropped because Rogers was drunk.

"Conniving John Rodgers conduct in regards to his conduct toward his son in the release of James Chisholm. I have talked to Rodgers who says that he was drunk at the time and his actions were due to his intoxication for which his is sorry. Grubbs trust that he will be forgiven."

Execution & Burial

The two men who carried out the execution of Doublehead on August 9, 1807, were Major Ridge and Alex Saunders. It is ironic that of the three men involved in the assassination of Doublehead, two were mixed-bloods and one was white. Alex Saunders was half Cherokee and Major Ridge was three fourths. John Rodgers was a white man married to a Creek Indian woman. Members of the Saunders family built Rocky Hill Castle and Saunders Mansion in Lawrence County after Doublehead's death. It was said that Thomas Jefferson actually did the house plans for the Saunders Mansion and Castle. John or Samuel Rogers, of the Roger's family, was the namesake of the Town of Rogersville on the north side of the Tennessee River in Lauderdale County, and later the Rogers Department stores.

Doublehead's black servant Kit Butler said that his spirit would rant and rave especially on stormy nights. He also stated that Doublehead was carefully brought back to his home by his friends and relatives, where he was buried on a hill overlooking the Blue Water Old Fields which is presently a polo club field. His grave is covered by a pile of stones and just east of Blue Water Creek on the north side of present-day highway 72 in Lauderdale County, Alabama. On the opposite side of the highway, a historic marker for Doublehead is on the south side of the highway 72 right-of-way near the polo field just a few hundred yards south of the unmarked grave site.

Doublehead's Estate

Doublehead controlled or owned several tracts of land given to him for signing treaties with the United States government officials. The largest tract controlled by Doublehead lay on the north side of the Tennessee River at Muscle Shoals and was bounded on the east by Elk River (Chuwallee) and on the west by Cypress Creek. This tract was given to Doublehead and his heirs for 99 years renewable for 900 years. It was known as Doublehead's Reserve which he and John D. Chisholm leased to white settlers under the name of the Doublehead Company.

The other large tract given to Doublehead, John D. Chisholm, and John Riley by the secret agreement consisted of three square miles and was located near South West Point downstream from the junctions of the Clinch River and the Tennessee River. Still another one square mile tract lay near the foot of the Cumberland Mountains; and, finally a one square mile tract on the north bank of the Tennessee River where Taluntuskee lived near the mouth of Blue Water Creek at Big Muscle Shoals.

In addition to vast tracts of land, Doublehead had a great deal of gold, silver, horses, cattle, and other valuables. In addition he and his relatives owned a large number of black slaves.

The following on Doublehead's Estate is the sworn oath given on June 8, 1838, by Catherine Spencer the niece of Doublehead and the only child of his brother, Pumpkin Boy:

Catherine Spencer's Version of Estate

Came Catherine Spencer and makes oath that she lived at the house of Doublehead the Chief when he was killed which was many years ago, she thinks it was about 27 years ago (actually Doublehead died August 9, 1807; therefore it was 30 years ago), and that she lived in his family about 12 years. Applicant is the niece of Old Doublehead, and is the only daughter and child of Eyahchutlee (Pumpkin Boy), a brother of Doublehead, and Chaueukah is her mother, and was then a grown woman about 19 years old and affiant states that the following described property was there and belonged to Doublehead the Chief when he was killed to wit,

One negro man named Andrew about 21 years old, very likely $1,000.00 One young negro man named Joe a Race Rider, very smart $650.00 One mullatto boy named

Ben, 16 years old $600.00 One brother of his named George, 14 years old $550.00 One negro boy named Jacob about 15 years old $550.00=$2,350.00

One negro man named Riddle about 22 years old $800.00 One negro woman named Phebe about 25 or 6 years old $500.00 and her four children, the oldest 10 and youngest 2 years old at $200.00 each on an average is $800.00 One negro woman named Mary or Polly about 23 years old $500.00 with her two children---$350.00

Austin, a man between thirty and 40 years old $600.00 and his wife Magon about 30 years old, a house woman, good cook, washer and Ironer $600.00 with five children the oldest a boy 12 years old and ranging from him down to the youngest about 2 years old, all worth on an average $200.00 each---$1,000.00 This man and woman came by the death of the applicants father to the Old Chief Doublehead with this affiant when she was moved to his quarters after the death of her father, and from this man and woman these 5 children were raised and all these seven negros were once the right of this applicant but affiant does not know where it is now=affiant declares most solemnly on her oath that she never sold them to anybody nor been paid one dollar for them—

All of the above described negroes were there before the Georgia negroes were brought there, and applicant states that a white man named John D.Chisholm was gone to Georgia to collect money due Old Doublehead when he was killed and shortly after that Chisholm returned with nine grown negroes from Georgia and left them there as a part of Doubleheads property and said he got those nine negroes in place of the money due unto Doublehead=affiant and the other Cherokees evidently then took these nine negroes and put them in the negro cabins with the other negroes and provided for them as for the other negroes of Doublehead and the remained there as a part of his estate until taken off by the white men; five of these Georgia negroes were men worth $700.00 each--?,00 and the other four women worth $500 each--$2,000.00 all stout able negroes and well grown, the names not recalled nor the ages==

There were 30 head of cows and calves worth $12.00 each--$360.00 and about 100 head of fine stock cattle, big and sturdy heifers all worth 5 to 8 dollars each $650.00 one fine stud horse at home worth as the people said $700.00 and one other stud horse, (Doublehead's favorite horse Postman was taken by Thomas Morris Clark of Kingston or West Piont.) at South West Point said by the people to be worth $1,000.00 and there were 8 other fine mares and geldings bought of Rik=e=ti=yah = John Christy's mother worth $100 each -- $800.00 and nine other head of common draw horses and colts worth about 50 or 60 dollars each, say 55 on an average $495.00 and five good horses called first rate and worth $500.00 Doublehead paid a fine negro named Mary for the 8 bought of John

236

Christy's mother with a view to increase his stock of horses, and that negro was not any of those housed here==this John Christy has gone to Sekausas.

50 head of sows and pigs and shoots and small stock hogs running about the house $3.00 each -- $150.00 one hundred head of large hogs running out in the woods worth $5.00 is--$500.00

4 large first rate beds and bedding and bedsteads worth $40 each --$160.00
6 weisdrar chairs at $2.00 each $12.00
12 common du, 50cts $6.00
1 case of bottles and liquor--$10.00
4 doz plates--$4.00
8 dishes, all large--$6.00
2 good tables--$8.00
1 fine du--$1.50
2 large pots--$10.00
3 large ovens--$9.00
2 smaller pots--$2.00
1 dinner pot--$2.00
1 brass kettle, common size $2.50
1 tea kettle--$1.50
3 pair of iron fire dogs $4.50
1 saddle and bridle and brace of pistols
a good saddle part worn=$15.00
the pistols first rate with a case and working $30.00

(Prince) according to her best (yu agreement) of the value of such articles of property and affiant states that Doublehead had a store there and a white man named Phillips was the clerk and (rate for ach) and the Cherokee people came there daily and bought goods for cash and Phillips refused to sell goods on a credit to the Cherokees. It was commendable stock worth about two or three thousand dollars, and Doublehead told affiant just before he was killed that he had three thousand dollars in a trunk in the store room=affiant says large quantites of money in Phillips hands but cannot state how much as she never counted it; affiant did not know of her uncle buying anything after that time and thinks there would have been as much as more than $3,000 cash on hand==affiant admits it to be true that she does not know so well about the store and the money because Phillips the white man had the entire IOU that of it when Doublehead was died and did not show the money anymore and did not communicate the situation of it to affiant==that year a white man named Samuel(Riley, Doublehead's double son-in-law) (Llebarrinan alrevcee d) for Doublehead and was making a good crop and (anocianally) all the big negroes (icraekill) out.—The (Observer) quit there loan after Doublehead was killed==Bird

Doublehead and his brother(Tassel) were sent to school and boarding at the Thomas Norris Clark and Peggy Peggy and Sucunnah and (Fley) (Doublehead's daughters, Peggy Wilson, Susannah Chisholm, and Alcy McNulty) *will (aff aho) None of the children of Doublehead were there nor does affiant recollect of their coming there==they were all very young. Bird was the eldest and many years younger than this affiant and no claims came through to protect their rights or secure their property==(lit surrued) that after their father was killed by his people that the children were also endangered by the nation==this affiant (averried) and managed as well as she could do.*

Affiant states that as soon as the news came that Doublehead was killed Phillips shut up the store (Trading post at the mouth of Bluewater Creek, Lauderdale County, Alabama) *and kept it shut up and quit selling goods==The crop was continued working by the negroes the others (heuinep) of Doublehead went on until towards fall when four white men came there and stayed four or five days,--these white men talked to Phillips a good long time and they seemed to be counseling together but affiant could not understand them—these white men after talked to the negroes and after about four days councelling the white men asked affiant and her Aunts and (Soney) Thau=ti=ne- all Doublehead and Wah=hatch a brother of Doublehead to (guerite) a (loam) and these one of the white man named Black proposed that all the negroes and horses and cattle and hogs and all the removable property should be taken care off for the children of Old Doublehead this Black* (Probably James Black who was teaching Bird Tail and Tassel) *was the man with whom Bird Doublehead had been and was there boording and whoal = It was asked by the whites whether this should be done or not and none of the Cherokees countered to it, but Phillips the store keeper gave his consent to it and he went off with the three white men and they carried all the goods boxes and trunks and all belongings to the store (off with them) and all the above described articles of property and negroes, and cattle and horses and hogs off with them and they (neuii) and paid for (norletuiua) any more==one of the negroes named Andrew who could speak and understand both English and Cherokee stated to affiant that he understood what the white men said and he told this affiant that these white men were not meaning to save the negroes and the other property for the children of Doublehead and that they were meaning to get it all for their own use and fixing to steal it and that if the white men did act so with the property he Andrew would run away and come back to the nation again. The other negroes seemed to be concerned that these white men would take them where Bird Doublehead was and went cheerfully and the negroes assisted the white men in collecting the stock and loading up the wagon and one of the negroes drove off the team and the plantation was left without and human being on it but her aunts and Wah=hatihi. It was the understanding with all the Indians that the children were to have all this property at last. Wah=hatih* (Wahatchie – Doublehead's Brothers) *got some Indians to (aprint hein) and they gathered the crops and put it away and no more white men came there to (couriett) for the goods of the heirs of Old Doublehead, and this affiant and her two Aunt Sorrey* (Doublehead's daughter Susannah

238

that married George Chisholm) *and Ks=ti=e=ie=ah*(Doublehead's daughter that married Thomas Jeferson Dishman) *Doublehead and Wah=hatih (mode urea it thermires)==Black and these other white men did not say that Doublehead owed them money, but only said that the property should be taken care of for the use of his heirs and this affiant and other kinfolks did not consent (uren) to that for this affiant these thoughts are known at the time that this affiant and the other Cherokees could have taken as good (coreafit) as these friendly white men could do.*

Sworn and transcribed
Before me this 8th *June 1838*
(Leirniz Lieiculf)
Commissioner

                                                                                    her
                                                                Catherine X Spencer
                                                                        Mark

Bird Tail Doublehead's Version of Estate

Testimony of Bird Doublehead re: Estate of Doublehead

Cherokee Agency East

Bird Doublehead, Son of Doublehead, a Cherokee Chief, makes that he had for some years previous to the time his father was killed as well as after and recalls its about 29 years ago he had been living at Thomas Norris Clark's at Kingston, Tennessee (South West Point) for the purpose of going to school and was living at Clark's at the time his father was killed. In the fall prior to his death affiant went home to his father's at the Muscle Shoals (mouth of Bluewater Creek in Lauderdale County, Alabama) *him as affiant sometime in the year 1812 and was residing there at the time of his father's on the Tennessee River on a visit and remained at his father's house about 3 months, and again at the expiration of that time affiant returned to Clark's and continued to reside with death. At the time affiant was at his father's last before his father's death and at during another time which affiant lived at home.*

Affiant recollects well to have seen a considerable quantity of property belonging to his father. Consisting of a large stock of horses, he thinks 30 or 40 head, old and young. Among them one brown stud horse purchased by affiant's father from Old Peelin for the sum of $1000, one thousand dollars. This horse [mah] a stand at South West Point. Affiant's father was a stock raiser and had some fine breed mares and was trying to improve his stock of horses. There was also a large stock of cattle of which affiant's father had given affiant 20 head as part of the cattle belonging to affiants step mother the wife (Kateeyeah Wilson) of the Chief Doublehead which part affiant presumes Thomas Wilson her brother (Doublehead's brother-in-law) got at Doublehead's death, but Doublehead still owned a considerable stock of cattle besides. He had as affiant believes also a large stock of hogs he is unable to say how many. He also had a large quantity of valuable household and kitchen furniture worth as affiant believes at least $600. Affiant states there was a store there but affiant is unable to give any account of the quantity or value of the goods therein but thinks there was a pretty general apportionment.

Affiant remembers that when affiant went home the fall before his father carried down the [money] in the boat an [abhtimal] stock of goods and after [setting/selling] some of them in the boat he put the balance in the store with the other goods and a white man called Phillips kept the store. Affiant thinks there could not have been less than $3000 worth of goods in the store. Affiant thinks the goods were not sold on a credit. Doublehead had also a considerable stock of Negroes besides those afterwards brought from Georgia. Those Negroes he had owned many years [torn part] of time before the recollection of affiant. Others were born there, and [Ms yellow boyz Bins oGimjyd] very likely were bought by Doublehead a few years before his death but affiant cannot recollect the precise numbers but believes there were at least 20 perhaps more at and before the time of Doublehead's death. Affiant's brother Tassel also went with him and boarded at Clark's. Affiant thinks $100 per year was the sum agreed to be paid to Clark for boarding each of us affiant and Tassel. Tassel died at Clark's about 2 weeks after Doublehead was killed. Affiant was then about 12 years of age, continued boarding at Clark's and did not go home but remained there at school. Affiant had no guardian appointed for him, nor did he directly or indirectly take upon himself the control or management of the property of his father's estate. Affiant had 3 sisters none of whom were at home when Doublehead was killed. One of them, Peggy, was living with her mother in what is now McMinn Co, Tennessee. The others, Ms Susannah and Alcy were at Hiwassee Garrison at school,(Doublehead's daughter, Peggy Wilson, Susannah Chisholm and Alcy McNulty).

The next fall after Doublehead was killed Clark went to the Muscle Shoals and to the late residence of affiant's father he did not inform affiant when he started what was his beliefs or where he was going. After an absence of some weeks Clark returned home to Kingston and brought with him 21, twenty one, Negroes and some horses. Phillips the store keeper also came back with Clark. Phillips informed affiant that Clark had got the Negroes and horses at the residence of affiant's father and that some other Negroes had also been taken that belonged to Doublehead [torn part] and had been by him delivered over to some other men, one of them to [Wau hatchy] one to [Ulau hatchy] his brother, two Cherokees, and one to Chisholm a white man, and the balance to some person or persons who are not recalled at present. Affiant was confident Phillips statement in

240

relation to the property was true from the fact that of the Negroes brought by Clark there were several affiant had himself known to have been in his father's family many years Jarrit, Austin, Magin, Andrew and Pheby and Peter Dempsy and some others which affiant understood had come from Georgia. Affiant understands that Clark has disposed of the property which he took of the estate of affiant's father and has applied the [proceeds] to his own use [some] of the property affiant knows he sold one Negro, Peter, to Sam [Martin] and other portions of the property affiant is informed he sold of which is one negro, Dempsy, a [brother?] to [Crozing] of Knoxville. Affiant remained at Clark's for upwards of two years perhaps three years after his father's death. The latter part of which time, Clark did not send affiant to school but put him in the field to plough and about six months of the time in a black smith shop to blow and strike. When affiant's mother came after him and took him away. When affiant started Clark let him have one [Roane] pony five or six years old to ride away with his mother and an old saddle and bridle worth in all not exceeding $32 or 40. Clark never let affiant have any of the property or money of said estate except the pony, bridle, saddle, not even money to bear affiant's expenses home. Nor did affiant believe Clark ever accounted to affiant's said sisters for one cent of the proceeds of the property of said estate. Nor has he to the knowledge of affiant ever accounted in any way for said property.

Affiant further states that in the year [1827] he employed Colonel Zacharah Sims to assist affiant to get his property or compensation for it from Clark and procured him to come on for that purpose to Jackson's [Troly?] where he and affiant were about to make an effort for that purpose when a complaint was made against Sims and he was ordered to be driven by the Light Horse out of the Cherokee Nation. Affiant recollects that John Benge then living as affiant thinks on Battle Creek was Captain of the Light Horse and had Sims arrested. Affiant don't recollect how he obtained his release but remembers that he left the Nation. Affiant then became discouraged and did not then further [implicate] his claim but the next fall immigrated to Arkansas where he remained until recently. He has returned to again assert his rights. Affiant has now two sisters surviving namely Susannah the wife of George Chisholm and Alcy the wife of Giles McNulty. Affiant's other sister Peggy has departed this life leaving four children surviving [her hissy at laws] by her husband William Wilson who is also dead. The eldest named Jane Wilson, the second Elzrah Wilson, the third George Wilson, and the fourth Bird Wilson.

[Signed] Bird Doublehead Sworn to oath inscribed before me this 21st June 1838 David [Sauam-ate.: C]

Caleb Starr's Version of Estate

The following is sworn testimony of Caleb Starr who was also an eyewitness to Doublehead's death. This part of the affidavit was describing part of Doublehead's estate and was given on August 11, 1838.

*John D. Chisholm was going to Georgia to collect money due Doublehead in Negroes. The number I do not remember. A man named Joseph Phillips, a small man and a keen land speculator come on with Chisholm and there was one other of the company came on besides Phillips and Phillips after told affiant that several Negroes had been sent on the _____ road to the Muscle Shoals to pay up for portions of the reservation, which was called and known as the Doublehead Reservation and the Negroes were called Doublehead's Negroes, and all the _____ served to be in the name and for the benefit of Doublehead. Affiant knew Samuel Riley (*Doublehead's Double son-in-law*) and knew he did not have more than two or three Negroes before Doublehead's death and did not know of his having any more afterwards. Affiant understands from everybody that Doublehead kept a dry goods Indian trading store at the reservation (*Located at the mouth of* Bluewater Creek in present-day Lauderdale County, Alabama*) and it was a great place to trade, for it was near to the Creeks, near to the Chickasaws, and in the Cherokee Nation, and a good supply of goods at that place, such as the place and times _____ without _____ have been equal to all the stores now in this place and it was when goods were sold to Cherokees for money and skins and no auditing.*

Sworn t) o and subscribed before me,
11th of August 1838
James / Liddel
Caleb Starr
(Signature)

Division of Doublehead's Estate

Upon news of Doublehead's death, several white business associates of the old chief rushed to his settlement at Muscle Shoals, to remove as much portable property such as livestock, trade goods, and slaves as they could. One of these men was Samuel Riley who was Doublehead's double son-in-law since he had married two of Doublehead's daughters, Nigodegiya and Gulustiyu. Samuel Riley's wives and the Riley grandchildren of Doublehead were the legitimate heirs of Doublehead and deserved a portion of the property. It is unclear how much Samuel took on behalf of Doublehead's heirs.

242

John D. Chisholm and James Chisholm, who was the son of John D. Chisholm and Patsy Brown, had no direct blood connection to Doublehead's children or the fortune he had accumulated. It is not known exactly how much of Doublehead's estate the Chisholms took for their personal benefit, but for sure Doublehead's sister Nancy and John D. Chisholm fought a legal battle over some of Doublehead's slaves.

Thomas Norris Clark from South West Point provided schooling and boarding for two of Doublehead's children, Bird Tail Doublehead and his brother Tassel. Clark was not blood kin to Doublehead or a legal heir to his estate, but probably took more of Doublehead's wealth than anyone. Clark was also known as the founder of Kingston, Tennessee. Thomas Norris Clark appears to have had great personal benefits that he stole from Doublehead's estate by taking some 21 slaves and numerous horses. According to Bird Tail Doublehead's testimony, neither he nor his siblings were given any of their father's wealth taken by Clark save one pony and saddle. Among the booty was Doublehead's prized race horse, "Postman." Doublehead had given $1,000.00 for the horse.

Conclusion

During the days of Doublehead, the rugged and raging waters of the Muscle Shoals of north Alabama stretched some 40 miles along the Tennessee River. These emense rapids created barriers to transportation, limited crossings to low water periods, and provided its occupants an abundance of fresh water mussels for food. In addition to mussels, game flourished along the banks of the river while the flood plains provide rich soils for growing crops of all kinds. Doublehead's slaves along with those of his brother-in-law John Melton farmed vast areas of the Tennessee Valley growing cotton, corn, tobacco, sugar cane, potatoes, and other crops with the surplus available for sale. Doublehead's trading post at the mouth of Blue Water Creek was catering to all tribal people in the area along with the white settlers that had leased large tracts of land from the old chief. Doublehead had advanced from a fearless warrior to a modern day plantation owner of some 40 black slaves, selling his cattle to the United States government to supply their troops, having a huge stock of some 50 horses, hundreds of hogs, and other items normally found in association with southern plantations. Doublehead had paid $1,000.00 for his prized stud horse, Postman, and $700.00 for his riding horse in the early 1800's.

Doublehead's people were not savage or heatherns, stupid or dumb, backward or illerate, and they were not in the stone-age at Doublehead's death. Many Scots-Irish people had married into the tribe and were well educated for the day. Doublehead's father-in-law, Christian Priber, was a German genius. Irishman John Melton was Doublehead's brother-in-law and had some 60 slaves farming a large plantation in Limestone and Lawrence Counties of north Alabama. Doublehead's son-in-law George Colbert owned some 150 blacks slaves at his death and was one of the richest men in the Chickasaw Nation. Many other well informed Scots-Irish people were related to Doublehead through the intermarriage with his siblings and children; therefore, Doublehead's kinfolks and other Cherokees were well informed and very successful for the early 1800's.

By the beginning of the early 1800's, the once flourishing Cherokee towns along the Little Tennessee River were practically abandoned by the Cherokee people. By 1817, even the lands controlled by the powerful Chickamauga Chief Doublehead along the Tennessee River's Great Bend of the Muscle Shoals were taken by the Turkey Town Treaty. Then, in 1830, the Indian Removal Act created tremendous hardships for many Cherokee families who wanted to stay in their eastern lands. Two years after the Treaty of New Echota in 1836, the Army of Winfield Scott attempted to remove all the Cherokee remaining east of the Mississippi River. Many Cherokee Indian people were forced from their southern homelands, but a substantial number of mixed bloods assimilated into the general population and avoided removal by denying their true heritage. Many of those remaining in the east were Scots-Irish and Cherokee mixed bloods whose love for their homes was worth more than acknowledging their true Indian heritage. They referred to themselves as Black Dutch or Black Irish in their years of denial, and today a remnant of Doublehead's Chickamauga band descendants still live in north Alabama, northwest Georgia, and southeast Tennessee.

Presently, in Lawrence County, Alabama, at the Shoal Town site which was the largest Cherokee town along the Great Bend of the Tennessee River, is Doublehead Resort. The resort is near the mouth of (Shoal) Town Creek about one mile before it empties into the Tennessee River. Just to the west of Doublehead Resort is a small creek running into Town Creek known Kattagisky Creek, named in honor of Doublehead's friend and fellow Cherokee leader among the Chickamauga Cherokees. Kittagisky lived on the south side of the Tennessee River near the mouth of the creek that is his namesake. Doublehead would be honored to know that he and his friend are immortalized by their names attached to a beautiful creek and recreational development near their native home sites.

Today, Doublehead Resort offers a world-class family destination on the outstanding recreational waters of Wilson Lake at Tennessee River Mile272.2. The resort embraces some 1,100acres of woodland which at one time was part of Shoal Town. The resort's complex stretches along a pine and hardwood covered peninsula where the mouth of Town Creek joins the Tennessee River at Wilson Lake. The mouth of Town Creek was the site of some of the largest aboriginal Indian mounds that were inundated by the backwaters of Wilson Dam. This site was the final home of the last Chickamauga Cherokee Chief Doublehead.

Doublehead Resort is on a small portion of the 15, 930 acres that make up Wilson Lake which is some 15 miles in length and lies between Wheeler Dam and Wilson Dam on the Tennessee River. The backwaters of Wilson Lake cover the majority of Big Muscle Shoals where many aboriginal shell middens were located and where Doublehead lived from 1802 until his death on August 9, 1807. The Cherokee village of Shoal Town where Doublehead lived his final years was located near the present-day site of at Doublehead's Resort. A large stand of cedar trees found on the resort property were in such abundance they were used in part of the construction. These cedars were probably seedlings or small trees when Doublehead's Chickamauga band lived at Shoal Town.

From sunrise to long after sunset, there are countless reasons why families vacation at Doublehead Resort. However, these visiting families may not have a clue about the story of the man that is the resort's namesake-Doublehead: Last Chickamauga Cherokee Chief.

References

Albright, Edward, *Early History of Middle Tennessee*, Brandon Printing Company, 207 pages, 1909.

American States Papers, *Indian Affairs*. Washington, D.C. 7th Congress, 1st session, Number 95.

American State Papers, *Indian Affairs*, Washington, D.C., 1832, Volume IV, page 754.

Belue, Ted Franklin, *The Long Hunt: Death of the Buffalo East of the Mississippi*, Stackpole Books, 1996.

Bishop, W. Jeff, *John McDonald of Chickamauga: Double Agent*, trailofthetrail.blogspot.com/2010/10/john-mcdonald-double-agent-of.html, October 5, 2010.

Brown, John P., *Old Frontiers: The Story of the Cherokee Indians from Earliest Times to the Date of Their Removal to the West,1838*, Southern Publishers, Kingsport, Tennessee, 1938.

Bullman, James A., *John Jolly (Ooluntuskee)*, The Lunch Counter, www.MyTown Franklin.com, Franklin, North Carolina, 2007-2009.

Carter, Clarence Edwin, editor, *The Territorial Papers of the United States: Alabama 1817-1819*. Washington: United States Government Publishing Company, 1952.

Carter, Clarence Edwin, editor, *The Territorial Papers of the United States: Mississippi Volumes V and VI.* United States Government Publishing Company, 1938.

Claiborne, J.F.H., Life & Times of General Sam Dale, Harpers and Brothers Publications, 1860.

Clark, Thomas D. and John D. W. Guice, *The Old Southwest 1795-1830, Frontiers in Conflict*, University of Oklahoma Press, Norman and London, 1989.

Hathorn, Stacye and Robin Sabino, *Views and Vistas: Traveling Through the Choctaw, Chickasaw, and Cherokee Nations in 1803*, The Alabama Review, Volume 54, Number 3, The University of Alabama Press, July, 2001.

246

Hatley, Tom, *The Dividing Paths. Cherokees and South Carolinians Through the Era of Revolution*, Oxford University Press, New York, New York, 1995.

Hendrix, Tom, *If the Legends Fade,* Country Lane Printing, Florence, Alabama, 2000

Haywood, *John, Civil and Political History of the State of Tennessee*, 1823.

Heiskell, S. G., *Andrew Jackson and early Tennessee History*, Knoxville, Tennessee, Pages 56-57 and 64-65, 1918.

Leftwich, Nina, *Two Hundred Years at Muscle Shoals,* Northport, Alabama, The American Southern Printing Company, 1935.

M.A.H., *Historical Traditions of Tennessee, The Captivity of Jane Brown and Her Family*, The American Whig Review, Volume 15, Issue 87, Cornersville, Tennessee, December 25, 1851, Published at 120 Nassau Street, New York, 1852.

Malone, Henry Thompson, *Cherokees of the Old South, A People in Transition,* The University of Georgia Press, Athens, 1956.

Manasco, Jim, *Walking Sipsey: The People, Places, and Wildlife*, Lawrence County Schools' Indian Education Program, 1992.

McDonald, William Lindsey, *Lore of the River…The Shoals of Long Ago*, Third Edition, Bluewater Publications, 2007.

Mize, Joel S., *Unionists of the Warrior Mountains,* Volume B, Dixie Historical Research and Education Publications, Lakewood, CO, 2005.

Mooney, James, *Myths of the Cherokee*, Dover Publications, Inc. New York, NY, 1900

Moore, John Trotwood and Austin P. Foster, *Tennessee, The Volunteer State 1769-1923*, Chicago, Illinois, The S. J. Clarke Publishing Company, 1923

Moulton, G. E., *John Ross, Cherokee Chief*, University of Georgia Press, Athens, Georgia, 1978.

Ownsby, Ted and David Warton, *Georgia's Old Federal Road,* University of Mississippi Press, 2007.

Pate, J. P., *The Chickamauga: A Forgotten Segment of Indian Resistance on the Southern Frontier,* Doctoral Dissertation, Mississippi State University, Mississippi, 1969.

Pickett, Albert James, *History of Alabama,* 1851.

Powell, John Wesley, Matthew Williams Stirling, Jesse Walter Fewkes, Frederick Webb Hodge, William Henry Holmes, *Annual Report, Volume 5, Parts 1883-1884,* Library of American Civilization PCMI Collection, Smithsonian Institution, Bureau of American Ethnology, Government Printing Office, Pennsylvania State University, page 272, 1887.

Puryear, Bill, *History of Old Sumner,* 2011

Proffatt, John, *The American Decisions: containing all the cases of general value and authority decided in the courts of the several states, from the earliest issue of the state reports to the year,* Bancroft – Whitney Publishers, 1886.

Ramsey, James Gettys McGready, *The Annals of Tennessee to the end of the eighteenth century comprising its settlement, as the Watauga Association, from 1769 to 1777; a part of North-Carolina, from 1777 to 1784; the state of Franklin, from 1784 to 1788; a part of North-Carolina from 1788 to 1790; the territory of the United States,* John Russell Publishing, 1853.

Rozeman Vicki, <u>Footsteps of the Cherokees</u>, John F. Blair Publisher, Winston-Salem, North Carolina, 1995.

Royall, Anne Newport, <u>Letters from Alabama 1817-1822</u>, University of Alabama Press, Tuscaloosa, Alabama, 1969.

Saunders, Colonel James Edmonds, *Early Settlers of Alabama,* Southern Historical Press, 1977, reprint of the original 1899 edition.

Stone, James H., *Surveying the Gaines Trace, 1807- 1808,* Alabama Historical Quarterly, Summer 1971.

Street, Oliver D., *Indians of Marshall, County,* Transactions of Alabama Historical Society, Volume IV (1899-1903) Montgomery, Alabama, 1866.

Sugden, John, *Tecumseh: A Life,* New York, New York, Henry Holt and Company, 1998.

Summers, L. P., *History of Southwest Virginia 1746-1786, Washington County 1777-1870*, J. L. Hill Printing Company, Richmond, Virginia, 1903.

Swanton, John R., *The Indians of the Southeastern United States*, Smithsonian Institution Press, Washington, D.C., 1987.

Tankersley, Kenneth Barnett, *Native American Studies*, Northern Kentucky University, 2004-5.

Tanner, Helen Hornbeck, *Cherokees in the Ohio Country*, Journal of Cherokee Studies, Volume III, Number 2, pp. 95–103. Cherokee: Museum of the Cherokee Indian, 1978.

United States American Ethnology Bureau, *Annual Reports*, Volume 5, New York Public Library, Page 213, 1887.

United States American Ethnology Bureau, *Annual Reports*, Volume 5, New York Public Library, Pages 191-195, 1887.

Walker, Rickey Butch and Lamar Marshall, *Indian Trails of the Warrior Mountains*, Southern Printing, Moulton, Alabama, June 2005.

Walsh, Robert, *The American Register, or General Repository of History, Politics, and Science*, Volume 6, C. and A. Conrad, Indiana University, Page 317, 1810.

Watts, C. Wilder, *Indians at the Muscle Shoals*, The Journal of Muscle Shoals History, Volume 1, 1973.

Wilkins, Thurman, *Cherokee Tragedy: The Ridge Family and the Decimation of a People*, University of Oklahoma Press, Second Edition, 1986.

Williams, Samuel C., *The Father of Sequoyah: Nathaniel Gist*, Chronicles of Oklahoma, Oklahoma Historical Society, Volume 15, Number 1, Johnson City, Tennessee, March 1937.

Worcester, Reverend Samuel A., From an account prepared by Rev. S. A. Worcester On Information obtained from Chief John Ross, Indian Advocate, Page 3, Column 1, January 1853.

Index

Black, John Junr, 212
Black, John Senr, 212
Black, Levi, 211
Black, Wm., 211
Blackburn, Gideon, 226, 227
Blair, James, 224
Blair, Jonathan, 211
Bledsoe, Anthony, 92, 94, 95, 127, 129, 132
Bledsoe, Isaac, 83, 88, 107, 118, 129
Blevins, Jonathan, 54
Blevins, Tarlton, 54
Blithe, Andrew, 212
Blithe, Jacob, 212
Blount, William, 143, 170
Blue Water Creek, 16, 69, 72, 74, 77, 91, 146, 147,
    155, 159, 179, 190, 234, 235
Bob Benge, 25, 26, 98, 99, 103, 125
Boggs, John, 134
Bonds, Nelson, 162
Bone Polisher, 221, 224, 225, 227
Bonnefoy, Antoine, 41
Boren, Abner, 212
Boren, James, 212
Boren, Nicholess, 212
Bosley, John, 136
Boudinot, Elias, 229
Bowen, William H., 172
Bowling, Damarias, 212
Bowling, Wm Jr, 209
Bowling, Wm Sen, 209
Braden, Jas., 212
Bradley, Hoseph, 209
Bradley, Samuel, 209
Bradon, Hugh, 212
Brady, Charles, 50
Brady, Earl, 50
Brady, Elizabeth, 50
Brady, Isaac Lewis, 50
Brady, James Monroe, 50
Brady, Lucinda, 50
Brady, Malinda, 50
Brady, Owen, 50
Brady, Rachel, 50
Brady, Sallie, 50
Brady, Samuel Riley, 50
Brandon, Jaret, 211
Bratton, Charles, 129
Brewer, Mathew, 212
Brighton, Thomas, 212
Brock, John, 19, 21
Brown, Abraham, 209
Brown, George, 209
Brown, Isham, 209

Brown, James, 209, 218, 222
Brown, John, 26, 72, 140, 154, 170
Brown, John P., 137, 158
Brown, Joseph, 118, 120
Brown, Moses, 87
Brown, Richard, 154, 158, 170
Brown's Ferry, 12, 14, 16, 69, 72, 73, 74, 155, 157,
    158, 159, 160, 161, 170, 179
Brunson, Joseph, 212
Brunson, Joshua, 211
Brunston, Mathew, 211
Bruntson, Josha, 211
Buchanan, Alex, 85
Buchanan, Samuel, 86
Buffington, Jo, 223
Bullman, James A., 23
Burleson family, 37, 163
Burleson, Edward, 162, 163
Burleson, James, 162, 163
Burleson, John, 162, 163, 211
Burleson, Jonathan, 211
Burleson, Joseph, 162, 163
Burleston, James, 163
Burlston, James, 211
Burney, Adam, 212
Burney, James, 212
Burney, William, 205
Burrell McLemore, 21
Butler County, Alabama, 31
Butler, Gabriel, 205
Butler, John, 205
Butler, Kit, 233
Butler, Richard, 205
Butler, Thomas, 205
Byers, Nicholas, 180, 181

C

Caffrey, John, 82
Caldwell, James, 209
Calvert, Joseph, 210
Calwell, John, 209
Cameron, Alexander, 67
Camnon, Abner, 212
Campbell, Arthur, 60, 140
Campbell, Dianna, 49
Campbell, William, 123
Candon, William, 210
Caney Creek, 14, 161
Caney Fork, 5, 109, 128
Caney Fork River, 109
Capshaw, David, 211
Capshaw, William W., 212

251

253

McMurry, William, 86
McNary, John, 49
McNary, Margaret, 49
McNulty, Alay, 238
McNulty, Aley, 240
McNulty, Armstead Blevin, 57
McNulty, Elisa, 57
McNulty, George Washington, 57
McNulty, John, 57
McNulty, Mary, 57
McNulty, Sallie, 57
McRavey, Christiana, 212
McRory, John, 96, 111
Medders, Drankey, 212
Meigs, Return J., 58, 155, 168, 174, 176, 177, 182, 184, 190, 192, 197, 198
Melton Bluff, 15, 37, 38, 69, 155, 159, 160, 161, 162, 165, 166, 167, 169, 177, 178
Melton, Barbara, 38
Melton, Charles, 37, 161, 162
Melton, David, 37, 161, 166
Melton, Elick, 37, 161, 162
Melton, James, 38, 161
Melton, John, 36, 37, 38, 154, 159, 160, 161, 164, 165, 166, 167, 169, 178
Melton, Lewis, 37, 168
Melton, Merida, 38
Melton, Moses, 37, 161, 167, 168
Melton, Ocuma, 36
Melton, Thomas, 37
Methoataske, 11
Miller, Abraham, 210
Miller, Alex, 211
Miller, David, 210
Miller, Henry, 210
Miller, Jas, 210
Miller, John, 211
Milliken, John, 80
Mills, Joel, 86
Milstead, James, 205
Milton, Daniel, 50
Milton, John, 50
Minor Hill, Tennessee, 71
Mississippi River, 2, 10, 18, 26, 51, 55, 68, 157, 172, 202, 228
Mitchell, 8, 19, 71, 159, 204, 210
Mitchell, John Jnr, 211
Mitchell, John Snr, 210
Mize, Joel, 19
Moccasin Gap, Virginia, 99
Monee Town, 154, 155, 159
Monroe County, Tennessee, 25, 30, 33, 39, 47
Moonshaw, Joseph, 85

Moor, Alexander, 211
Moor, Amos, 210
Moor, Robert, 211
Moore, Lodwich, 205
Morgan County, Alabama, 37, 57
Morres, Shadrach, 211
Morse, George, 112
Mossy, James, 210
Moulton Valley, 15
Moulton, Alabama, 71, 249
Mounce, Margaret, 46
Mouse Town, 37, 69, 154, 155, 159, 162, 163
Mowery, John, 210
Moytoy, 19, 39, 40, 43
Mulherrin, William, 86
Mullens, James, 211
Mullin, Thomas, 211
Mullin, Wm, 211
Mungle, Daniel, 83
Murrell, Benj., 209
Murrell, Isaac, 209
Murrell, Richard, 209
Murrell, William, 212
Murry, Solomon, 82
Muscle Shoals, 1, 2, 3, 5, 6, 7, 8, 9, 10, 12, 13, 14, 15, 16, 17, 18, 57, 59, 61, 69, 70, 71, 72, 73, 74, 76, 77, 78, 79, 80, 90, 98, 133, 147, 154, 155, 162, 165, 168, 169, 171, 172, 178, 179, 180, 184, 190, 191, 195, 198, 203, 214, 225, 235, 239, 240, 242, 247, 249
Muscogee Creek, 11
Myers, John, 210
Myrick, Mary, 31

N

Nashville, Tennessee, 52, 69, 71, 78, 82, 90, 91, 98, 99, 102, 103, 147, 190, 206
Natchez Trace, 16, 47, 48, 69, 71, 74, 75, 80, 99, 178
Neely, William, 81, 119
Negro Fox, 37, 162
Neill, James, 209
Nelson, John, 209
Nelson, Samuel, 211
Nelson, Wm., 209
Nenetooyah, 25
Nigodigeyu, 46, 49, 51
Nina Leftwich, 16
Nolan, Joseph, 86
Nolan, Thomas, 86
Norman, James, 212
Norrington, Joshua, 86

260

O

Obongpohego, 135
Oconee Mountain, 150
Ocuma, 36, 38, 159, 160, 164, 165, 166
Odaniell, Michael, 209
Ogel, George, 212
Ohio Valley, 15, 34
Old Hop, 33, 54
Old Tassel, 32, 93
Olde Charles Town, South Carolina, 15, 21
Ollie, 30
O'Neel, Hirram, 212
O'Neel, Mitchell, 212
O'Neel, Tiery, 212
Oolootsa, 30
Ore, James, 121, 143
Osbourn, Benjimen, 209
Ostenaco, 34
Overall, William, 86, 128
Overhill Cherokee Towns, 21
Overhill Towns, 33, 60

P

Paine, John, 210
Panton, Jesse, 210
Panton, John, 210
Park V., Ezekiel E., 204
Parker, David, 211
Parmerly, John, 212
Pates, John, 117
Path Killer, 16, 146, 147, 156, 158, 159, 160, 218
Pathkiller, 154, 156, 158
Patrick, James, 98
Paul, James, 112
Payne, Wiliam, 209
Pearson, John, 40
Peeler, Frederick, 205
Peeler, Fredrick, 205
Pendleton, Frances, 98
Pennington, Isaac, 107
Perkins, Joshua, 210
Perrett, Isaac, 212
Perry, Rachel, 48
Pettegrew, John, 133
Pettegrew, William, 133
Peyton, John, 88
Peyton, Thomas, 88
Philips, Beverly, 210
Philips, Joel, 211
Phillips, Clement, 31
Phillips, Joel, 206

Phillips, Joseph, 204, 232, 233, 242
Phillips, Soloman, 82
Phillips, William, 162
Phillips, Zach, 204
Pickett, Albert James, 73
Pickins, Andrew, 212
Pickins, James, 213
Pigeon, 29, 34, 117, 125
Pool, Thomas, 210
Porter, Oliver, 204
Potier, Guillaume, 41
Preed, James, 209
Preed, Sammell Jun, 209
Preed, Sammul, 209
President George Washington, 6, 8, 25, 41, 140, 141,
    142, 143, 144, 145, 146, 147
Priber, Christian G., 39, 41
Priber, Christian Gottleib, 39, 46
Priber, Christian Gottlieb, 39
Priber, Susan, 21, 39, 46
Price, Elijah, 209
Price, Looney, 23
Price, Thos, 211
Prigman, Polly, 212
Professor Henry Sale Halbert, 12, 15
Pruett, Daniel, 87
Pugh, Thomas, 88
Pumpkin Boy, 35, 36, 68, 124, 126, 235
Pyeatt, Jacob, 211
Pyeatt, James, 211

R

Radish, James, 206
Rainbolt, Elisha, 210
Rains, John, 82, 120
Rains, Patsy, 86
Rains, William, 162
Ramsey, James Gettys McGready, 124
Randal, William, 204
Randal, Willis, 204
Randolph, Hugh, 206
Ransom, Francis, 120
Ray, John, 211
Rays, Benjamin, 205
Read, John, 212
Read, Thomas, 212
Reasons, Thomas, 135
Red Bird, 19, 20, 21, 36, 39, 46, 68
Red Bird Carpenter, 19, 21
Red Bird II, 20
Redey, James, 210
Redus, Thomas, 209

261

Rickey Butch Walker is a life long native son of the Warrior Mountains. He descends from Cherokee, Creek, and Celtic (Scots-Irish) people who migrated into the hills and coves of the mountainous region of north Alabama some 250 years ago. He, as was his father, is a member of the Echota Cherokee Tribe of Alabama. His Indian name is Fish Bird in honor of his fifth, fourth, and third great grandmothers-Catherine Kingfisher, Experience Fish, and Elizabeth Bird.

The kingfisher and fish bird (Osprey) love to fish and so does Butch. In addition, the osprey is of contrasting colors of black and white which identify Butch's character. Things that rule his life are true or false, yes or no, and black or white with virtually no gray areas; therefore, he lives his life somewhat as an open book. Also, according to Indian legend, the birds of prey soar high in the sky and carry the prayers of the earthly creatures to the great spirit. Fish Bird (Butch) has his entire adult life been an advocate to preserve and protect the environment for all the earthly creatures that are unable to speak for themselves.

As a young boy, Butch was born and raised in the shadows of the Warrior Mountains where he was taught by his grandpa the ways of the wild. He squirrel hunted on Brushy Mountain, trapped in Sugar Camp Hollow, searched for ginseng in Indian Tomb Hollow, and fished in West Flint Creek. He walked with his grandparents on old Indian trails including Black Warriors' Path, Sipsie Trail, and many others. He explored the deep canyons, rolling hills, steep bluff lines, and vast hollows containing beautiful waterfalls where he would stand in the spray to cool off on a hot day. He was nourished by the subsistence of West Flint Creek and surrounding hardwood bottoms, and molded from traveling the trails and paths his people once trod. He grew up with a fierce love for the Warrior

Mountains in which his ancestors lived, died, and are buried.

In 1966 because of the love of his mountainous homeland, Butch became an advocate to stop the clear cutting of old growth woodlands that he roamed and hunted as a youngster. He worked to help establish the Sipsey Wilderness Area which was dedicated in 1975 and wrote weekly articles about the forest for the Moulton Advertiser. In 1992, Butch teamed up with Lamar Marshall and helped begin the Bankhead Monitor to fight the clear cutting and destructive practices by the United States Forest Service taking place in the sacred Indian Tomb Hollow. The Monitor became Wild Alabama and later Wild South. Butch served as Chairman of the Board of Directors until Wild South merged with the Southern Appalachain Biodiversity Project in 2006.

Rickey Butch Walker retired after some 35 years with the Lawrence County Board of Education during which he earned post graduate degrees in science, education, and supervision. He taught high school science for 11 years and served as Director of Lawrence County Schools' Indian Education Program and Oakville Indian Mounds Education Center until his retirement in 2009. In addition to his Masters Thesis, he has written several books including *High Town Path, Warrior Mountains Folklore, Indians of the Warrior Mountains, Indian Trails of the Warrior Mountains, Warrior Mountains Indian Heritage, Warrior Mountains Indian HeritageStudent Edition* and currently completing *Chickasaw Chief George Colbert: His Family and His Country.*

You can find Butch's book at Amazon.com or www.Historicaltruth101.com.

You can also subscribe to his weekly blog at www.RickeyButchWalker.com or

http://rickeybutchwalker.blogspot.com to receive Butch's weekly updates ofn the historical research he is currently writing.

Bluewater Publications is a multi-faceted publishing company capable of meeting all of your reading and publishing needs. Our two-fold aim is to:

1) Provide the market with educationally enlightening and inspiring research and reading materials.
2) Make the opportunity of being published available to any author and or researcher who desire to be published.

We are passionate about preserving history; whether through the re-publishing of an out-of-print classic, or by publishing the research of historians and genealogists. Bluewater Publications is the *Peoples' Choice Publisher*.

For company information or information about how you can be published through Bluewater Publications, please visit:

www.BluewaterPublications.com

Also check Amazon.com to purchase any of the books that we publish.

Confidently Preserving Our Past,
Bluewater Publications.com

CPSIA information can be obtained
at www.ICGtesting.com
Printed in the USA
BVHW091413240619
551802BV00007B/124/P